Modelling Sustainable Development

THE FONDAZIONE ENI ENRICO MATTEI (FEEM) SERIES ON ECONOMICS, THE ENVIRONMENT AND SUSTAINABLE DEVELOPMENT

Series Editor: Carlo Carraro, *University of Venice, Venice and Research Director, Fondazione Eni Enrico Mattei (FEEM), Milan, Italy*

Editorial Board

The Fondazione Eni Enrico Mattei (FEEM) was established in 1989 as a non-profit, non-partisan research institution. It carries out high-profile research in the fields of economic development, energy and the environment, thanks to an international network of researchers who contribute to disseminate knowledge through seminars, congresses and publications. The main objective of the Fondazione is to foster interactions among academic, industrial and public policy spheres in an effort to find solutions to environmental problems. Over the years it has thus become a major European institution for research on sustainable development and the privileged interlocutor of a number of leading national and international policy institutions.

The Fondazione Eni Enrico Mattei (FEEM) Series on Economics, the Environment and Sustainable Development publishes leading-edge research findings providing an authoritative and up-to-date source of information in all aspects of sustainable development. FEEM research outputs are the results of a sound and acknowledged co-operation between its internal staff and a worldwide network of outstanding researchers and practitioners. A Scientific Advisory Board of distinguished academics ensures the quality of the publications.

This series serves as an outlet for the main results of FEEM's research programmes in the areas of economics, the environment and sustainable development.

Titles in the series include:

Modelling Sustainable Development

Transitions to a Sustainable Future

Edited by

Valentina Bosetti
Fondazione Eni Enrico Mattei, Italy

Reyer Gerlagh
*University of Manchester, UK and VU University,
The Netherlands*

Stefan P. Schleicher
Austrian Institute of Economic Research, Austria

THE FONDAZIONE ENI ENRICO MATTEI (FEEM) SERIES ON
ECONOMICS, THE ENVIRONMENT AND SUSTAINABLE
DEVELOPMENT

Edward Elgar
Cheltenham, UK • Northampton, MA, USA

Published by
Edward Elgar Publishing Limited
The Lypiatts
15 Lansdown Road
Cheltenham
Glos GL50 2JA
UK

Edward Elgar Publishing, Inc.
William Pratt House
9 Dewey Court
Northampton
Massachusetts 01060
USA

A catalogue record for this book
is available from the British Library

Library of Congress Control Number: 2009924304

Mixed Sources
Product group from well-managed
forests and other controlled sources
www.fsc.org Cert no. SA-COC-1565
© 1996 Forest Stewardship Council

ISBN 978 1 84720 905 4

Printed and bound by MPG Books Group, UK

Contents

Contributors

Terry Barker, University of Cambridge, UK.

Christoph Böhringer, University of Oldenburg, Germany.

Valentina Bosetti, Fondazione Eni Enrico Mattei, Italy.

Barbara K. Buchner, International Energy Agency, France.

Carlo Carraro, University of Venice and Fondazione Eni Enrico Mattei, Italy.

Sebastian De-Ramon, Experian Ltd, UK.

Marzio Galeotti, Centre for Research on Energy and Environmental Economics and Policy (IEFE) and University of Milan, Italy.

Reyer Gerlagh, University of Manchester, UK and VU University, The Netherlands.

Frédéric Ghersi, Centre National de la Recherche Scientifique, France.

Jean-Charles Hourcade, Centre National de la Recherche Scientifique, France.

Walter Hyll, Klagenfurt University, Austria.

Ger Klaassen, European Commission, Belgium.

Ray Kopp, Zentrum für Europäische Wirtschaftsforschung (ZEW), Germany.

Andreas Löschel, Zentrum für Europäische Wirtschaftsforschung (ZEW), Germany.

Gerard Martinus, Energy Research Centre of the Netherlands (ECN), The Netherlands.

Hector Pollitt, Cambridge Econometrics, UK.

Thomas F. Rutherford, ETH Zürich, Switzerland.

Stefan P. Schleicher, Austrian Institute of Economic Research, Austria

Koen Smekens, Energy Research Centre of the Netherlands (ECN), The Netherlands.

Gregor Thenius, Austrian Institute of Economic Research, Austria.

Richard S.J. Tol, Economic and Social Research Institute, Ireland; VU University, The Netherlands and Carnegie Mellon University, USA.

Bob van der Zwaan, Energy Research Centre of the Netherlands (ECN), The Netherlands and Columbia University, USA.

Foreword: Challenges of Sustainability to Economics

Ger Klaassen

Sustainable development can be defined as a better quality of life for everyone, now and for generations to come. This is about meeting the needs of present generations without jeopardising the needs of future generations. It implies development that links economic development, protection of the environment and social justice in an integrated and mutually reinforcing way. Sustainable development focuses on:

- high levels of employment and social cohesion;
- a high level of environmental protection and responsible use of natural resources;
- balanced and equitable economic development;
- coherent policy-making in an open, transparent and accountable political system;
- effective international cooperation to promote sustainable development globally.

The European Council of the European Union adopted in June 2006 a renewed Strategy for Sustainable Development (SDS) for an enlarged EU. It builds on the Gothenburg strategy of 2001 and is the result of a review process that started in 2004. The renewed EU SDS sets out a single, coherent strategy on how the EU will more effectively live up to its long-standing commitment to meet the challenges of sustainable development. It recognises the need to gradually change our current unsustainable consumption and production patterns and move towards a better integrated approach to policy-making. It reaffirms the need for global solidarity and recognises the importance of strengthening our work with partners outside the EU, including those rapidly developing countries which will have a significant impact on global sustainable development.

The Council decisions of June 2006 were based on a Communication from the European Commission on the Review of the Sustainable Development

Strategy of 13 December 2005. This built upon the (Gothenburg) strategy adopted in 2001 that provided a first step, but since the challenges remained, the revised strategy recognised the need to make greater efforts in implementing the real changes needed to achieve sustainability. The new text identifies six key challenges: (i) climate change and clean energy; (ii) public health; (iii) social exclusion, demography and migration; (iv) management of natural resources; (v) sustainable transport; and (vi) global poverty and development.

Part of the strategy on sustainable development is about investing in the future. That also entails investing in research and development as is being done under the Framework Programmes for Research, Technological Development and Demonstration funded by the European Community. The 5th European Community Framework Programme for Research and Development funded the project TranSust (The Transition to Sustainable Economic Structures). This book is based on the results of that project, a project I had the pleasure to supervise when working at the Directorate General for Research at the European Commission.

What makes this project and book so interesting and worthwhile for policy-making on sustainable development? First and foremost, the book deliberately takes a practical approach to sustainable development, aiming at including contributions that address the practical implications of sustainable development and the various ways to operate the concept for day-to-day policy-making.

Secondly, this book is relevant since it addresses a wide range of issues relevant for sustainable development at a European level at considerable depth. The book includes an overview of the use of economic models, extending the debate to include the three dimensions of sustainable development – environment, economic development and social cohesion – while assessing the use of tax reforms in Africa to alleviate poverty, improve the environment and support economic growth. The book includes a fine, concise survey of the strategy on sustainable development of the EU noting the relevance of a broader view on welfare, the institutional context, and the occurrence of co-benefits and the role of innovation.

The book also includes a survey of energy–economy–environment models and the indicators for sustainable development that they cover. There is a chapter on the notion of abatement costs of climate policies, their use in partial and general equilibrium modelling and the appropriate translation of this information to decision-makers. There is a contribution on progress being made in including innovation as an endogenous process rather than 'manna from heaven' in economy–environment models. The contribution on tax revenues that can be recycled if carbon prices are raised over time compares nine different models to assess in particular the employment impacts. In doing so it gives guidance to the recent decision (March 2007) of the Council of the EU to reduce greenhouse gas emissions by 20 per cent in 2020 (compared to 1990) while trying to maintain high levels of employment. Another contribution provides a comparison of how the different economy–energy–environment models simulate carbon capture and storage and renewable energy technologies and the risks associated with carbon capture and storage. This is a timely topic in view of current discussions on the inclusion of carbon capture and storage in the EU's emissions trading scheme for CO_2 emissions, and the Council conclusion from 8–9 March 2007 setting an EU target of a share of 20 per cent renewable energy by 2020. A final chapter explores the impact of the same set of taxes on carbon emissions, energy use and gross domestic product (GDP), closely examining the mechanisms at work in the set of underlying models thus examining the idea of decoupling energy use from economic development.

In sum, this book makes a fine contribution to the linking of economic development, protection of the environment and social justice in an integrated way and deserves credit for its explicit focus on practical ways of handling the notion of sustainable development for policy-making purposes.

Acknowledgements

As editors, we are grateful for the contribution of all project participants who not only shared their ideas, but were also willing to spend many days in writing them up in an easily accessible way. We are very thankful to the European Commission for their financial support. European integration of research would remain a dream without material support. Special thanks go to Richard Tol and Ray Kopp who offered us challenging and sometimes provoking thoughts that helped us shape our own ideas and research plans. We hope this book will prove a valuable contribution to policy-makers who want to understand what researchers can do, cannot do, and should not want to do with their models, and to researchers who work on the modelling of sustainability policies.

Valentina Bosetti, Reyer Gerlagh and Stefan P. Schleicher

Introduction: Modelling Sustainability – The TranSust Project

Valentina Bosetti, Reyer Gerlagh and Stefan P. Schleicher

INTRODUCTION

This book collects contributions on sustainable development (SD) in its more operative and applied sense. Although many papers have been written to elaborate on the potential interpretations and definitions of the concept of sustainable development, many of these papers are too abstract, and policy-makers and researchers alike call for more practical, and effective, guidelines. If we want to develop actual policies that aim at sustainability, we first need to find practical means that can help us to assess whether policy proposals, specific decisions or targeted scenarios are sustainable. Assessment of sustainability is often approached through various indicators and aggregate measures, and one wants to know whether and how these can be included in models that are used for decision-making support.

PART I: DEFINING SUSTAINABILTY

In the first part the book starts with a brief address of broader issues related to the application of the sustainable development concept to the policy process and to economics. Its contributors are Richard Tol, Barbara Buchner and Ray Kopp. Tol discusses the connections between sustainable development as a policy issue and economic models as tools for policy analysis. With a wide view and clear opinion he discusses differences in objectives and the meaning of the terms we use in the sustainability debate. An important element in his chapter is the distinction between strong and weak sustainability, and their counterparts in applied terms as cost-effectiveness analyses and cost–benefit analysis. Tol takes the argument beyond a simple listing of the two visions by showing how both concepts face similar problems when confronted with the uncertainty that is characteristic for real global sustainability issues. Also, Tol links the environmentally oriented concepts with the broader sustainability concept that includes social justice. He concludes that from a theoretic point of view, economics seems capable of addressing the major sustainability issues. In practice, it is still to be seen whether an applied economic analysis can be sufficiently broad to capture all issues while at the same time being sufficiently specific to do so rigorously.

Barbara Buchner discusses the design of sustainable policy from a European perspective. She describes the need for sustainability policy in EU policy design and the trade-off between detailed specification of (sub) targets versus setting 'good examples' that invite broad imitation. She is concerned with changes in the economic structures and the policy settings that can support sustainability and economic welfare in the long run, and as a case study she analyses the EU Sustainable Development Strategy (SDS), adopted in 2006. She finds that the EU SDS acknowledges the need for a broad interpretation of welfare, it integrates different issues in common policy, it recognises the need to first capture so-called low-hanging fruit, and it correctly understands the role of technological change for long-term sustainable development. At the same time, the EU SDS often does not reach beyond recommendation and its effectiveness is still unproven.

Ray Kopp provides us with some practical counterweight, presenting a fine explanation of the US perspective on sustainability. In the US, though many understand and appreciate the concept of sustainability well, it is not deployed in policy language as it is in the EU. Also, the concern for sustainability is typically restricted to environmental and resource issues, whereas social concerns are considered to be part of a different domain. Sustainability is understood to be about (correcting) market failures, and most of US legislation that we could interpret as part of the sustainability agenda is directed to the inclusion of prices for environmental resources in other economic markets. As an example, the proposed Lieberman and Warner legislation for climate change requires deep cuts in US greenhouse gas (GHG) emissions through auctioning decreasing amounts of emission permits. Notably, the term 'sustainability' only enters the proposal when referring to sustainable energy, meaning renewable energy. Yet, the proposal echos the concept of sustainability as it makes an implicit balance between present costs and long-term benefits.

PART II: ISSUES IN MODELLING SUSTAINABILTY

The second part of the book is devoted to specific issues that arise when sustainability is incorporated in applied models and the concept is used for assessing policies. It discusses the choice of indicators, their role in different models, the relevance of the sustainability concept for the broader debate on climate change and the interpretation of costs of environmental policy, the relationship between sustainable development and new technologies, the role of revenue recycling in reducing costs of environmental policy, and the role of carbon capture and storage in climate policy. Many of these issues have been analysed as part of the TranSust project, and this part of the book reflects the outcomes of the process of ongoing discussion between colleague researchers. It starts with a central concept in the applied sustainability literature: the use of indicators.

The first chapter in Part II by Christoph Böhringer and Andreas Löschel presents a comprehensive survey of different indicators that the EU has outlined and that, together, are supposed to capture the concept of sustainability. The authors discuss these indicators and their inclusion in those models that have been used in the TranSust project.

The second chapter, by Jean-Charles Hourcade and Frédéric Ghersi, discusses the intricacies surrounding the definition and meaning of climate policy costs. The meaning of policy costs has been much debated following the publication of the Stern Review and the recent 4th IPCC Assessment Report WG3. Each model predicts different types of policy costs depending on model structures and key assumptions underlying the model baseline. To compare cost calculations from different models, it is essential to have a common understanding of the measurement and meaning of costs and the main drivers for each specific model. The difficulties that arise when comparing annual costs with one-time costs, on the basis of net present value analysis, has received considerable attention; one only needs to think of the heated debate on ethical versus positive discounting that followed the presentation of the Stern Review. Hourcade and Ghersi, however, show that the problem of discounting is only one of many problems encountered when comparing results from different model calculations.

Technological progress, its implications for the prospect of sustainable development and how it can be modelled, is the subject of the third chapter by Valentina Bosetti and Marzio Galeotti. The chapter provides a comprehensive review of modelling efforts in this area. A key area of research in this field is the potential of technological change to decouple economic growth from GHGs emissions.

The fourth chapter in Part II, by Terry Barker, Sebastian De-Ramon and Hector Pollitt, focuses on green tax recycling and labour markets, a subject that has gained popularity as part of the double dividend literature. This subject is of direct relevance to policy-makers who can choose between various green fiscal and non-fiscal instruments, each with different potential for recycling. In some circumstances, a win–win solution is feasible where the environment benefits, employment rises and costs are spread evenly, leading to an improvement in equity. The subject has gained much attention in the theoretic literature, and this chapter provides an overview of its cover in applied models, its relation to various modelling techniques and how these issues are treated in different models used within the TranSust project.

The last chapter in this second part of the book is by Bob van der Zwaan. He addresses a timely issue, the modelling of carbon dioxide capture and storage (CCS) and renewable energy technologies. Indeed, if a greenhouse gas emissions reduction policy is to be successful, then both CCS and renewables will probably need to play a crucial role in the process of decarbonising our energy infrastructure. Introducing these technologies into energy–environment–economy (EEE) models is thus essential, and allows for more accurately estimating the costs associated with reducing the carbon intensity of economies. Somewhat surprisingly, however, CCS and renewable energy technologies have not been integrated to many of the TranSust project models. This chapter reviews some CCS and renewables modelling techniques as well as main results, and thereby presents a concise guide to modellers for future CCS and renewables simulation.

PART III: MODEL DESCRIPTIONS

The third part of the book has a more technical focus. In this part of the book all models used within the TranSust project are described in detail, thus providing an easy technical guide for anybody interested in using or simply better understanding any of these models. Rather than a mere appendix, this accessible description of some European models that are used to integrate the science of climate change with economic policy represents a major merit of the book. The model described are MARKAL, DEMETER, IMACLIM-S, E3ME, FEEM-RICE and PACE.

PART IV: SYNTHESIS OF TRANSUST

Part IV of the book concludes. Reyer Gerlagh, Stefan Schleicher, Walter Hyll and Gregor Thenius present an overview on a set of climate change policy exercises performed with the TranSust models and discuss the differences in outcomes based on different models. Specifically, the first chapter in this part explores the effects of CO_2 taxes on CO_2 emissions, energy use, and gross domestic product (GDP) in the different TranSust models. The book ends with a conclusion by Valentina Bosetti and Carlo Carraro who wrap up the main policy conclusions drawn from the project.

PART I

Defining Sustainability

1. Economic Models for Sustainable Development

Richard S.J. Tol

1.1 INTRODUCTION

This chapter is about how economic models can be used to advise policy-makers on sustainable development. Van den Bergh and Hofkes (1998) and Moffat et al. (2001) devote whole books to this topic. In a single chapter, I cannot match them for detail. Instead, I highlight and classify the broad connections between sustainable development as a policy issue and economic models as tools for policy analysis. In Section 1.2, I first interpret sustainable development. This is to acquaint the reader with my view on this issue, and to help the reader interpret what I write later. In Section 1.3, I turn to the use of economic models – distinguishing between cost–benefit analysis and cost-effectiveness analysis for setting targets, and policy implementation. Sections 1.2 and 1.3 focus on the environment. Section 1.4 extends the discussion by including all three pillars of sustainability: environmental quality, economic well-being and social cohesion. Section 1.5 concludes.

1.2 SUSTAINABILITY

Sustainable development is development that meets the needs of the present generation without compromising the ability of future generations to meet their needs (WCED, 1987). It is hard to be against sustainable development. It spares future generations without compromising the present. There is no trade-off. You can have your cake and eat it. Sustainable development is like motherhood and apple pie.

It is therefore no surprise that Brundtland's magnificent definition took the world by storm. Coined in 1987, every nation and every large company in the world has supported sustainable development, at least on paper.[1] The strength of sustainable development lies in its mix of specificity and vagueness (note that Palmer et al., 1997, would disagree). Intuitively, it is pretty clear what is meant by sustainable development: the planet we will leave to our children should be a planet on which we would like to live too. But, sustainable development does not proscribe any specific action. The many weasel words in Brundtland's definition leave infinite scope for interpretation. What are 'needs'? What is a 'compromised ability'?

Sustainable development has intuitive appeal, and there is no sanction to signing up to it. So, many have. However, many also sing, with Neil Young and Johnny Rotten, that 'it is better to burn out, than to fade away'.[2] To my knowledge, no one has ever surveyed the general public as to which slogan is preferred.

Many have tried to make the definition of sustainable development more specific (for example, Brown et al., 1987), even if that might come at the expense of its appeal. Rather than listing the great many definitions, they can be grouped into weak sustainability and strong sustainability (for example, Ayres et al., 2001). Of course, there are also people who argue for in-between sustainability. In the weaker definitions of sustainability, human well-being is the prime concern. Environmental resources can be substituted for one another and for human-made capital. In the stronger definitions, humans are but one of many species, and substitution is much more difficult.

The issue of specism is void. We are human, and we can only look at the world through the eyes of humans. Sustainable development was introduced to help human decision-makers make the right decisions. As such, what matters is how much value we accord to other species. We cannot know how much value other species give to themselves, or to us.

The issue of substitutability is, at first sight, an empirical question. However, it cannot be answered by empirical means. To date, we have survived. Therefore, no essential, non-substitutable input to human life was ever lost. The point of sustainable development is to ensure that things remain this way – the fact that something did not happen in the past does not mean it will never happen in the future. Besides, the issue of essentiality and substitutability is of course defined relative to a goal. The human race has survived, but life has not been uniformly comfortable. John Stuart Mill (1848) expressed this very clearly:

> If the earth must lose that great portion of its pleasantness which it owes to things that the unlimited increases of wealth and population would extirpate from it, for the mere purpose of enabling it to support a larger, but not a happier or better population, I sincerely hope, for the sake of posterity, that they will be content to be stationary long before necessity compels them to it.[3]

Sustainability is therefore a matter of ethics (Farrow, 1998; Gerlagh and Keyzer, 2001; Padilla, 2002; Yohe and van Engel, 2004). Most people restrain their sexual and violent urges – including in situations where they would have the power to follow their impulses. For some, this is because they are afraid of the legal and social consequences. For others, this is because they are convinced that living out their fantasies is wrong, immoral or repugnant. This development is relatively recent, reversible, and has yet to reach all corners of the world.

Humans have only recently acquired the power to do lasting, large-scale damage to the environment. Sustainable development is about restraining our power to do damage to other generations and other species. This is a moral question. Different people draw the line between use and abuse elsewhere. Reasonable people have different opinions about what restraint would be appropriate. Nonetheless, sustainability is about not destroying the planet just because we can.

Note that sustainable development is about all of development and all of the environment. It is not about a specific environmental problem, such as eutrophication or acidification. It is not about a specific development problem, such as education for girls or enforcement of property rights. This helps to explain the popularity of sustainable development: it is everything to everyone. However, policy and policy analysis are reductionist, addressing one issue at the time.

1.3   TOWARDS SUSTAINABILITY

For policy, the issue of what is sustainability is perhaps less important than the question of how to make society sustainable, that is, how to 'sustainabilize' society. The ability to do this may be called 'sustainabilizability'.[4] Economic models can be used to support decisions for sustainabilization and inform on issues of sustainabilizability.

If one's heart goes out to strong sustainability, the first issue is to draw a line. The environment can be used or contaminated up to this point, but no further. Drawing this line is a thoroughly unscientific affair, even though scientific information on cause, exposure and effect should be used (see Funtowicz et al., 1998). For some issues, there are even pseudo-objective standards. For instance, a dose is deemed safe if less then 0.5 per cent of rats die when fed ten times the amount. This removes the actual target-setting from politics, but the choice of rats, the 0.5 per cent and the factor of ten are of course arbitrary except that they represent 'a small fraction', 'an order of magnitude', and 'an animal that is sufficiently like us to be a model, but sufficiently unlikable to be used in experiments'.

As soon as the target is set, standard economic analyses can be used to investigate the cheapest way of meeting the goal (for example, Manne and Richels, 1998; Polasky et al., 2001; Schiemann et al., 2002) and the best policy instruments used to change the behaviour of people (for example, Eskeland and Jimenez, 1992; Parry and Williams, 1999; Zabel et al., 1998). Standard as the general principles of these analyses may be, there are plenty of nuances and complications to occupy an applied economist.

If one's heart goes out to weak sustainability, one would have to measure human welfare (for example, Boadway, 1976; Sen, 1982), and find a way to put humanity on a path of increasing, or at least not decreasing welfare (Hamilton, 1995). The second part, finding the optimal trajectory towards the target, is as with strong sustainability, albeit with a different target. The first part, finding the target, is standard economics too. However, the definition of the optimal target is muddled by the difficulties of measuring and aggregating welfare and changes in welfare (Fankhauser et al., 1997). This problem is pronounced as many of the relevant goods and services are not traded at markets (for example, Bateman et al., 2002; Braden and Kolstad, 1991; Champ et al., 2003), or are traded on markets that do not function particularly well (Bradford and Hildebrandt, 1977).

Sustainabilizability therefore poses no fundamental challenge to economic science or economic models. There are a great many practical challenges, however, some of which are generic to economics (for example, welfare), while others are specific to environmental and resource economics (for example, valuation).

A particular problem of sustainability is that so few problems are in fact problems of sustainability. Stronger forms of sustainability are often unattainable (for example, Meadows, 1995). For instance, even if all emissions of greenhouse gas were to cease today, sea level rise would continue for another thousand years (Nicholls and Lowe, 2004) – with impacts on land, wetlands, freshwater, and so on (Nicholls and Tol, 2006). In practical terms, the questions are which fraction of the damage should be avoided, and how much effort should be spend on that.

One may argue that large-scale disruptions of the earth system should be avoided at all cost, or perhaps only at considerable cost. Examples include the shutdown of the thermohaline circulation (Clark et al., 2002; Gregory et al., 2005; Link and Tol, 2004; Rahmstorf, 1999; Vellinga and Wood, 2002), the melting of Greenland (Greve, 2000; Hvidberg, 2000; van de Wal and Oerlemans, 1997), or the collapse of the West Antarctic Ice Sheet (Mercer, 1978; Oppenheimer, 1998; Vaughan and Spouge, 2002). However, this only works if the thresholds not to be crossed are known with a fair degree of certainty. In actual fact, we do not know for sure that climate change would lead to such events, and that emission abatement would reduce the probability. Emission abatement, no matter how stringent, would not reduce the probability to zero – it may be that emission reduction has no effect, as the events have been triggered already, and it may even be that emission reduction increases the probability. The absolute guidance of strong sustainability disappears with such uncertainty. If humanity is doomed anyway, the best policy may be to party like there is no tomorrow. Or, policy may turn to geoengineering, unpalatable in all but desperate circumstances (Crutzen, 2006).

Problems with meeting the criteria of weaker sustainability are not regularly observed either. It is only rarely the case that environmental pollution is strong enough to offset the positive welfare effects of economic growth, or the technological progress that drives growth. In most cases, environmental degradation is a problem of efficiency, not (weak) sustainability. In principle, Pigouvian taxes can be used to internalize the externalities.

For instance, in an earlier paper (Tol, 2005), I reviewed the literature on the marginal damage costs of carbon dioxide emissions. I found that, depending on the discount rate used, the median estimate is somewhere between $7 and $33 per tonne of carbon. Global average emissions are one tonne of carbon per person per year, so the damage per tonne is about the same size as the damage per person. This reflects the estimates for the total, annual damage done by a doubling of the atmospheric concentration of carbon dioxide, which range up to 1.5 per cent of world income. This number is substantial enough, but is in fact lower than growth rate of the world economy. Indeed, Fankhauser and Tol (2005) show that climate change would slow economic growth, but is unlikely to reverse it.

Poverty traps are a possible exception, but little explored. In a poverty trap, the reason that one is poor is caused by poverty itself. A poverty trap is a vicious circle (Azariadis, 1996; Bloom et al., 2003). Health is an example. Poor people cannot afford high-quality health care, and therefore often suffer from bad health. Unhealthy children miss out on their education, and unhealthy adults are less productive. A relatively large part of the meagre income is spent on health care. Unhealthy people are therefore poor (Adams et al., 2003; Fuchs, 2004; Meer et al., 2003; Strauss and Thomas, 1998). In the jargon of economic growth models, a poverty trap is a stable equilibrium at low income, or perhaps an equilibrium that circles around that, leading to repeated boom and bust in time. Older growth models all have stable equilibria at exponential growth, but more recent models have poverty traps too (Becker and Murphy, 1990; Galor and Weil, 1999). As environment and climate affect human health (for example, McMichael et al., 2003), one could argue that a deteriorating environment or a warming climate widens or deepens poverty traps by exacerbating health problems. I am aware of only one such study. I found in Tol (2008) that this is probably not true for malaria and climate change. If it were true, then climate change would reverse economic growth – and be a true problem of weak sustainability.

Freshwater may be seen as an area where weak sustainability meets the strong variety. People are very unhappy when thirsty. In many places, groundwater is pumped at a rate that is far higher than the rate at which it is replenished (Rosegrant et al., 2002a, 2002b). Groundwater use violates the Feenstra rule of sustainability, not to use more than is produced.[5] The expected lifetime of some fossil water resources is less than ten years. A believer in strong sustainability would cry foul, but an adherent of weak sustainability would point to desalinated seawater as an option (Zhou and Tol, 2005).

Above, I argue that problems of sustainabilization can often be reinterpreted as problems of cost minimization or welfare maximization, and as problems of policy implementation. At a conceptual level, nothing is new and the standard economics toolbox is applicable to environmental issues. At the practical level of model building, things are different. In the mainstream, economists prefer models with analytical solutions. Analytical solutions require regularity conditions. A substantial part of the body of environmental economics hinges on such conditions (or attention is limited to such conditions), but it is rarely checked whether 'the environment' behaves as is assumed. The result is elegant but irrelevant matemathics. Possible exceptions include the work of Tschirhart (2000, 2002, 2003, 2004), Finnoff and Tschirhart (2003a, 2003b), Pethig and Tschirhart (2001) and Gerlagh (1999), who try to honour both environmental realism and economic rigour.

Rules have exceptions. Some economists are trying to include in their models representations of the environment that actually match reality – or at least some stylized facts. This started with acidification (ApSimon and Warren, 1996; Gough et al., 1995; Hordijk and Kroeze, 1997; Warren and ApSimon, 2000), has progressed most for climate change (Edmonds and Wise, 1998; Manne et al., 1995; Nordhaus, 1991; Nordhaus and Yang, 1996; Peck and Teisberg, 1992; Tol, 1997), and is now spilling into other fields, such as nutrients (Ayres, 1997; van der Veeren and Tol, 2001), water (Pahl-Wostl, 2002) and infrastructure (Dey, 2002). The resulting models often have numerical solutions only, and are often large, cumbersome and intransparent – the very reasons why theoretical economists dislike this line of work. Unfortunately, numerical research being somewhat of a stepchild of economics, standards are not uniformly high and simple rules of good practice (for example, systematic sensitivity analysis, model code in the public domain) are too often violated.

This research has now started to push against the frontier of economics. A faithful representation of the environment may imply non-convexity – a formidable conceptual and numerical challenge. Keller et al. (2000, 2004) have shown a way to include this in a rigorous manner. Environmental problems are often spatially explicit, and geographical economics only a recent addition to the economist's toolkit. Darwin et al. (1996; Darwin, 2004; Lewandrowski et al., 1999) combined a spatially explicit representation of land with a computable general equilibrium model. Environmental goods and services are often not traded on markets. In many cases, the environment directly affects utility and behaviour only indirectly. Then, the issue is one of measuring preferences. In other cases, the environment is a factor of production, but one that is unaccounted for as nature does not demand payment for its services. Issues of measurement are here confounded with issues of the consistency of accounts and models. Water is a prominent example (Berrittella et al., 2005a, 2005b).

1.4 THREE PILLARS

Originally, sustainable development was about the environment. Later, economic growth and social justice have been added to environmental quality. Sustainable development is often said to have three pillars (Lehtonen, 2004; Santaholma, 2003). For companies, this has been called the triple bottom line: people, profits and the planet (for example, Zwetsloot, 2003). Above, I used the traditional equation of sustainability with environmental quality. Below, I introduce economic development and equity.

Equity and growth are, of course, worthwhile goals. From the perspective of those working to achieve either (or both), it is a clever strategy to jump the successful bandwagon of sustainable development. However, this has further blurred the notion of sustainable development, which now encompasses all that is good, like motherhood and apple pie. This further explains why virtually everybody is in favour of sustainable development. However, putting all criteria under one header hides real trade-offs. Often, there is a choice between faster economic growth and better environmental quality. Also, environmental care may be at the expense of an egalitarian income distribution. For instance, an energy tax would reduce climate change, slow economic growth and, as all consumption taxes on necessary goods, worsen the income distribution. Is an energy tax in line with sustainable development or not?

The tools of economic analysis outlined in Section 1.3 address two of sustainability's three pillars. In a cost-effectiveness analysis, environmental degradation is limited at a minimum cost to the economy. In a cost–benefit analysis, the notion of welfare is expanded to include the environment; and this welfare is maximized.

Economists have more trouble with the third pillar: equity. Although economics is often defined as being about the allocation of scarce resources, most economists have little to say about the resulting distribution – apart from the largely irrelevant question of whether a policy is potentially Pareto improving (Farrow, 1998). Coase (1960) showed that, under certain circumstances, the issues of efficiency and equity are separated. Many an economist uses this as an excuse to limit the analysis to efficiency only – and some would declare equity as being beyond (economic) analysis.

I do not share this opinion. Issues of equity cannot be avoided when dealing with impacts on different people, from different countries and generations. Attempts to ignore equity in fact imply implicit assumptions on equity. It would be better to make these assumptions explicit and perform sensitivity analyses. It may happen that seemingly opposite moral positions lead to the same policy advice; or that apparently close positions are in fact distant (Rose and Stevens, 1993; Tol, 2001). Equity analyses can illuminate this – but like all decision support, analysis does not replace decision-making.

A desirable policy would improve on all three main criteria of sustainable development.[6] There are few analyses of this sort. Recently Van Heerden et al. (2006) and Letsoalo et al. (2007) published two studies on South Africa, the former on energy, the latter on water. Both studies use a computable general equilibrium (CGE) model to study tax reform. Earlier studies already looked at whether it is possible to reform taxes such that emissions fall and economic growth accelerates. The answer is yes, provided that the budgetneutral tax reform reduces the overall distortionarity of the tax system.

The South African studies take this a step further. The CGE model distinguishes 44 different household types. Beside overall economic growth and emissions/resource use, the analyses also checked whether tax reform would increase real consumption of the poorest households. This is also possible. However, the set of possible tax reforms is smaller if more criteria are imposed. Only a few, very specific tax reforms would have the desired effect of improving sustainability for all three pillars. See Figure 1.1. Particularly, any energy or water tax would reduce carbon dioxide emissions or water consumption, even if accounting for the rebound effect of tax recycling. Recycling tax revenues through lower income tax might stimulate economic growth, but it does so only in a few scenarios. Poverty is not reduced (as the poor do not pay income tax), and in fact worsens as the rich get richer and the poor are further marginalized. Recycling by reducing value added tax (VAT) is slightly better for economic growth, and slightly better for poverty reduction. However, most scenarios foresee a worse situation. Recycling by reducing the VAT on food only stimulates economic growth and reduces poverty, as this tax falls disproportionally on the poor, and they are so many that the demand stimulus is substantial. These results are, of course, specific to South Africa. For other countries, similar analyses would lead to different insights.

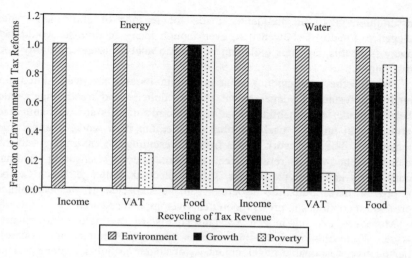

Note: The fraction of tax reforms that improve the environment (left, green), economic growth (middle, red) , and poverty (right, blue), for 'energy taxes' (that is, carbon tax, fuel tax, electricity tax, or energy tax) and water taxes (on forestry, all mining, gold mining, coal mining, other mining, irrigated agriculture, field crops, or horticulture) and for three alternative ways to recycle the tax revenues (reducing the income tax, VAT, VAT on food).

Figure 1.1   Dividends of Environmental Tax Reform

1.5   CONCLUSIONS

In this chapter, I have discussed the role of economic modelling in policy analyses of sustainable development. I began by arguing that sustainability is an ethical matter; it is a choice for self-restraint. As in all ethical matters, reasonable people disagree, in this case about the appropriate amount of self-restraint and the appropriate trade-offs between worthwhile but disparate goals. I then argued that strong sustainability maps to cost-effectiveness analysis – that is, choosing a path towards an exogenous goal so as to maximize welfare. Weak sustainability maps to cost–benefit analysis – that is, choosing a goal and a path towards that goal so as to maximize welfare. Both cost-effectiveness analysis and cost–benefit analysis are standard economic tools. Both suffer from the problems of defining and measuring welfare, but this is more pronounced with cost–benefit analysis. In both cases, the analysis of policy instruments is part of the overall assessment, and again this analysis is standard. Although the main lines of analyses are not novel, many details still need to be sorted out. I argued that a realistic representation of the environment requires economists to release some of the assumptions that are frequently made for reasons of convenience and elegance. Finally, I showed that, even though many economists would shy away from this, rigorous tools can be used to analyse issues of equity and distribution.

Overall, the conclusion is that economic models are well suited for analysing sustainable development and for policies and trends that would help or hinder sustainability. That is, economic models are well suited in principle. In practice, useful applications require hard work, intellect and inspiration. The hard work comes from representing the environment in the model such that it reflects reality. Simultaneously ensuring internal consistency and rigorous analysis is an intellectual challenge. Much can be improved here, but little progress can be expected if the economics profession continues to prefer theoretical over applied research.

Moreover, existing models are tailored towards a single environmental issue. While this is defensible from a pragmatic, 'horses for courses' perspective, sustainable development is, of course, a holistic concept. This suggests that a true economic analysis of sustainable development would require a 'model of everything'. It remains to be seen whether a model can exist that is sufficiently broad without being uselessly shallow.

ACKNOWLEDGEMENTS

Financial support by the Hamburg University Innovation Fund and the ESRI Energy Policy Research Centre is gratefully acknowledged. Valentina Bosetti and Reyer Gerlagh had useful comments on an earlier version.

NOTES

1. This may be a myth. I have often said this, and heard others say this, without opposition. It is true for every country and company I ever checked, but this is a small number only. I have been unable to find a systematic study that shows this, although I was able to find studies that claim this.
2. One may counter that these two gentlemen are fading rather than burning. Neil Young is an ardent environmentalist.
3. Note that Mill (1848), like Malthus (1803) but unlike Simon (1983), did not believe in growth in the long term.
4. This term was coined by Huib Jansen, an unsung pioneer of environmental economics.
5. Jan Feenstra was another unsung pioneer.
6. Note that a desirable policy is by no means optimal.

REFERENCES

Adams, P., M.D. Hurd, D. McFadden, A. Merrill and T. Ribeiro (2003), 'Healthy, wealthy, and wise? Tests for direct causal paths between health and socioeconomic status', *Journal of Econometrics*, **112**, 3–56.

ApSimon, H.M. and R.F. Warren (1996), 'Transboundary air pollution in Europe', *Energy Policy*, **24**(7), 631–40.

Ayres, R.U. (1997), 'Integrated assessment of the grand nutrient cycles', *Environmental Modeling and Assessment*, **2**, 107–28.

Ayres, R.U., J.C.J.M. van den Bergh and J.M. Gowdy (2001), 'Strong versus weak sustainability: Economics, natural sciences, and "consilience"', *Environmental Ethics*, **23**(2), 155–68.

Azariadis, C. (1996), 'The economics of poverty traps – Part one: Complete markets', *Journal of Economic Growth*, **1**, 449–86.

Bateman, I.J., R.T. Carson, B. Day, W.M. Hanemann, N. Hanley, T. Hett, M. Jones-Lee, G. Loomes, S. Mourato, E. Özdemiroglu, D.W. Pearce, R. Sugden and J. Swanson (2002), *Economic Valuation with Stated Preference Techniques*, Cheltenham, UK and Northampton, MA, USA: Edward Elgar.

Becker, G.S. and K.M. Murphy (1990), 'Human capital, fertility and economic growth', *Journal of Political Economy*, **98**(5), S12–S37.

Berrittella, M., A.Y. Hoekstra, K. Rehdanz, R. Roson and R.S.J. Tol (2005a), 'The economic impact of restricted water supply: A computable general equilibrium analysis', Working Papers FNU–93, Research Unit Sustainability and Global Change, Hamburg University and Centre for Marine and Atmospheric Science, Hamburg.

Berrittella, M., K. Rehdanz, R. Roson and R.S.J. Tol (2005b), 'The economic impact of water pricing: A computable general equilibrium analysis', Working Papers FNU–96, Research Unit Sustainability and Global Change, Hamburg University and Centre for Marine and Atmospheric Science, Hamburg.

Bloom, D.E., D. Canning and J. Sevilla (2003), 'Geography and poverty traps', *Journal of Economic Growth*, **8**, 355–78.

Boadway, R. (1976), 'Integrating equity and efficiency in applied welfare economics', *Quarterly Journal of Economics*, **90**(4), 541–56.

Braden, J.B. and C.D. Kolstad (eds) (1991), *Measuring the Demand for Environmental Quality*, Amsterdam: Elsevier.

Bradford, D.F. and G.G. Hildebrandt (1977), 'Observable preferences for public goods', *Journal of Public Economics*, **8**, 111–31.

Brown, B.J., M.E. Hanson, D.M. Liverman and R.W. Merideth, Jr. (1987), 'Global sustainability: Toward definition', *Environmental Management*, **11**(6), 713–19.

Champ, P.A., K.J. Boyle and T.C. Brown (eds) (2003), *A Primer on Nonmarket Valuation*, Dordrecht, Boston, MA and London: Kluwer Academic Publishers.

Clark, P.U., N.G. Pisias, T.F. Stocker and A.J. Weaver (2002), 'The role of the thermohaline circulation in abrupt climate change', *Nature*, **415**, 863–9.

Coase, R.H. (1960), 'The problem of social cost', *Journal of Law and Economics*, **3**, 1–21.

Crutzen, P.J. (2006), 'Albedo enhancement by stratospheric sulfur injections: A contribution to resolve a policy dilemma?', *Climatic Change*, **77**, 211–19.

Darwin, R. (2004), 'Effects of greenhouse gas emissions on world agriculture, food consumption, and economic welfare', *Climatic Change*, **66**, 191–238.

Darwin, R.F., M. Tsigas, J. Lewandrowski and A. Raneses (1996), 'Land use and land cover in ecological economics', *Ecological Economics*, **17**(3), 157–81.

Dey, P.K. (2002), 'An integrated assessment model for cross-country pipelines', *Environmental Impact Assessment Review*, **22**, 703–21.

Edmonds, J.A. and M.A. Wise (1998), 'Building backstop technologies and policies to implement the framework convention on climate change', *Energy and Environment*, **9**(4), 383–98.

Eskeland, G.S. and E. Jimenez (1992), 'Policy instruments for pollution control in developing countries', *World Bank Research Observer*, **7**(2), 145–69.

Fankhauser, S. and R.S.J. Tol (2005), 'On climate change and economic growth', *Resource and Energy Economics*, **27**, 1–17.

Fankhauser, S., R.S.J. Tol and D.W. Pearce (1997), 'The aggregation of climate change damages: A welfare theoretic approach', *Environmental and Resource Economics*, **10**, 249–66.

Farrow, S. (1998), 'Environmental equity and sustainability: Rejecting the Kaldor–Hicks criteria', *Ecological Economics*, **27**, 183–8.

Finnoff, D. and J. Tschirhart (2003a), 'Harvesting in an eight-species ecosystem', *Journal of Environmental Economics and Management*, **45**, 589–611.

Finnoff, D. and J. Tschirhart (2003b), 'Protecting an endangered species while harvesting its prey in a general equilibrium ecosystem model', *Land Economics* **79**(2), 160–80.

Fuchs, V.R. (2004), 'Reflections on the socio-economic correlates of health', *Journal of Health Economics*, **23**, 653–61.

Funtowicz, S., J. Ravetz and M. O'Connor (1998), 'Challenges in the use of science for sustainable development', *International Journal of Sustainable Development*, **1**(1), 99–107.

Galor, O. and D.N. Weil (1999), 'From Malthusian stagnation to modern growth', *American Economic Review*, **89**(2), 150–54.

Gerlagh, R. (1999), *The Efficient and Sustainable Use of Environmental Resource Systems*, Amsterdam: Thela Thesis.

Gerlagh, R. and M.A. Keyzer (2001), 'Sustainability and the intergenerational distribution of natural resource entitlements', *Journal of Public Economics*, **79**, 315–41.

Gregory, J.M., K.W. Dixon, R.J. Stouffer, A.J. Weaver, E. Driesschaert, M. Eby, T. Fichefet, H. Hasumi, A. Hu, J.H. Jungclaus, I.V. Kamenkovich, A. Levermann, M. Montoya, S. Murakami, S. Nawrath, A. Oka, A.P. Sokolov and R.B. Thorpe (2005), 'A model intercomparison of changes in the Atlantic thermohaline circulation in response to increasing atmospheric CO_2 concentration', *Geophysical Research Letters*, **32**(L12703), 1–5.

Greve, R. (2000), 'On the response of the Greenland ice sheet to greenhouse climate change', *Climatic Change*, **46**(3), 289–303.

Gough, C.A., M.J. Chadwick, B. Biewald, J.C.I. Kuylenstierna, P.D. Bailey and S. Cinderby (1995), 'Developing optimal abatement strategies for the effects of sulphur and nitrogen deposition at European scale', *Water, Air, and Soil Pollution*, **85**, 2601–6.

Hamilton, K. (1995), 'Sustainable development, the Hartwick rule and optimal growth', *Environmental and Resource Economics*, **5**, 393–411.

Hordijk, L. and C. Kroeze (1997), 'Integrated assessment models for acid rain', *European Journal of Operational Research*, **102**, 405–17.

Hvidberg, C.S. (2000), 'When Greenland ice melts', *Nature*, **404**, 551–2.

Keller, K., B.M. Bolker and D.F. Bradford (2004), 'Uncertain climate thresholds and optimal economic growth', *Journal of Environmental Economics and Management*, **48**, 723–41.

Keller, K., K. Tan, F.M.M. Morel and D.F. Bradford (2000), 'Preserving the ocean circulation: Implications for climate policy', *Climatic Change*, **47**, 17–43.

Lehtonen, M. (2004), 'The environmental–social interface of sustainable development: Capabilities, social capital, institutions', *Ecological Economics*, **49**(2), 199–214.

Letsoalo, A., J. Blignaut, T. de Wet, M. de Wit, S. Hess, R.S.J. Tol and J. van Heerden (2007), 'Triple dividends of water consumption charges in South Africa', *Water Resources Research*, **43**(W05412), doi:10.1029/2005WR004076.

Lewandrowski, J., R.F. Darwin, M. Tsigas and A. Raneses (1999), 'Estimating costs of protecting global ecosystem diversity', *Ecological Economics*, **29**, 111–25.

Link, P.M. and R.S.J. Tol (2004), 'Possible economic impacts of a shutdown of the thermohaline circulation: An application of FUND', *Portuguese Economic Journal*, **3**, 99–114.

Malthus, T.R. (1803), *An Essay on the Principle of Population*, London: Echo Library.

Manne, A.S., R.O. Mendelsohn and R.G. Richels (1995), 'MERGE: A model for evaluating regional and global effects of GHG reduction policies', *Energy Policy*, **23**(1), 17–34.

Manne, A.S. and R.G. Richels (1998), 'On stabilizing CO_2 concentrations: Costeffective emission reduction strategies', *Environmental Modeling and Assessment*, **2**, 251–65.

McMichael, A.J., D.H. Campbell-Lendrum, C.F. Corvalán, K.L. Ebi, A.K. Githeko, J.D. Scheraga and A. Woodward (eds) (2003), *Climate Change and Human Health: Risks and Responses*, Geneva: World Health Organization.

Meadows, D.L. (1995), 'It is too late to achieve sustainable development, now let us strive for survivable development', *Journal of Global Environment Engineering*, **1**, 1–14.

Meer, J., D.L. Miller and H.S. Rosen (2003), 'Exploring the health–wealth nexus', *Journal of Health Economics*, **22**, 713–30.

Mercer, J.H. (1978), 'West antarctic ice sheet and CO_2 greenhouse effect: A threat of disaster', *Nature*, **271**, 321–25.

Mill, J.S. (1848), *Principles of Political Economy, with some of their Applications to Social Philosophy*, London: Parker.

Moffat, I., N. Hanley and M.D. Wilson (2001), *Measuring and Modelling: Sustainable Development*, New York and London: Parthenon Publishing Group.

Nicholls, R.J. and J.A. Lowe (2004), 'Benefits of mitigation of climate change for coastal areas', *Global Environmental Change*, **14**, 229–44.

Nicholls, R.J. and R.S.J. Tol (2006), 'Impacts and responses to sea-level rise: A global analysis of the SRES scenarios over the 21st Century', *Philosophical Transaction of the Royal Society A: Mathematical, Physical and Engineering Sciences*, **361**(1841), 1073–95.

Nordhaus, W.D. (1991), 'To slow or not to slow: The economics of the greenhouse effect', *Economic Journal*, **101**, 920–37.

Nordhaus, W.D. and Z. Yang (1996), 'RICE: A regional dynamic general equilibrium model of optimal climate-change policy', *American Economic Review*, **86**(4), 741–65.

Oppenheimer, M. (1998), 'Global warming and the stability of the West Antarctic ice sheet', *Nature*, **393**, 325–32.

Padilla, E. (2002), 'Intergenerational equity and sustainability', *Ecological Economics*, **41**, 69–83.

Pahl-Wostl, C. (2002), 'Towards sustainability in the water sector: The importance of human actors and processes of social learning', *Aquatic Sciences*, **64**, 394–411.

Palmer, J., I. Cooper and R. van der Vorst (1997), 'Mapping out fuzzy buzzwords: Who sits where on sustainability and sustainable development', *Sustainable Development*, **5**(2), 87–93.

Parry, I.W.H. and R.C. Williams III (1999), 'A second-best evaluation of eight policy instruments to reduce carbon emissions', *Resource and Energy Economics*, **21**, 347–73.

Peck, S.C. and T.J. Teisberg (1992), 'CETA: A model for carbon emissions trajectory assessment', *Energy Journal*, **13**(1), 55–77.

Pethig, R. and J. Tschirhart (2001), 'Microfoundations of population dynamics', *Journal of Bioeconomics*, **3**(1), 27–49.

Polasky, S., J.D. Camm and B. Garber-Yonts (2001), 'Selecting biological reserves cost-effectively: An application to terrestrial vertebrate conservation in Oregon', *Land Economics*, **77**(1), 68–78.

Rahmstorf, S. (1999), 'Rapid transitions of the thermohaline ocean circulation', in F. Abrantes and A.C. Mix (eds), *Reconstructing Ocean History: A Window into the Future*, New York: Plenum Press, pp. 139–49.

Rose, A. and B. Stevens (1993), 'The efficiency and equity of marketable permits for CO_2 emissions', *Resource and Energy Economics*, **15**, 117–46.

Rosegrant, M.W., X. Cai and S.A. Cline (2002a), *Global Water Outlook to 2025 – Averting an Impending Crisis*, Washington, DC: International Food Policy Research Institute.

Rosegrant, M.W., X. Cai and S.A. Cline (2002b), *Water and Food to 2025 – Policy Responses to the Threat of Scarcity*, Washington, DC: International Food Policy Research Institute.

Santaholma, J. (2003), 'Economic responsibility, responsibility for the environment, and social responsibility: The three pillars for responsibility in sustainable development', *Corporate Environmental Strategy*, **10**(1), 2–15.

Schmieman, E., W. de Vries, L. Hordijk, C. Kroeze, M. Posch, G.J. Reinds and E. van Ierland (2002), 'Dynamic cost-effective reduction strategies for acidification in Europe: An application to Ireland and the United Kingdom', *Environmental Modeling and Assessment*, **7**, 163–78.

Sen, A. (1982), *Choice, Welfare, and Measurement*, Cambridge, MA: Harvard University Press.

Simon, J.L. (1983), *The Ultimate Resource*, Princeton, NJ: Princeton University Press.

Strauss, J. and D. Thomas (1998), 'Health, nutrition, and economic development', *Journal of Economic Literature*, **36**, 766–817.

Tol, R.S.J. (1997), 'On the optimal control of carbon dioxide emissions: An application of FUND', *Environmental Modeling and Assessment*, **2**, 151–63.

Tol, R.S.J. (2001), 'Equitable cost–benefit analysis of climate change', *Ecological Economics*, **36**(1), 71–85.

Tol, R.S.J. (2005), 'The marginal damage costs of carbon dioxide emissions: an assessment of the uncertainties', *Energy Policy*, **33**, 2064–74.

Tol, R.S.J. (2008), 'Climate, development and malaria: An application of FUND', *Climatic Change*, **88**(1), 21–34.

Tschirhart, J. (2000), 'General equilibrium of an ecosystem', *Journal of Theoretical Biology*, **203**, 13–32.

Tschirhart, J. (2002), 'Resource competition among plants: from maximizing individuals to community structure', *Ecological Modelling*, **148**, 191–212.

Tschirhart, J. (2003), 'Ecological transfers replace economic markets in a general equilibrium ecosystem model', *Journal of Bioeconomics*, **5**, 193–214.

Tschirhart, J. (2004), 'A new adaptive system approach to predator–prey modeling', *Ecological Modelling*, **176**, 255–76.

van de Wal, R.S.W. and J. Oerlemans (1997), 'Modelling the short-term response of the Greenland ice-sheet to global warming', *Climate Dynamics*, **13**, 733–44.

van den Bergh, J.C.J.M. and M.W. Hofkes (eds) (1998), *Theory and Implementation of Economic Models for Sustainable Development*, Dordrecht: Kluwer Academic Publishers.

van der Veeren, R.J.H.M. and R.S.J. Tol (2001), 'Benefits of a reallocation of nitrate emission reductions in the Rhine river basin', *Environmental and Resource Economics*, **18**, 19–41.

Van Heerden, J., R. Gerlagh, J. Blignaut, M. Horridge, S. Hess, R. Mabugu and M. Mabugu (2006), 'Searching for triple dividends in South Africa: Fighting CO_2 pollution and poverty while promoting growth', *The Energy Journal*, **27**(2), 113–41.

Vaughan, D.G. and J.R. Spouge (2002), 'Risk estimation of collapse of the West Antarctic Ice Sheet', *Climatic Change*, **52**(1–2), 65–91.

Vellinga, N. and R.A. Wood (2002), 'Global climatic impacts of a collapse of the Atlantic thermohaline circulation', *Climatic Change*, **54**, 251–67.

Yohe, G.W. and E. van Engel (2004), 'Equity and sustainability over the next fifty years: an exercise in economic visioning', *Environment, Development and Sustainability*, **6**, 393–413.

Warren, R.F. and H.M. ApSimon (2000), 'Application of limiting marginal abatement costs in optimised strategies to reduce acidification and eutrophication in Europe: Illustrations using the abatement strategies assessment model (ASAM)', *Journal of Environmental Assessment Policy and Management*, **2**(1), 119–66.

WCED (World Commission on Environment and Development, The Brundtland Commission) (1987), *Our Common Future*, Oxford: Oxford University Press.

Zabel, T.F., K. Andrews and Y. Rees (1998), 'The use of economic instruments for water management in selected EU member countries', *Journal of the Chartered Institution of Water and Environmental Management*, **12**(4), 268–72.

Zhou, Y. and R.S.J. Tol (2005), 'Evaluating the costs of desalination and water transport', *Water Resources Research*, **41**(3), W03003.

Zwetsloot, G.I.J.M. (2003), 'From management systems to corporate social responsibility', *Journal of Business Ethics*, **44**(2–3), 201–7.

2. Designing Sustainability Policy[1]

Barbara K. Buchner

2.1 SUSTAINABLE DEVELOPMENT POLICY IN THE EU

How can we meet today's needs without diminishing the capacity of future generations to meet their own? This question characterises the challenge of sustainability, which during the last decades has become a more and more important guideline for economic, social and environmental processes. Indeed, the concept of sustainable development was from its very beginning meant to be relevant for a comprehensive philosophy including – apart from environmental aspects – a variety of social issues. The pioneering work of the World Commission on Environment and Development (WCED, 1987) refers to sustainable development as 'development that meets the needs of the present without compromising the ability of future generations to meet their own needs'. With this famous report, *Our Common Future*, the Brundtland Commission placed sustainability on international political and scientific agendas.

Notwithstanding this broad definition, many political discussions initially have adopted a relatively narrow focus, concentrating mainly on areas where sustainability can be defined directly or exclusively in terms of specific environmental problem (see for example discussion in Pezzey, 2001). However, in order more comprehensively to implement the concept and to lead the world towards a sustainable path, the wider notion of sustainability needs to be taken into account, acknowledging thus the original intention of the WCED pioneers.

For more than a decade, the European Union (EU) has taken a leading role in the promotion of sustainable development (SD), as is emphasised by various key political decisions starting from the Treaty of Maastricht (1992). At the Lisbon Summit in March 2000, a new strategic goal for the European Union was established. The European Council formulated a ten-year strategy to make the EU the world's most dynamic and competitive economy. Under the strategy, a stronger economy is assumed to drive job creation alongside social and environmental policies that ensure sustainable development and social inclusion. The Lisbon Strategy touches on most of the EU's economic, social and environmental activities, strengthening the objective of sustainable development with a special focus on competitiveness. In the subsequent Gothenburg Summit in June 2001, the European Strategy for Sustainable Development (European Commission, 2001) was adopted. This strategy aims at a restructuring of the European economy by means of integrating economic welfare, environmental integrity and social coherence. The transition to these innovative economic structures poses a major challenge to economic policy design. Sustainability is also high on the policy agenda outside of Europe. The World Summit on Sustainable Development in September 2002 emphasised the links to economic development, economic security, dissemination of technologies, and the social issues of health and ageing in a world that is growing in population. These goals overlap with the targets put forward by the United Nations Millennium Project.

After decades of research on sustainable development, the euphoria for sustainability appears thus to experience a new peak in policy circles. Yet, recent experiences show that the implementation of all these sustainability strategies is difficult and that unsustainable trends persist. An example of the friction is highlighted in the context of the Lisbon Strategy, which is a commitment to bring about economic, social and environmental renewal in the EU. The European Commission's annual Spring Report examines the main problems encountered in implementing this strategy as well as its effect so far in detail. The recent 2004 report acknowledges progress in certain domains, emphasising however significant problems that hold back the implementation of other major parts of the strategy. The need for a vigorous implementation of reform in all the different areas through integrated strategies is stressed. Insufficient implementation of the Lisbon Strategy could produce significant net costs for Europe, for example in terms of reduced economic welfare and a growing gap with some of the large industrial partners in the fields of education and R&D, even though the extent of these costs is very uncertain. In order to progress towards the Lisbon targets, a broad view of sustainability is required, and synergies among the different objectives and the strategies to achieve them have to be exploited.

The European Commission acknowledged the difficulties of putting Europe on a sustainable path. Faced with persisting potentially unsustainable trends, such as continuously stronger indications for climate change, the ageing of societies in developed countries, and a widening gap between the rich and the poor in the world, the Commission and the European Council launched in 2004 an extensive review process of the EU sustainability strategy. The Renewed EU Sustainable Development Strategy (EU SDS) was adopted by heads of state and governments at the European Council in June 2006. Building on the Gothenburg Strategy of 2001, this strategy promises a comprehensive approach to help the EU more effectively live up to its long-standing commitment to meet the challenges of sustainable development.

The objective of this chapter is to explore a potentially successful strategy to design sustainability policies, taking into account broader sustainability aspects and preconditions required to pave the way for sustainability policies appropriately. For this purpose, Section 2.2 briefly discusses the reasons that justify the increased focus on sustainability. Section 2.3 outlines the key elements that a sustainability policy should incorporate. Section 2.4 verifies how the recent Renewed EU Strategy takes these elements into account. Section 2.5 concludes.

2.2   WHY DO WE NEED MORE SUSTAINABILITY?

During recent years, the notion of sustainability has become more prevalent in public and political discussions and in scientific research. The reason might be the perceived increasingly unsustainable situation in the industrialised countries. The continuous growth of these countries has led to serious environmental problems, including biodiversity loss, desertification, an increase in overall pollution[2] and in transboundary problems as well as a higher frequency of environmental disasters such as droughts, storms and floods. One well-known example of this unsustainable development regards climate change: the continued global rise in carbon dioxide emissions is likely to result in an increase in global temperatures in the 21st century. This phenomenon could induce adverse impacts including deterioration with respect to health as well as floods, and damage to slowly adapting ecosystems. Apart from the environmental problems, there are worrying trends regarding the ageing of societies in developed countries and a widening gap between the rich and the poor in the world. These trends suggest that the developing programme of the rich countries should not serve as a simple template for helping the developing world to reach a higher living standard. Rather, more sustainable strategies need to be discovered which enable a higher development in these countries without encountering the same problems as the industrialised world.

However, development has also brought huge achievements apart from the overall increase in per capita income: a strong decrease in infant mortality and in adult illiteracy. The industrialised countries have achieved a level of per capita consumption and prosperity higher than at any time before in history. A further continuation of this upward trend, and a successful move of developing countries in the same direction, automatically implies higher consumer expenditures. A comparison between the actual and the past standard of living suggests that investments in research, education and capital goods indeed induce a higher real living standard of the follow-up generation, and as such, it provides a powerful argument in favour of the continuation of the current growth path. The argument is also supported by early growth theories, which demonstrate that a monotonic increase in the standard of living is possible as long as the interest rates exceed the population growth rate (Arrow et al., 2002). More recent analysis of the role of technological change provided similar insights. Technological change can induce increases in outputs without the need of increasing productive inputs. Furthermore, technological knowledge, research and development (R&D) efforts and learning-by-doing (LBD) embody public-goods aspects, increasing returns and spillover effects. These insights helped to establish an even more optimistic outlook. Various observed trends support the optimistic view. One example is the overall increase in energy efficiency. Another example is the series of resources for which scarcities were foreseen many times, while these have not yet occurred.

Nevertheless, the continued growth clearly puts pressure on the environment and its fixed factors, and therefore, the fall in wealth could just be a matter of time. In both industrialised countries and the developing world some common 'sense of environmental urgency' is emerging. It becomes clear that the development programme of the industrialised world cannot be copied one-to-one to developing countries. Developing countries already suffer a number of serious problems, such as extreme poverty and related inequality conflicts. In the future, they might also be the most affected by climate change. Various of these problems may be aggravated if the developing countries copy the development path taken by the currently rich countries. As noted by William Easterly:

> the evidence that life gets better during growth is surprisingly uneven, while the cross-country relationship between income and diverse indicators of the quality of life remains strong. (Easterly, 1999, p. 26)

Therefore – although economic growth is without any doubt the key to improving the quality of life in developing countries – solutions to combat poverty must involve elements complementary to economic growth. Also, industrialised countries recognise the 'sense of urgency'. Recent happiness research demonstrates that aggregate economic growth does not necessarily lead to more happiness. People feel vulnerable, and security has become more important in the industrialised world.

2.3   CRUCIAL ASPECTS ON THE WAY TO SUSTAINABLE ECONOMIC STRUCTURES

Where the environment is concerned, current trends suggest that the developed world currently lives beyond its means. In order to guarantee a world that allows future generations to meet their own needs in an unconstrained way, the challenge is to develop structures for sustainability. The analysis has to be careful since – although it is generally accepted as important – there are many difficulties related to the concept of sustainability.

After the Brundtland Report (WCED, 1987), a variety of definitions of sustainability concepts have appeared.[3] However, these definitions are diverse and sometimes induce criticisms.[4] The core ethic of intergenerational equity, underlying most sustainability concepts, requires that future generations are entitled to at least as high a welfare as the present generation. The specification of welfare poses a major challenge: it comprises various aspects beyond per capita consumption of marketed goods and services, more into the broader concepts of 'needs' and 'quality of life'. A common definition of sustainability, according to which welfare of future generations should not be less than the welfare of the current generation ('utility should not decline'), only requires that overall welfare remains non-decreasing, but the trade-offs between various aspects of life or utility components are intrinsically difficult. The provision of equal welfare to future generations can also be framed as a sharing of the resources with future generations. These resources are traditionally viewed as 'a common heritage of mankind to which every generation should have the same right of access' (Asheim et al., 2001, p. 3), but for many resources, it is not obvious what the sharing between generations in practice means.

As a consequence of these and a number of other problems, one strand of literature has tried to specify sustainability accurately, claiming that the use of a sustainability concept must be coupled to a detailed definition and a clear specification of the geographical and temporal contexts in order to avoid misunderstanding and confusion. At the same time, a second strand of research has preferred 'to allow a meaning of sustainability to emerge from … examples or general context' (Pezzey and Toman, 2002), saying that due to the different approaches it is difficult to combine the notions of economic, environmental (or ecological) and social sustainability into one integrated, common sustainability concept. More generally, Stavins et al. (2002) suggest that the notion of sustainability can be better understood and thus addressed by breaking it into two components, dynamic efficiency and intergenerational equity. This argument is in particular true for an economic perspective: in order to achieve dynamic efficiency, the total welfare needs to be maximised while it is at the same time essential that this maximised total welfare does not decrease over time, taking thus intergenerational equity into account. Stavins et al. (2002) thus define sustainability in economic terms:

> an economy is sustainable if and only if it is dynamically efficient and the resulting stream of maximised total welfare functions is non-declining over time. (Stavins et al., 2002, p. 4)[5]

This chapter will not contribute to the already vast literature on the strengths and weaknesses of sustainability definitions, but wants to explore changes in the economic structures and the policy settings that are able to support sustainability and economic welfare in the long run without creating burdens on social, economic and environmental resources. We can now move to the elements that can bring these economic and policy-related structures around: a focus on the contribution of both flows and stocks to welfare, on institutional settings and technological change, as well as on multiple benefits of integrated policies.[6]

A Broader View of Welfare

Welfare as measured by gross domestic product (GDP) focuses on economic flows: streams of paid commodities and services. In contrast to conventional flow-oriented paradigms, sustainable development emphasises the interaction of stocks and flows in providing economic welfare. To a large extent, material flows (such as energy) can be substituted by services provided by stocks (such as improved thermal stock of buildings).[7] The flow–stock ratios represent an aspect of the economic structure. Given the empirical evidence of widely dispersed flow–stock ratios (such as energy intensities), overall material use can be substantially reduced by following best practice examples, setting guidelines for these flow–stock relationships that are compatible with sustainability criteria. But economic structures can adjust only slowly. Shifting from existing structures to those that are closer to sustainability criteria has a major impact on the existing capital stocks.

The concept of welfare therefore needs to be seen from a broader viewpoint than is traditionally applied in the economic, environmental or social sciences, in order appropriately to reflect the priorities towards a more sustainable future. Given problems with respect to the specification of welfare, measures of welfare need to be designed that are compatible with the above-mentioned sustainability aspects and basic requirements for sustainability.[8]

More Focus on the Institutional Setting

Institutions and institutional design play a crucial role in guaranteeing a satisfactory performance of the economy. In particular, given the great uncertainties, effective institutions for implementing credible compliance and enforcement systems are needed in order to put policies into force and to maintain the two key factors that are decisive in minimising expected regrets, namely robustness and flexibility (Schmalensee, 1996).

Robust institutional mechanisms are especially important in the area of sustainability policy, due to the fact that complex problems are involved, ranging from issues related to economic growth and general development needs, to both local and global environmental degradation. These issues have a variety of common drivers and causes and are often characterised by public good characteristics and free-riding incentives as well as other market failures. In addition, the situation is aggravated by the lack of a supranational authority able to enforce global sustainability policies. The different areas are usually treated by different institutional bodies, rendering a comprehensive approach difficult.[9]

More Focus on Technological Change

There is overwhelming evidence that technological change is not an exogenous phenomenon but driven by corporate investments in research and development, spillovers from these activities, and by learning processes. Technical progress is in general considered an important force for improving competitiveness and stimulating new opportunities for economic growth.[10] Efficiency improvements induced by technological progress appear to play a key role in the transition towards sustainability.[11] The advance of technology is supposed to enable us to maintain the present level of welfare, or living standard, or even increase it, while at the same time reducing the employment of resources. Economic policy is increasingly searching for options to stimulate technological progress in a desired direction. Special attention shall therefore be given to policies that stimulate technological change aimed at inducing sustainable structures.

At the same time, technological progress need not only be a blessing. There are also path-dependence, lock-in phenomena and rebound effects of technological progress on sustainable development that need to be taken into account, since technological improvements can evoke behavioural and strategic responses[12] (Arthur, 1989; Binswanger, 2001; Grubb et al., 1995; Ha-Duong et al., 1997).[13]

Paying More Attention to the Benefits

For a long time the debate in environmental policy has focused on the cost-effectiveness of potential measures and policies. This is in particular true when environmental policies are framed in terms of short-term policy targets, as policy-makers are primarily interested in the current impact of policies on their economies while benefits will occur in the longer term and thus fall beyond the current policy horizon.

Yet, recently more emphasis is put on the potential side-effects that are induced by environmental policy measures.[14] Within recent years the interest in these so-called 'ancillary' or co-benefits and costs has continually been growing and they gained special attention through the Intergovernmental Panel on Climate Change (IPCC) Third Assessment Report (IPCC, 2001), which focused on side-effects of climate change policy. But, as has been pointed out among others by Davis et al. (2000) and Pearce (2000), the concept of additional policy effects is not unique to climate policy. Notwithstanding the large uncertainties and other difficulties surrounding the assessment of ancillary effects, there is compelling evidence that mitigation policies are indeed accompanied by positive side-effects and that the inclusion of ancillary effects can affect the geographic, sectoral and even technological focus of policy-making by altering the balance of costs and benefits of specific measures.[15]

Though the magnitude of side-effects that has been specified in various case studies differs substantially due to different methodologies, data restrictions and country-specific characteristics, nevertheless the early impression achieved by Ekins (1996) seems most often confirmed by the recent studies; ancillary benefits appear to be 'a significant fraction of, or even larger than the mitigation costs', whereas the ancillary costs are likely to have a smaller scale (Davis et al., 2000). A challenging question concerns the policy implications of side-effects. If it is true that environmental policy mostly has additional benefits, benefits inclusion could change the way in which this policy is viewed. Rather than perceiving environmental policy as a cost, it may be understood as a policy with multiple benefits, some in the shorter term, others in the longer term.

This section has provided a tentative overview on issues that are important for policies directed to sustainable structures. Let us attempt to provide some conclusions and lessons from this discussion for concrete policy design:

- The transition to more sustainable economic structures requires a search for incentive strategies that provide a supportive environment for directed technological change and substitution of services through the consumption of flows by services provided through stocks.
- Policy instruments should be evaluated, including the additional impacts that they have, in order to verify whether the chosen policy approach remains appropriate in the light of the more comprehensive understanding of activities. As part of this, a broader perspective on welfare needs to be taken.

Combining a mixture of incentive strategies as mentioned above could move the economy closer towards a long-term approach to key problems such as poverty, inequality, conflict and environmental degradation, accounting for the interactions between economic, social and environmental problems at local, national and global levels. This implies at the same time that attention needs to be paid to a portfolio of issues when designing sustainability policies. The broader context of sustainable development has to be taken into account, acknowledging the strong linkages between sustainability issues and a number of specific environmental, economic and social aspects.

The next section verifies whether recent policy-making lives up to these expectations.

2.4   AN OVERVIEW AND DISCUSSION OF THE RECENT RENEWED EU SDS

The overall motivation of the Renewed EU SDS appears to recognize the sense of urgency described above (Council of the European Union, 2006, p. 2). Indeed, the main motivation to strengthen the EU sustainable development strategy launched in 2001 is the fact that Europe continues to face unsustainable trends, ranging from climate change to the ageing of societies, aggravated by new challenges arising from the EU enlargement, terrorist threats and violence, and further globalisation and changes in the EU and world economies. This situation made clear that the initial EU sustainability strategy was not strong enough to cope with the changed circumstances. As a consequence, the revised strategy was proposed, claiming to be more coherent with a stronger focus, a clearer division of responsibilities, a better integration of the international dimension and more effective implementation and monitoring. Let us now provide an overview on the overall approach and specific components embodied by the EU SDS.

The overarching objective of the Renewed EU SDS is:

> to identify and develop actions to enable the EU to achieve continuous improvement of quality of life both for current and for future generations, through the creation of sustainable communities able to manage and use resources efficiently and to tap the ecological and social innovation potential of the economy, ensuring prosperity, environmental protection and social cohesion. (Council of the European Union, 2006, p. 3)

Correspondingly, the revised strategy first sets four key objectives capturing the different facets of sustainability:

- environmental protection;
- social equity and cohesion;
- economic prosperity;
- meeting our international responsibilities.

Based on these objectives, the revised strategy outlines a number of policy-guiding principles that cover a wide range of aspects helpful for implementing a sustainability policy. Given this framework, seven key priority challenges to enable a transition to a sustainable path are identified:

- climate change and clean energy;
- sustainable transport;
- sustainable production and consumption;
- conservation and management of natural resources;
- public health;
- social inclusion, demography and migration;
- global poverty and sustainable development challenges.

For these priority areas, which cover the economic, social and environmental components of sustainability with a light bias towards the latter, targets, operational objectives and concrete targets are set. Also, concrete actions are promised, which however in various cases do not appear to be very concrete but instead somewhat suggestive. In addition, some of the priority areas receive more attention than others, as for instance the fifth.

A particular premise of the Renewed EU Strategy is to make use of the synergies of the EU SDS and the Lisbon Strategy for growth and jobs and to integrate sustainability aspects in all, both internal and external, areas of EU policy-making in order to improve all potential synergies and reduce trade-offs. The approach proposed in the EU SDS to improve policy-making is based on two components. First, better regulation is envisaged through the requirement of high-quality impact assessment (IA) of policy proposals and *ex post* assessment of policy impacts as well as public and stakeholder participation. Second, the principle that sustainable development is to be integrated into policy-making at all levels is reinforced for all levels of government, calling also upon business, non-governmental organisations (NGOs) and citizens to become more involved in advancing the sustainability debate. For this purpose, a key role is attributed to communication activities and ways to mobilise actors. Clearly, the Renewed EU Strategy attempts to become as comprehensive as possible, putting sustainable development on the agenda of all policies and all levels of government.

To implement this approach successfully, emphasis is given to cross-cutting policies like education and training as well as research and development. In addition, to facilitate the transition towards a more sustainable path, the Renewed EU Strategy also stresses the key role of financing and making use of the most appropriate economic instruments, with an emphasis on enhancing synergies between the various EU funding channels.

Finally, the EU SDS outlines a strong governance cycle to implement the proposed strategy effectively, which consists of both continuous monitoring and well-defined follow-up activities. In particular, it stipulates that the Commission will produce a progress report on the implementation of the strategy every two years (starting in 2007). This report will form the basis for discussion at the December European Council, which will provide general orientations to the next steps in the implementation of the EU sustainability strategy. The monitoring approach suggested by the EU SDS draws strongly on a comprehensive set of sustainable development indicators (SDIs), including the EUROSTAT SD Monitoring Report, and is supposed to take the latest scientific evidence as well as developments in relation to key EU activities into account.

2.5   SOME POLICY INSIGHTS FOR A SUCCESSFUL TRANSITION TOWARDS A SUSTAINABLE FUTURE BASED ON RECENT EU EXPERIENCES

The meaning of sustainable development is far from being fully agreed upon either in a political or in an economic perspective, but the objective of sustainable development appears to be unquestioned worldwide, and consensus seems to be emerging on a few basic aspects that need to be taken into consideration in order to ensure a sustainable future setting. Above all, more attention needs to be paid to incentive-based strategies, which create the preconditions for institutions capable of providing guidance for sustainability policies, stimulate a supportive environment for technological change, and appropriately account for a comprehensive assessment of activities.

This increasing consensus is also evident from the great weight sustainability aspects receive in policy discussions, especially in Europe. Yet, has policy-making really embraced the key aspects that are needed to pave the way for sustainable development? In this chapter, we have tackled this question by taking a closer look at the Renewed EU sustainability strategy. The EU SDS clearly incorporates the main ingredients for a successful transition towards sustainability, as emerges from the following brief assessment:

- The EU SDS acknowledges the need to approach welfare from a broader perspective, as is shown through the emphasis on a wide set of sustainability indicators, which are used for monitoring purposes but also continuously updated, further developed and reviewed.
- The EU SDS also pays attention to the integration of sustainable development in a broader context, acknowledging the strong linkages

between sustainability issues and a number of specific environmental, economic and social aspects and aiming therefore for a truly integrated approach that makes use of the synergies between a portfolio of different areas. The strategy of aligning policies in the three specific fields (that is, economic, environmental and social) with the overall objective of sustainable development seems to be a promising way of improving the long-term performance of each specific area, as well as of their implications in terms of sustainability impacts.[16] The EU SDS endorses this approach, and through it aims to spread the notion of sustainability as far as possible. The EU SDS acknowledges the broader challenge of implementing sustainable development, aiming for sustainability to become a guideline not only for the larger political and economic decisions but also for the everyday decisions by the citizens. Behavioural changes are therefore a major issue, and a number of communication strategies to mobilise actors at all global, national and local levels are envisaged.

- Given the difficult changes needed to bring about sustainable development, the EU SDS recognises that it is important as a first step to grasp the low-hanging fruit. Sustainability policies may appear easier if the multiple benefits of policies and measures are appropriately taken into account, and the EU strategy promotes this insight.

- Throughout all areas, particularly in the context of its priority challenges, the EU SDS emphasises the role of technical change as a means to stimulate an endogenous transition to sustainability. For this purpose, emphasis is also given to education and training as well as to research and development, with the specific objective of further developing the positive role of technology to enable so-called 'smart' growth patterns.

- Finally, a strong signal is given by the EU SDS to implement an effective governance circle, ensuring both appropriate monitoring and follow-up activities to reinforce the long-term intentions of this policy. To facilitate the strategy's implementation, a range of policy instruments is proposed, including various funding channels and economic instruments.[17]

Notwithstanding the generally positive framework of the EU SDS, the real actions envisaged appear to be insufficient to enable the transition to sustainability in the different key areas. Often, actions do not reach beyond recommendations, which makes it difficult to foresee the real impact of the strategy on the key challenges. Related to this limitation, few details on compliance are provided. Finally, the important role of uncertainty in the whole sustainability debate seems to be under-represented. More focus on the identification and the specific design of effective incentive strategies that implement all the aspects sustained by the EU SDS could represent the missing piece to bring Europe definitively on the path towards sustainability.

The European way of designing sustainability policies thus highlights the difficulties one has to cope with when actually implementing a concept as complex as sustainable development. But it also demonstrates the progress that policy-making has made over the last three decades to understand comprehensively the vision of sustainability. It therefore is a step in the right direction, and the experiences from this experiment will help policy design to better address the challenge of bringing about sustainable development.

Despite all difficulties related to the understanding, designing and executing of sustainability policies, a few policy guidelines have emerged that are hardly debated any more: current economic structures should be stimulated towards increasing the productivity of all resources, above all energy resources, by investing heavily into new technologies and human capital. These structures in turn could generate a certain level of welfare with lower flows of products, income and greenhouse gas emissions, thus de-emphasising the conventional measures of economic welfare in favour of a more comprehensive understanding of economic well-being that is valid also for intergenerational comparisons.

NOTES

1. This chapter is part of the research work being carried out by the Climate Change Modelling and Policy Unit at Fondazione Eni Enrico Mattei and draws upon the PhD thesis of the author. The author is grateful to Valentina Bosetti, Carlo Carraro, Reyer Gerlagh and Stefan Scheicher for helpful suggestions and remarks and the participants of the TranSust project for valuable discussions. The usual disclaimer applies.
2. However, one needs to emphasise that the highly developed countries have also made considerable progress in addressing their environmental problems, most evident by the sometimes strong reductions in local air pollution.
3. For a survey on different definitions of sustainability concepts see for example Pezzey (2001).
4. One point of the general sustainability concept which is often criticised regards intragenerational equity: sustainability does not take distributional issues explicitly into account.
5. The criterion of dynamic efficiency need not be necessary, nor is it a sufficient condition for achieving sustainability if interpreted in distributional terms. But it is helpful: if an economy fulfils dynamic efficiency, it can in principle be made sustainable in the sense of a non-declining total welfare path by applying appropriate intergenerational transfers. In order to contribute to the solution of the challenges posed by sustainability it may therefore be better for economists to use their economies' comparative advantages and focus on dynamic efficiency, leaving the final allocation to the political process. For a further discussion of this argument see Stavins et al. (2002).

6. See for example Chichilnisky (1997), Chichilnisky (1998), a collection of research papers in Chichilnisky et al. (1998) and Schleicher (2002) for a survey of critical aspects related to the sustainability paradigm.
7. Economic theory can easily take account of the services provided by stocks as part of welfare, but actual accounting easily neglects or undervalues them.
8. See for example Dasgupta (2002) who suggests the use of 'wealth' as an aggregate measure, based on a comprehensive list of assets including manufactured capital, human capital and natural capital.
9. Amongst others, the case of climate change control highlights that a successful climate policy is strongly dependent on the effective design of institutions which govern the management of this global common (see Barrett, 2002; Carraro, 2001; Carraro and Siniscalco, 1998; Schmalensee, 1996, for a few surveys).
10. Technologies are likely to play a key role in moving the economy towards sustainability. Examples in practice demonstrate that a number of extremely innovative technologies, both production and consumption technologies, are emerging, as can for example be seen in the transport sector. For a more detailed discussion of arguments in the context of technological change see for example a recent survey by Löschel (2002).
11. An excellent survey on the treatment of technological change in economic models of environmental policy is provided by Löschel (2002), who emphasises the key role of technological change, concluding that: 'the direction and extent of technological change proves crucial for the environmental impact of future economic activities' (Löschel, 2002).
12. For example, efficiency improvements induced through technological progress can set an incentive for a higher consumption of resources and energy.
13. Not only does the sequence of historical events influence future possibilities, but various elements, such as investment costs, uncertainty or infrastructure, can also create de facto standards for technology. In addition, efficiency improvements also affect the demand for energy, and therefore the so-called rebound effects can arise: an increase in efficiency can induce a less than proportional decrease in resource use or even a rise in resource use.
14. For an overview on research studies in the context of climate change control see for example OECD (2000) and for a discussion of the main issues arising in this research field see for example Buchner (2001).
15. Nilsson and Huhtala (2000) show for the case of the Swedish environmental target that the obvious gain from international emissions trading almost vanishes if the secondary benefits are taken into account.
16. For example, see Buchner (2007) for the analysis of how sustainable development objectives can be promoted by appropriately designing policies to reduce the risk of climate change.
17. In particular, the objective is to use the 'most appropriate economic instruments ... to promote market transparency and prices that reflect the real economic, social and environmental costs of products and services (getting prices right)' (Löschel, 2002, p. 31). Taxation should be further shifted from labour to resource and energy consumption and/or pollution while a reform of subsidies that have considerable negative effects on the environment and are incompatible with sustainable development is envisaged, with a view to gradually eliminating them. Finally, a closer coordination between member states and the Commission is suggested to enhance complementarities and synergies between various strands of Community and other co-financing mechanisms such as cohesion policy, rural development, Life+, Research and Technological Development (RTD), the Competitiveness and Innovation Programme (CIP) and the European Fisheries Fund (EFF).

REFERENCES

Arrow, K., G. Daily, P. Dasgupta, P. Ehrlich, L. Goulder, G. Heal, S. Levin, K.-G. Mäler, S. Schneider, D. Starrett and B. Walker (2002), 'Are we consuming too much?', Beijer International Institute of Ecological Economics Discussion Paper 151.

Arthur, B. (1989), 'Competing technologies, increasing returns, and lock-in by historical small events', *Economic Journal*, **99**, 116–31.

Asheim, G.B., W. Buchholz and B. Tungodden (2001), 'Justifying sustainability', *Journal of Environmental Economics and Management*, **41**, 252–68.

Barrett, S. (2002), *Environment and Statecraft*, Oxford: Oxford University Press.

Binswanger, M. (2001), 'Technological progress and sustainable development: What about the rebound effect?', *Ecological Economics*, **36**(1), 119–32.

Buchner, B. (2001), 'Ancillary benefits and costs of climate change policies', Fondazione Eni Enrico Mattei.

Buchner, B. (2007), 'CDM – A policy to foster sustainable development?', in M.L. Gullino, I. Musu, C. Clini and Y. Xiaoling (eds), *Sustainable Development and Environmental Protection: Experiences and Case Studies*, New York: Springer.

Carraro, C. (2001), 'Institutional design for managing global commons', presentation at the 4th FEEM-IDEI-INRA Conference on Property Rights, Institutions and Management of Environmental and Natural Resources, Toulouse, 3–4 May.

Carraro, C. and D. Siniscalco (1998), 'International environmental agreements: Incentives and political economy', *European Economic Review*, **42**, 561–72.

Chichilnisky, G. (1997), 'What is sustainable development?', *Land Economics*, **73**(4), 467–91.

Chichilnisky, G. (1998), 'Consumption for human development. Background papers', in *Human Development Report 1998*, New York: UNEP.

Chichilnisky, G., G.M. Heal and A. Vercelli (eds) (1998), *Sustainability: Dynamics and Uncertainty*, Dordrecht: Kluwer Academic Publishers.

Council of the European Union (2006), 'Review of the EU Sustainable development strategy (EU SDS) – Renewed strategy', 10117/06.

Dasgupta, P. (2002), 'Economic development, environmental degradation, and the persistence of deprivation in poor countries', mimeo.

Davis, D., A. Krupnick and G. McGlynn (2000), 'Ancillary benefits and costs of greenhouse gas mitigation: An overview', presented at the expert workshop on Ancillary Benefits and Costs of Greenhouse Gas Mitigation Strategies, Washington, DC, 27–29 March.

Easterly, W. (1999), 'Life during growth', World Bank Working Paper No. 2346.

Ekins, P. (1996), 'The secondary benefits of the CO_2 abatement: How much emission reduction do they justify?', *Ecological Economics*, **16**, 13–24.

European Commission (2001), 'A sustainable Europe for a better world: A European Union strategy for sustainable development', communication from the Commission, COM(2001(264) final.

Grubb, M., T. Chapuis and M. Ha-Duong (1995), 'The economics of changing course: Implications of adaptability and inertia for optimal climate policy', *Energy Policy*, **23**(4/5), 417–31.

Ha-Duong, M., M. Grubb and J.-C. Hourcade (1997), 'Influence of socio-economic inertia and uncertainty on optimal CO_2 emission abatement', *Nature*, **390**, 270–73.

IPCC (Intergovernmental Panel on Climate Change) (2001), *Climate Change 2001: Mitigation*, Cambridge: Cambridge University Press.

Löschel, A. (2002), 'Technological change in economic models of environmental policy: A survey', FEEM Working Paper 04.02.

Nilsson, C. and A. Huhtala (2000), 'Is CO_2 trading always beneficial? A CGE-model analysis on secondary environmental benefits', Working Paper No. 75, The National Institute of Economic Research, Stockholm.

OECD (2000), 'Ancillary benefits and costs of greenhouse gas mitigation', presented at the expert workshop on Ancillary Benefits and Costs of Greenhouse Gas Mitigation Strategies, Washington, DC, 27–29 March.

Pearce, D. (2000), 'Policy frameworks for the ancillary benefits of climate change policy', presented at the expert workshop on Ancillary Benefits and Costs of Greenhouse Gas Mitigation Strategies, Washington, DC, 27–29 March.

Pezzey, J.C.V. (2001), 'Sustainability policy and environmental policy', Australian National University.

Pezzey, J. and M. Toman (2002), 'Making sense of "sustainability"', Issue Brief 02–25, Washington, DC: Resources for the Future.

Schleicher, S.P. (2002), 'On the economics of climate change and the climate change of economics', in K.W. Steininger and H. Weck-Hannemann (eds), *Global Environmental Change in Alpine Regions*, Cheltenham, UK and Northampton, MA, USA: Edward Elgar, pp. 41–52.

Schmalensee, R. (1996), 'Greenhouse policy architectures and institutions', MIT Report No. 13, MIT Joint Program on the Science and Policy of Climate Change.

Stavins, R.N., A.F. Wagner and G. Wagner (2002), 'Interpreting sustainability in economic terms: Dynamic efficiency plus intergenerational equity', Harvard University.

WCED (World Commission on Environment and Development, The Brundtland Commission) (1987), *Our Common Future*, Oxford: Oxford University Press.

3. An American View of Sustainability

Ray Kopp

3.1 INTRODUCTION

Does the concept of sustainable development as originally defined by Brundtland et al. (WCED, 1987) and embodied in the EU Sustainable Development Strategy (Council of the European Union, 2006) play a central role in American public policy?[1] How does the American view of sustainability compare to the European view? Do Americans use the concept as a guiding principle in the development of public policy beyond issues of the environment and natural resources? Unfortunately, I cannot hope to provide definitive answers to these questions in this brief chapter, but I will share my opinions and let the reader decide whether they contain the elements of credible answers.

If opinions are to be the substance of this chapter, then readers should be afforded the means to assess the author. I am an economist and I have spent my entire research career (30-plus years) focused on environment and natural resource issues and have done so at a single research institution whose sole mission is to improve policy-making with respect to those issues. That American institution, Resources for the Future (RFF), was created in 1952, some 35 years before the introduction of the sustainability concept credited to Brundtland.

Over the past five decades, RFF researchers have struggled with the very same issues now associated with sustainable development. My opinions are based on my research, those of my colleagues at RFF, and the wider community of scholars working in both applied welfare economics and environmental and resource economics. I have long focused my research in order to contribute to the public policy development process. Currently, I am examining how sustainability has affected the character of American public policy with respect to environment and natural resource issues.

3.2 SUSTAINABLE DEVELOPMENT AND ITS ROLE IN AMERICAN PUBLIC POLICY

Is sustainable development a center-stage concept in American public policy? The simple answer to this question is no – at least at the present time. Those Americans familiar with it view it as an economic concept that balances actions today with impacts tomorrow. Such a view recognizes an explicit trade-off among generations. While I believe the concept is properly understood in America, it is not deployed broadly as it seems to be in the European Union (EU). For example, it does not play a role in non-discrimination policies affecting race, age and gender as it might in the EU. The American view is that these policies assign 'rights', barring any notion of economic trade-off, and therefore are distinct from policies where trade-offs are possible. Thus, if sustainability is based on some notion of balancing, it is not immediately relevant in the United States for these issues of rights.

Trade-offs are considered in the area of the environment and natural resources and it is here where one might expect to find the concept of sustainability. Consider for example the current debate in the US Congress regarding climate change. While the United States has not signed on to the Kyoto Protocol and accepted legally binding emissions targets, it is in the process of developing domestic legislation that will impose mandatory limits on greenhouse gas (GHG) emissions. At the current time (winter 2008) the leading legislative proposal is that of Senators Lieberman and Warner (S. 2191). The legislation is broad and economy-wide, very long-term, specifying emissions targets out to 2050, would require deep cuts in emissions, and is premised on the belief that costs incurred now are necessary to protect the well-being of future generations. In short, it sounds very much like a policy that could be based on the concepts of sustainable development. Yet there is no mention of the phrase 'sustainable development' in the legislation. The term 'sustainable' is used in reference to renewable energy technologies, referring to this group of electricity generation technologies as 'sustainable energy', but the term is used solely as an adjective not as a meaningful concept.

It is perhaps possible to argue that the Lieberman and Warner legislation is really sustainable development policy, just not recognized as such, but in a sense that is my point. This potentially landmark legislation is not viewed by its authors, nor I would argue by other legislators, as sustainable development policy. Rather, the legislation is viewed as a logical extension of traditional US environmental regulations, dating to the Clean Air Act of the 1970s and the important 1990 Amendments to the Act.

One may argue that legislation is not the best place to look for the presence of sustainable development as a paradigm of public policy development. Rather, one should look to the manner in which broad policy goals contained in legislation are turned into on-the-ground actions and to the guidance provided Executive Branch agencies as they conduct analysis of regulatory options.

The US Environmental Protection Agency (EPA) provides detailed guidance for the analysis of environmental regulation, specifying both the metric by which the performance of regulations is to be measured as well as the techniques used to perform the measurements.[2] Both Executive Orders and statutes require adherence to this guidance by the EPA in its continuing analysis of regulations under its jurisdiction.

The EPA Guidelines are over 200 pages long and not once is the concept of sustainable development or sustainability mentioned.[3] It seems only reasonable to conclude that as a paradigm for the development or implementation of regulatory policy with respect to the environment, the concept of sustainable development has not had the same impact in the United States as it has had in the EU. Moreover, it seems unlikely that it will displace the existing US paradigms of cost–benefit analysis and cost-effectiveness any time soon.

If sustainable development is not an integral part of US policy-making, does the concept resonate with Americans at all? In this case I believe the answer is yes. The popularized notion of sustainability has increased awareness among policy-makers, private business and the general public of environmental and natural resource problems that are intertemporal and importantly intergenerational. However, I do not believe American policy-makers are convinced (at least not today) that a new paradigm is required to deal properly with these issues.

3.3   SUSTAINABLE DEVELOPMENT AND WELFARE ECONOMICS

The formulation of American public policy with respect to the environment and natural resources has been heavily influenced by economic thinking,[4] which is grounded in a century of theoretical development and empirical application of welfare economics. In terms of welfare theory, I do not believe it is unfair to say that there is nothing new in the idea of sustainable development. Indeed, one can argue that the concept of sustainability is already embodied in existing welfare theory,[5] particularly when sustainability is confined to environmental and natural resource issues. Once sustainability is expanded to include 'economic, social and environmental renewal' as noted by Buchner (Chapter 2 in this book), the concept steps away from economics and toward politics where the role played by welfare economics fades rapidly. In all that follows, I address what one might term 'narrow' sustainability to refer to only those issues that arise with the services provided by the environment and natural resources.

From an American perspective, concerns raised by sustainability for the most part reflect underlying market failures. As I explain below, these failures are well known at all levels of US policy-making. To the extent that the issues raised by sustainable development arise because of market failures, I hope to convince the reader that US policy-making does address those issues, but it does not use the term 'sustainability' to describe its actions.

Sustainability is often given operational meaning by equating it to intergenerational equity, or non-decreasing intergenerational welfare over time (Pezzy, 1992). In Chapter 1 of this book, Tol goes further and discusses weak and strong sustainability citing Ayres et al. (2001). Ayers et al. consider weak sustainability to imply perfect substitution between natural and manufactured capital, although it seems the less restrictive assumption of some substitution is all that is required. Ayres et al. state that strong sustainability implies some minimum amount of natural capital as an essential input for the production of human welfare which therefore cannot be completely substituted for by manufactured capital, and that 'very strong' sustainability implies no possible substitution of manufactured capital for natural capital.[6]

If 'very strong' sustainability is the concept at issue which welfare economics has little to say. I tend to agree with Tol that the underpinnings of strong sustainability may be entirely ethical in nature and 'rights' based, in which case economic analysis of any type has limited applicability. Very strong sustainability may have adherents in the United States, but few can be found in the US Congress.

This leaves us with weak and strong sustainability which I view on a continuum defined by the degree to which one can substitute manufactured capital for natural capital, both in the production of goods and services (and here I include non-priced as well as priced goods and services) and in the direct production of utility.[7] While at some ratios of manufactured capital to natural capital there is a good deal of substitution, it is a straightforward neoclassical result that the degree of substitution (in both production and consumption) falls as that ratio grows. This is the weak form of sustainability. At extreme input ratios, some component of the natural capital vector becomes 'limitational' in either production of consumption.[8] This is the strong form of sustainability.

Assume that one element of the natural capital vector is crude petroleum. As one substitutes increasing amounts of manufactured capital for crude petroleum its marginal product rises along with its market price. The rising price has three effects: the increasing petroleum price causes conservation of its use (standard demand effect); the higher price incentivizes substitution away from petroleum (the substitution effect); and the higher prices fosters new research and development directed toward the development of new substitutes (technical change). It matters little whether at some point crude petroleum becomes limitational given current techniques of production. A competitive market for crude petroleum will ensure the price rises enough to foster the optimal amount of conservation and innovation long before the input becomes limitational or exhausted.[9]

The example above refers to an exhaustible natural resource that trades on a reasonably competitive market where price can signal scarcity. If such markets exist, and one believes in markets and the ingenuity of humans, then sustainability with respect to these natural resources is not an issue.[10] However, suppose we are talking about natural resources and the services they provide that are not traded on markets and where no price exits.[11] Under such circumstances, sustainability is a very real problem, but one well recognized by welfare economics as a classic market failure, and importantly, equally well recognized by policy-makers.

The problems for optimal resource allocation posed by non-market environmental goods and services have been the topic of intense study by environmental and resource economists worldwide for decades. The academic journals are full of studies that describe the theoretical foundations for the economic valuation of non-market goods and the empirical application of that theory.[12] The widely used US Environmental Protection Agency's guidance document that describes procedures for conducting cost–benefit analyses of environmental and natural resource policy provides detailed instructions for the design and execution of non-market valuation studies (US Environmental Protection Agency, 2000). Similarly, US government guidance for the assessment of damage to natural resources due to releases of hazardous substances also contains detailed instructions with respect to non-market valuation studies.[13]

3.4   MARKET FAILURE AND IMPENDING US CLIMATE POLICY

The idea that problems of narrowly defined sustainability are largely due to market failures, most importantly the lack of market prices needed to signal impending scarcity of non-renewable resources and the degradation of the quality and quantity of services provided by the environment, is seemingly well accepted among economists on the American side of the Atlantic.[14] My guess is that the same is true in the EU.

At the present time (summer of 2009), the US Congress is debating a sweeping new piece of legislation that will impose strict limits on the emissions of GHGs for at least the next 40 years.[15] It is hard to know how the political machinations will play out, but what does seem clear is the political will to enact legislation to curb emissions. While one cannot know whether this US legislation will match the level of effort the EU will undertake to limit its emissions post-2012, the tone and character of the two debates seem on a par. What is perhaps different is the perceived role of sustainability in the formulation of the two future policies.

To be sure, sustainability is a prominent component of the EU design, but as I have previously stated, sustainability as a paradigm for policy formulation is non-existent in the US legislation. This is not to say that the issues posed by sustainable development are ignored in the United States. Rather, the issues are recognized and dealt with, using tools and paradigms that are familiar to US policy-makers, and have proven to be extremely effective in the past. These are tools that focus on market failures, and Lieberman and Warner (S. 2191) is a perfect example of their application.

The Lieberman and Warner bill is complex and has many distinct features; however the two most important components address the two greatest failures of the market when it comes to GHG emissions – the absence of a price on emissions and the failure of private markets to incentivize the optimal amount of research and development. The legislation corrects the pricing failure with an economywide cap-and-trade program covering all six GHGs. If implemented as currently configured, about 80 percent of all US GHGs would be captured by the program and priced. A large portion of the allowances established by the cap would be auctioned and those revenues used to address the second market failure by providing a stable source of funds for a long-term and very large-scale research and development effort aimed at new low carbon technologies.[16]

One aspect of the legislation that does not directly rely on a welfare-theoretic market failure analysis is the choice of emissions reduction target. That is, no explicit and rigorous comparison of benefits and costs has been undertaken in setting the target. Given the enormous uncertainty that surrounds the quantification and economic valuation of climate change impacts, this is understandable. What will drive the final targets that are passed into legislation will be some political determination of the maximum willingness-to-pay by the current generation (or two) for a very uncertain payoff to future generations.

Certainly, each American's willingness-to-pay will involve ethical considerations regarding the proper environment to pass on to future generations. Consequently, a bit of the sustainability concept will slip unnoticed into the political calculus.

NOTES

1. Like other authors in this volume, I refer to the 'Brundtland Commission' for a workable definition of sustainability where sustainable development is 'development that meets the needs of the present without compromising the ability of future generations to meet their own needs'.

2. US Environmental Protection Agency (2000). The preface to the guidance states in part: 'The Guidelines for Preparing Economic Analyses (or EA Guidelines) is part of a continuing effort by the EPA to develop improved guidance on the preparation and use of sound science in support of the decision making process. The EA Guidelines provide guidance on analyzing the benefits, costs, and economic impacts of regulations and policies. The EA Guidelines have been updated to keep pace with the evolving emphases policy makers place on different economic and social concerns affected by environmental policies. ... An economic analysis can describe the implications of policy alternatives not just for economic efficiency, but also for the magnitude and distribution of an array of impacts'.

3. In fact, one sees a good deal more attention paid to the concept of sustainability within the business community than one sees within the US Congress or the halls of the nation's environmental agency. See, for example, the non-governmental organization, Business for Social Responsibility, whose stated mission is to 'help its member companies integrate sustainability into business strategy and operations'. Members are drawn from a wide range of business sectors and include companies as diverse as Coca-Cola, ExxonMobil, Ford and Wal-Mart.

4. See US Environmental Protection Agency (2000) and Office of Management and Budget (2003).

5. This is not meant to be taken in a derogatory manner, quite the opposite. To the extent that sustainability is a popularized and perhaps generalized articulation of welfare theory, it can properly lay claim to internal theoretical consistency. Such consistency is vital if one is to build credible empirical policy models resting on the sustainability concept. Without a sound theoretical structure assuring internal consistency, these models possess little value for policy-makers.

6. Robert Solow's vision of substitution and sustainability is instructive: 'It is of the essence that production cannot take place without some use of natural resources. But I shall also assume that it is always possible to substitute greater inputs of labor, reproducible capital, and renewable resources for smaller direct inputs of the fixed resource. Substitution can take place on reasonable terms, although we can agree that it gets more and more costly as the process of substitution goes on. Without this minimal degree of optimism, the conclusion might be that this economy is like a watch that can be wound only once: it has only a finite number of ticks, after which it stops. In that case, there is no point in talking about sustainability, because it is ruled out by assumption; the only choice is between a short happy life and a longer unhappy one' (Solow, 1992).

7. In the first case, I am referencing substitution possibilities in production functions, while in the second, I am referencing substitution within utility functions. The fact that natural capital enters utility functions is now a standard assumption in modern welfare theory and its empirical applications. The days when welfare depended only on the consumption of private market goods is long gone – at least since Krutilla (1967).

8. An element of the natural capital vector is limitational if an increase in its quantity (or quality) is a necessary, but not sufficient, condition for an increase in output or utility (Ferguson, 1969; Georgescu-Roegen, 1935).

9. This chain of economic reactions to rising price (and scarcity) of natural resources has been known and documented for more that half a century. Indeed, RFF was established in 1952 for the sole purpose of researching this chain of economic responses. See President's Materials Policy Commission (1952), the first major study of the chain of economic reactions.

10. Recall that this chapter describes a practical American view, recognizing that theoretically it is possible to have an unsustainable path without market failure.

11. In the late 1960s, researchers at RFF became increasingly worried about a class of natural assets that did not trade in markets – clean air and water are obvious examples. In these

cases, the market could not signal scarcity and therefore overuse and depletion of these resources could occur and the welfare of future generations be impaired. At the time, this was RFF's main concern about sustainability. RFF researchers were focused on two aspects of the problem that emanated from the lack of private markets. First, since these resources had no market price they could not be valued in a proper cost–benefit analysis, which meant that they were de facto valued at zero and ignored (Krutilla, 1967). Second, the lack of prices meant that there was no mechanism to signal scarcity and therefore no way for the economy to value the consumption of these resources. This in turn meant the power of markets could not be used to ration use and stimulate the development of new alternatives. To do so would require direct government regulation of natural resource use and with that regulation, the fear that without measures of value or prices the regulation could be highly inefficient.

12. The purpose of this research is to provide estimates of value to be used in lieu of market prices in the development of public policy concerning non-market environmental goods and services.

13. This guidance is embodied in US federal regulations for the conduct of natural resource damages assessments under the Comprehensive Environmental Response and Compensation and Liability Act (the 'Superfund' law). The guidelines are contained in US Government (1986).

14. See, for example, the comment of Nobel Laureate Robert Solow (1992).

15. See Lieberman and Warner (S. 2191).

16. Other sections of the legislation deal with additional market failures due to principal–agent problems and information asymmetries.

REFERENCES

Ayres, R.U., J.C.J.M. van den Bergh and J.M. Gowdy (2001), 'Strong versus Weak Sustainability: Economics, Natural Sciences, and "Consilience"', *Environmental Ethics*, **23**(2), 155–68.

Council of the European Union (2006), 'Review of the EU sustainable development strategy (EU SDS) – Renewed strategy', 10117/06.

Ferguson, C.E. (1969), *The Neoclassical Theory of Production and Distribution*, London: Cambridge University Press.

Georgescu-Roegen, N. (1935), 'Fixed coefficients of production and the marginal productivity theory', *Review of Economic Studies*, **2**, 40–49.

Krutilla, J.V. (1967), 'Conversation Reconsidered', *American Economic Review*, **47**, 777–86.

Office of Management and Budget (2003), 'Circular A-4: Regulatory analysis'.

Pezzy, J. (1992), 'Sustainable development concepts: An economic analysis', World Bank Environment Paper, Washington, DC: World Bank.

President's Materials Policy Commission (1952), 'Resources for Freedom'.

Solow, R. (1992), 'An almost practical step toward sustainability', invited lecture on the occasion of the fortieth anniversary of Resources for the Future, Washington, DC.

US Environmental Protection Agency (2000), 'Guidelines for preparing economic analyses', Office of the Administrator.

US Government (1986), 'US Government code of federal regulations', 43 CFR Part 11, Natural Resource Damage Assessments.

WCED (World Commission on Environment and Development, The Brundtland Commission) (1987), *Our Common Future*, Oxford: Oxford University Press.

PART II

Issues in Modelling Sustainability

4. Implementing the EU Sustainability Indicators[1]

Christoph Böhringer and Andreas Löschel

4.1 INTRODUCTION

In 1987, the report of the World Commission on Environment and Development (WCED or Brundtland Commission) defined sustainable development (hereafter: SD) as:

> development that meets the needs of the present without compromising the ability of future generations to meet their own needs. (WCED, 1987)

In June 1992, the Rio Earth Summit concluded that:

> the right to development must be fulfilled so as to equitably meet developmental and environmental needs of present and future generations. (UNCED, 1992a, Principle 3)

SD has meanwhile become one of the most prominent catchwords on the world's policy agenda. Nearly all governments and multinational firms have committed themselves to the overall concept of SD.

The ubiquity of SD as a yardstick for human activities is reflected in the growing importance of Sustainability Impact Assessment (hereafter: SIA) of governmental policies. Initially, the assessment of SD impacts concentrated on trade policy reforms (see, for example, Kirkpatrick and Lee, 1999, for the SIA of the World Trade Organization's Millennium Round proposal). More recently, SIA has been extended to other policy areas. Taking a lead role, the European Union (EU) meanwhile requires:

> careful assessment of the full effects of [any larger] policy proposal ... [that] must include estimates of its economic, environmental and societal inputs inside and outside the EU. (EC, 2001)

The argument behind this is that SIA can improve the SD coherence of policy initiatives across various areas by identifying spillovers and interlinkages.

However, SD, which is not just about the environment but also about the economy and society, has proven to be hard to define and rather susceptible to ambiguities. One reason for this is that SD explicitly incorporates a (normative) equity dimension, which is 'so hopelessly subjective that it cannot be analyzed scientifically' (Young, 1994). Another reason is that the scope of the concept seems prohibitively comprehensive and therefore too complex to make it operational in concrete practice.

Acknowledging the huge inherent difficulties in coming up with pragmatic approaches to the concept of SD and the need for SIA, the scientific community has focused in a first step on the identification of appropriate indicators. These efforts have included the development of qualitative tools (for example electronic checklists such as IASTAR, see http://iaplus.jrc.es) that can provide useful orientation for policy decision makers.

Yet, qualitative approaches are unable to commensurate different impacts. This constitutes a major shortcoming, since the three dimensions of SD, that is, environmental quality, economic performance (gross efficiency) and equity concerns, are inherently intertwined and subject to trade-offs. Accomplishing one objective frequently means backpedaling on another. Therefore, research activities on SIA increasingly aim at developing the quantitative tools for trade-off analysis along the SD dimensions. One example for this direction is the IQ.Tools project (Indicators and Quantitative Tools for Improving the Process of Sustainability Impact Assessment – see http://www.zew.de) which not only provides an updated guide to SIA indicators but also introduces numerical tools for quantitative impact assessment of policy regulation.[2]

Since economics is the study of trade-offs, there is plenty for economists to contribute in order to make the concept of SD operational. One important contribution of (environmental) economics over the last decade has been the thorough assessment of external costs, in particular for energy transformation and transport activities, as a prerequisite towards 'getting the prices right' (see, for example, EC, 1999; Friedrich and Bickel, 2001). Given external cost estimates, two aspects of SD, namely economic performance (gross efficiency) and environmental quality, can be merged to a comprehensive net efficiency dimension. Furthermore, while economics has little to say on equity per se, the sound economic quantification of distributional effects for different agents and trade-offs between equity and efficiency objectives are a prerequisite for any rational policy debate.

The quantification of trade-offs calls for the use of numerical model techniques in order to assess systematically and rigorously the interference of the many forces that interact in the economy, thereby affecting potential SD indicators. Compared to (stylized) analytical models, the numerical approach facilitates the analysis of complex (non-linear) system interactions and the impact assessment of structural policy changes. In the end, the decisions on how to resolve potential trade-offs must be taken on the basis of societal values and political decisions. However, model-based analysis puts decision-making on an informed basis concerning sustainable development rather than on fuzzy or contradictory hunches.

A major challenge in building quantitative SIA tools is the policy-makers' demand for comprehensive coverage of potentially important policy impacts. SIA tools must identify:

> the chain of significant cause-effect links from the ... [policy] measures ... through to any sustainability impact' and produce 'comparable indicators of the magnitude and dimensions of each sustainability impact. (EC, 2003a)

as an input into policy formulation and implementation. Obviously, quantitative SIA does not only require an adequate reduction of complex real-world relationships but – as a prerequisite – the translation of potentially vague policy proposals into a concrete policy impetus that can be 'processed' within an analytical model.

There is a wide range of quantitative models for assessing the causal chains between a proposed policy change and its potential economic, environmental and social impacts. Models mainly differ with respect to the emphasis placed on: (i) sectoral details versus economy-wide scope; (ii) econometric foundation of functional relationships; and (iii) the richness of behavioral assumptions for economic agents. Referring to criterion (i), there is a widespread distinction between bottom-up sector-level models and top-down macroeconomic models. Referring to criterion (ii), models can be classified as either econometrically estimated when driving equations are based on econometric techniques using mostly time-series data, or as calibrated when parameters of functional forms are simply selected to fit a single empirical observation. Referring to criterion (iii), models may be distinguished between micro-/macro-founded approaches and simple accounting frameworks.

While such taxonomy of models can be useful, it has its limits. For example, the commonly perceived dichotomy between top-down economy-wide models and bottom-up sectoral models can not be traced back to fundamentally different paradigms but rather relates to differences in the level of aggregation, the degree of endogeneity for system variables and the representation of market imperfections. Furthermore, among top-down models there is often an exaggerated divide between econometric demand-driven Keynesian models and computable general equilibrium (CGE) models. Popular arguments against the informational value of CGE models include that these models must be calibrated (and thus lack empirical evidence) and can reflect neither disequilibria (such as unemployment or underutilization of production capacities) nor transitional dynamics. In turn, econometric Keynesian models are often accused of a lack of micro-foundation. These claims ignore substantial developments during the last two decades to overcome such policy-relevant shortcomings.

The use of quantitative models for SIA of policy reforms requires the specification of indicators, instruments and analytical chains. First, both measurable sustainability indices covering the SD concerns of interest and instruments that may promote sustainability in different domains have to be identified. Then, the complete path from the application of the instrument to the impact on the sustainability indicator has to be modeled. Finally, policy explorations have to be carried out and implications on the sustainability indicators have to be assessed.

In general, there is no specific model which fits all requirements for comprehensive SIA, but rather a package of models (or methods) depending on the policy measure or issue to be assessed and the availability of data. The status quo and prospects of CGE models for SIA are assessed in Böhringer and Löschel (2006a). Boulanger and Bréchet (2005) consider six different model types frequently used in socio-economic policy-making and provide a framework to help decision-makers choose the most appropriate one (or a combination of models) by assessing their relative strengths and weaknesses. In the same vein, the TranSust activity which aims at stimulating economic modeling for policy advice on the transition to sustainable economic structures (http://www.transust.org), covers a variety of numerical models (see Schleicher and Hill, 2003). These models mainly differ in the coverage and depth of market representation as well as their assumptions on market design and mechanisms. Yet, they may be all classified as energy–economy–environment (E3) models since they are all concerned with linkages between economic activities, energy transformation and associated environmental impacts.

In this chapter, we investigate the use of energy–economy–environment (E3) models within the TranSust project for measuring the impacts of policy interference on policy-relevant economic, environmental and social (institutional) indicators. We find that operational versions of E3 models have a good coverage of central economic indicators. Environmental indicators such as energy-related emissions with simple direct links to economic activities are widely covered, whereas indicators with a complex natural science background such as water stress or biodiversity loss are hardly represented. Societal indicators stand out for very weak coverage, not least because they are vaguely defined or incommensurable. Our analysis confirms demand for future modeling activities in the field of integrated assessment that link standard E3 models to theme-specific complementary models with environmental and societal focus.

The structure of the chapter is as follows. Section 4.2 addresses the definition of SD indicators as a prerequisite for SIA. We present two highly policy-relevant indicator lists (Eurostat, 2004; EC, 2003b), distinguishing between: (i) indicators that are covered in the TranSust project; (ii) indicators that are in the scope of more or less straightforward extensions of the core models; and (iii) indicators that are rather difficult to address in quantitative analysis. Section 4.3 evaluates to what extent key indicators for SD are currently captured or subject to (feasible) extensions in operational E3 models of the TranSust project. Section 4.4 briefly illustrates the ideas to widen the scope for quantitative impact assessment and concludes.

4.2   INDICATORS FOR SUSTAINABLE DEVELOPMENT

Monitoring progress towards SD requires in the first place the identification of operational indicators that provide manageable units of information on economic, environmental and social (including institutional) conditions. The crucial role of SD indicators has been prominently emphasized by the United Nations Conference on Environment and Development (UNCED), held in Rio de Janeiro in 1992, that calls on individual countries as well as international governmental and non-governmental organizations to 'develop and identify indicators of SD in order to improve the information basis for decision-making at all levels' (UNCED, 1992b, Agenda 21, Chapter 40). Since the early 1990s a multitude of indicator lists has been developed; the Compendium of Sustainable Development Indicator Initiatives lists more than 500 sustainable indicator efforts (Parris and Kates, 2003).

The United Nations Commission on Sustainable Development (CSD), established in 1992 to ensure effective follow-up of the UNCED, has focused its work to date mainly on the development and testing of indicators that could be readily used in planning, policy formulation and evaluation at the national level. The initial work program on Indicators of Sustainable Development resulted in a list of 134 indicators, which covers social, environmental, economic and institutional aspects of SD. After voluntary national testing (within 22 countries) and expert group consultation, a reduced and revised set of 58 'core indicators' categorized within 15 themes and 38 subthemes for monitoring the progress towards SD was released (UN, 2001).

Efforts by the European Community (EC) to integrate environmental objectives into the different fields of policy-making date back to the early 1970s as manifested for example within the first Environmental Action Plan (EAP, 1973). The Amsterdam Treaty, signed in 1997, codified environmental policy integration as a central EU policy element within Article 6:

> environmental protection requirements must be integrated into the definition and implementation of the Community policies ... in particular with a view to promoting SD

and furthermore re-enforced Article 2, which defines SD as a fundamental objective for the European Community. The Gothenburg Summit in 2001 (European Council, 2001) came up with the definition of an European Union Strategy for Sustainable Development that combines the commitment to improved environmental performance (Helsinki European Council, 1999) with the objective:

> to become the most competitive and dynamic knowledge-based economy in the world capable of sustainable economic growth with more and better jobs and greater social cohesion. (Presidency Conclusions of the Lisbon European Council, see European Council, 2000)

An annual stocktaking of the progress towards SD – due at each Spring Summit – was agreed upon.

The European Union Strategy for Sustainable Development focuses on six themes which are enhanced by four other themes derived from further discussion on sustainability by the EU, UN and so on (Eurostat, 2004). Within each theme, a number of sub-themes and 'areas to be addressed' have been identified. The sub-themes encompass the relevant SD issues addressed in the basic policy documents. Generally, the sub-themes are closely linked to the headline objectives, which are also reflected in the labeling of the sub-themes. The 'areas to be addressed', which can be considered as an interface between indicators and policies, are closely linked to the measures announced in European Council's Communications (EC, 2001). However, a certain amount of balancing has been done between the sub-themes and the areas to be addressed to take account of the different levels of importance of the issues and to ensure consistency. Additional sub-themes have sometimes been included in order to increase the visual clarity of the overall framework and to group the areas to be addressed. The large number of 73 indicators (see Table 4.2) that have been put forward by the European Union Strategy for Sustainable Development made it rather difficult to draw a clear picture on SD progress. Therefore, the Spring Report 2004 (EC, 2003b) has been scheduled to report on only 14 structural indicators thereby balancing the importance of employment, innovation and research, economic reform, social cohesion and the environment (see Table 4.1).

4.3   E3 MODELS FOR SIA: EVIDENCE FROM TRANSUST

We asked the different modeling groups within TranSust to what extent key indicators for SD as listed in Tables 4.1 and 4.2 are currently captured or subject to (feasible) extensions in their operational E3 models. The modeling groups had to specify whether the indicators are currently measurable within

Table 4.1   Coverage of Structural Indicators by E3 Models

	Indicator	1	2	3	4	5	6	7	8	9	10
I	GDP per capita	■	■	■	■	■	■	■		·	·
II	Labor productivity	■	■	■	■	■	■	▫		·	·
III	Employment rate	■	■	■	■	■	▫	·	·	·	·
IV	Employment rate of older workers	▫	·	·	·	·	·	·	·	·	·
V	Spending on human resources (pub exp. on educ.)	■	■	■	▫	·	·	·	·	·	·
VI	Research and development expenditure	■	■	▫	▫	▫	·	·	·	·	·
VII	Information technology expenditure	▫	▫	·	·	·	·	·	·	·	·
VIII	Financial market integration	·	·	·	·	·	·	·	·	·	·
IX	At risk-of-poverty rate	▫	·	·	·	·	·	·	·	·	·
X	Long-term unemployment	▫	▫	·	·	·	·	·	·	·	·
XI	Dispersion of regional employment rates	▫	·	·	·	·	·	·	·	·	·
XII	Greenhouse gases emissions	■	■	■	■	■	■	■	■	■	·
XIII	Energy intensity of the economy	■	■	■	■	■	■	▫	·	·	·
XIV	Volume of transport	■	▫	▫	▫	·	·	·	·	·	·

Notes: ■ Core;   ▫ extended.

Source: Spring Report 2004 – EC (2003b).

their model (labelled 'core' in Tables 4.1 and 4.2) or could be measured after appropriate extensions (labelled 'extended' in Tables 4.1 and 4.2). Blank spaces indicate the modelers' assessment that the specific indicator is considered to be out of the current and extended model's scope. In total, our SIA questionnaire has been filled out by ten out of 12 modeling teams. Thus, the maximum score in our descriptive evaluation presented in Tables 4.1–4.2 amounts to 10.

We start with the assessment of responses on the coverage of the 14 EU structural indicators listed in the Spring Report on Sustainable Development (Table 4.1). Almost all operational versions of E3 models can quantify central economic indicators such as gross domestic product (GDP) per capita, labor productivity, or the level of employment. Indirect measures of economic potential such as research and development (R&D), information technology expenditure, or spending on human resources are hardly covered in most of the operational E3 models and also viewed with reserve as feasible extensions. Social indicators such as at-risk-of-poverty rates are not present in current model versions and hardly regarded as feasible future extensions within most E3 models.

With respect to the environmental dimension, the EC structural indicators

Table 4.2a   Coverage of Economic Indicators by E3 Models

Theme/Subtheme	Areas to be Addressed	1	2	3	4	5	6	7	8	9	10
ECONOMIC DEVELOPMENT											
Investment	1. Investment in R&D	■	■	■	■	⊡	⊡	⊡	⊡	·	·
	2. Investment in env. friendly technologies	■	■	■	■	⊡	·	·	·	·	·
	3. Consumption and inflation	■	■	■	■	■	·	·	·	·	·
	4. Saving and borrowing	■	■	■	·	·	·	·	·	·	·
Competitiveness	5. Labor productivity	■	■	■	■	■	■	■	⊡	·	·
	6. Unit labor costs	■	■	■	■	■	■	■	·	·	·
	7. Life-long learning	·	·	·	·	·	·	·	·	·	·
Employment	8. Employment rate	■	■	■	■	■	⊡	⊡	·	·	·
	9. Unemployment rate	■	■	■	■	⊡	⊡	⊡	·	·	·

Notes: ■ Core;   ⊡ extended.

Source: Eurostat (2004).

Table 4.2b   Coverage of Social Indicators by E3 Models

Theme/Subtheme	Areas to be Addressed	1	2	3	4	5	6	7	8	9	10
POVERTY AND SOCIAL EXCLUSION											
Monetary Poverty	10. Income inequality	■	⊡	⊡	·	·	·	·	·	·	·
	11. Non-monetary deprivation	⊡	·	·	·	·	·	·	·	·	·
Access to Labor Market	12. Poverty-in-work	·	·	·	·	·	·	·	·	·	·
Other Aspect of Social Exclusion	13. Access to education	·	·	·	·	·	·	·	·	·	·
	14. Access to health care	·	·	·	·	·	·	·	·	·	·
	15. Access to housing	·	·	·	·	·	·	·	·	·	·
	16. Social participation	·	·	·	·	·	·	·	·	·	·
AGING SOCIETY											
Pensions Adequacy/ Demographic Changes	17. Income of elder generations	⊡	·	·	·	·	·	·	·	·	·
	18. Life expectancy	⊡	·	·	·	·	·	·	·	·	·
	19. Fertility	⊡	·	·	·	·	·	·	·	·	·
	20. Migrations	⊡	·	·	·	·	·	·	·	·	·
Financial Sustainability	21. Age of withdrawal from labor market	·	·	·	·	·	·	·	·	·	·
	22. Pension expenditures	■	⊡	⊡	·	·	·	·	·	·	·

Table 4.2b   Coverage of Social Indicators by E3 Models (Continued)

Theme/Subtheme	Areas to be Addressed	1	2	3	4	5	6	7	8	9	10
PUBLIC HEALTH											
Human Health Protection and Lifestyles											
	23. Financial sustainability	⊡	·	·	·	·	·	·	·	·	·
	24. Disability-free life expect.	·	·	·	·	·	·	·	·	·	·
	25. Premature mortality	·	·	·	·	·	·	·	·	·	·
	26. Life styles	·	·	·	·	·	·	·	·	·	·
	27. Health and safety at work	·	·	·	·	·	·	·	·	·	·
	28. Infectious diseases and resistance to antibiotics	·	·	·	·	·	·	·	·	·	·
Food Safety and Quality											
	29. Pesticide residues	·	·	·	·	·	·	·	·	·	·
	30. Microbiological contamination	·	·	·	·	·	·	·	·	·	·
	31. Drinking water quality	·	·	·	·	·	·	·	·	·	·
Chemicals Management											
	32. Chemicals production and consumption	■	■	⊡	·	·	·	·	·	·	·
	33. Exposure to chemicals	■	·	·	·	·	·	·	·	·	·
Health Risks Due to Environmental Conditions											
	34. Air quality	■	⊡	·	·	·	·	·	·	·	·
	35. Noise exposure	■	·	·	·	·	·	·	·	·	·

Notes: ■ Core;   ⊡ extended.

Source: Eurostat (2004).

Table 4.2c   Coverage of Environmental Indicators by E3-Models

Theme/Subtheme	Areas to be Addressed	1	2	3	4	5	6	7	8	9	10
CLIMATE CHANGE AND ENERGY											
Climate Change											
	36. GHG emissions reduction	■	■	■	■	■	■	■	■	■	·
Energy											
	37. Energy taxes	■	■	■	■	■	■	■	■	⊡	·
	38. Energy efficiency	■	■	■	■	■	■	■	⊡	·	·
	39. Renewable energy resources	■	■	■	⊡	⊡	⊡	⊡	⊡	·	·
	40. Management of nuclear waste	■	·	·	·	·	·	·	·	·	·
	41. Air pollution from energy use	■	■	■	⊡	⊡	⊡	·	·	·	·
PRODUCTION AND CONSUMPTION PATTERNS											
Eco-efficiency											
	42. Decoupling economic growth and resource use	■	■	■	■	⊡	⊡	·	·	·	·
	43. Decoupling economic growth and emissions	■	■	■	■	■	■	■	■	■	·

Table 4.2c   Coverage of Environmental Indicators by E3 Models (Continued)

Theme/Subtheme	Areas to be Addressed	1	2	3	4	5	6	7	8	9	10
	44. Decoupling economic growth and waste	⊡	⊡	⊡	·	·	·	·	·	·	·
Agriculture											
	45. Pesticides use	⊡	·	·	·	·	·	·	·	·	·
	46. Nitrogen balances	■	⊡	·	·	·	·	·	·	·	·
	47. Environmentally friendly farming	·	·	·	·	·	·	·	·	·	·
Corporate Responsibility											
	48. Triple bottom line	·	·	·	·	·	·	·	·	·	·
Consumer Awareness											
	49. Consumer information	·	·	·	·	·	·	·	·	·	·
MANAGEMENT OF NATURAL RESOURCES											
Biodiversity											
	50. Protection of habitats and natural systems & biodiversity	·	·	·	·	·	·	·	·	·	·
	51. Maintaining the carrying capacity	⊡	·	·	·	·	·	·	·	·	·
Marine Ecosystems											
	52. Overfishing	⊡	·	·	·	·	·	·	·	·	·
Fresh Water Resources											
	53. Water extraction and use	⊡	·	·	·	·	·	·	·	·	·
	54. Protection of surface and ground water resources	·	·	·	·	·	·	·	·	·	·
Land Use											
	55. Land use change	⊡	⊡	⊡	⊡	·	·	·	·	·	·
	56. Soil degradation	·	·	·	·	·	·	·	·	·	·
	57. Forests	■	⊡	⊡	⊡	·	·	·	·	·	·
TRANSPORT											
Transport Growth											
	58. Decoupling of economic and transport growth	■	■	■	⊡	⊡	·	·	·	·	·
	59. Road to rail, water and public transport	■	■	⊡	⊡	·	·	·	·	·	·
	60. Land use by transport systems	⊡	·	·	·	·	·	·	·	·	·
Environm. Impact of Transport											
	61. Air pollutants	■	■	⊡	⊡	⊡	·	·	·	·	·
[GLOBAL PARTNERSHIP]											
Resource Management											
	70. Resource consumption	■	■	⊡	⊡	⊡	·	·	·	·	·
	71. Air emissions & Energy	■	■	⊡	⊡	·	·	·	·	·	·
	72. Water	⊡	⊡	·	·	·	·	·	·	·	·
	73. Waste	⊡	⊡	·	·	·	·	·	·	·	·

Notes: ■ Core;   ⊡ extended.

Source: Eurostat (2004).

Table 4.2d Coverage of Institutional Indicators by E3 models

Theme/Subtheme	Areas to be Addressed	1	2	3	4	5	6	7	8	9	10
GOOD GOVERNANCE											
Policy Coherence											
	62. Citizen's adherence and support to EU actions	·		·		·		·		·	·
	63. Sustainability of EU actions and measures	■		·		·		·		·	·
	64. Legislative compliance	·		·		·		·		·	·
Public Participation											
	65. Communication and mobilization	·		·		·		·		·	·
GLOBAL PARTNERSHIP											
Globalization of Trade											
	66. Market access for least developed countries (LDC)	·		·		·		·		·	·
Financing for SD											
	67. Foreign direct investments to developing countries	▫	▫	·		·		·		·	·
	68. Official Development Assistance (ODA)	·		·		·		·		·	·
	69. Other official financing	·		·		·		·		·	·

Notes: ■ Core;   ▫ extended.

Source: Eurostat (2004).

only cover greenhouse gas emissions, energy intensity and transport volumes. As E3 models are deliberately designed to link economic and energy flows, the comprehensive coverage of energy intensity and energy- related emissions is not surprising. Yet, it should be made clear that – at second glance – incorporation of greenhouse gas emissions mainly refers to carbon dioxide emissions from combustion of fossil fuels. Non-CO_2 greenhouse gases such as CH_4 or N_2O that cannot be directly linked in fixed proportions to input or output activities in economic sectors are only weakly represented. Surprisingly, only one operational E3 model within TranSust accounts for the volume of transport – the latter being a prime concern for several environmental themes, for example climate change.

Table 4.2 (featuring slight rearrangements of the original EUROSTAT indicator list) reveals in much more detail the shortcomings of existing E3 models with respect to the extensive wish-list on impact assessment. Whereas the theme 'economic development' (see Table 4.2a) with central indicators including consumption, saving, labor productivity, labor costs or employment rates, is broadly represented, societal aspects (see Table 4.2b) addressed in the themes 'poverty and social exclusion', 'ageing society', or 'public health' are more or less missing in current E3 models; insightful in this respect is that nearly all social indicators are considered to be out of scope of feasible (reasonable) model extensions. On the one hand, these deficiencies can be explained by the explicit focus of E3 models on non-societal dimensions. On the other hand, various indicators – for example social participation – are very vaguely defined and difficult if not impossible to measure quantitatively. Within the environmental dimension of SIA (see Table 4.2c), the thematic field 'climate change and energy' is widely covered which reflects the policy demand and research focus in applied modeling during recent decades. In fact, concerns on climate change and energy use have driven the development of E3 models. Other central aspects of sustainable environmental management including consumer awareness, biodiversity, water and land use are considered to be outside the scope of most current E3 models. Finally, there are various indicators to characterize good governance of global partnership that are absent from the investigated E3 models (Table 4.2d), again owing to the specific objectives of E3 models but also due to inherent measurement problems.

4.4   DISCUSSION AND CONCLUSIONS

The evaluated E3 models cover only a few indicators for SIA. Central economic indicators like GDP per capita, labor productivity or the level of employment are quantified by almost all models. However, while research, development and diffusion of new technologies are of paramount importance for the measurement of sustainability, indicators such as R&D expenditure, investment in environmentally friendly technologies, information technology expenditure, or spending on human resources are hardly covered in most of the operational E3 models and are also viewed with reserve as feasible extensions (see Löschel, 2002). Many of the models do not take into account the empirical evidence that technological change is to an important degree endogenous, that is, responding to socio-economic (policy) variables. As, for example, environmental policy implicitly or explicitly increases the price of energy, firms invest in R&D with the intention of producing profitable new (energy-efficient) products and processes (Otto et al., 2008, Löschel and Otto, 2009). The omission of measures of the direction and extent of technological change poses a major shortcoming of E3 models.

Larger gaps also exist in the field of environmental impact analysis and in particular with respect to social impact assessment. However, there are many complementary quantitative models that feature substantially more details of technological conditions (for example engineering bottom-up energy system models), socio-economic household behavior (for example micro-simulation models) or natural science relationships (for example climate models, water stress models, land-use models). This raises the question to what extent and in what manner different models can be linked towards a more comprehensive coverage of SIA requirements. In principle, there are two basic approaches for model linkages which are loosely termed soft-link and hard-link. Roughly speaking, the soft-link approach involves combination of two or more models that have been developed independently from another and can be run stand-alone. Due to the heterogeneity in complexity and accounting methods across different models, the soft-link approach stands out for substantial problems in achieving overall consistency and convergence of iterative solution approaches. On the other hand, it allows for maintaining detailed information embodied within the various (often interdisciplinary) models without requiring comprehensive expertise. Furthermore, linkages can be based on established models rather than requiring modeling work from scratch. These rather pragmatic advantages may outweigh to some degree impending deficiencies in overall consistency. The hard-link approach puts strong emphasis on internal consistency and therefore makes use of a single integrated modeling framework. Information from other models is directly fed into the core model. This means that data and functional relationships from other models must be condensed and synthesized in a way compatible to the structure of the core model.

In practice, there have been several examples of soft links between macro-economic models and energy system models in order to enrich macroeconomic analysis of energy or environmental policies with bottom-up technological details (see, for example, Bergman and Lundgren, 1990). Beyond soft-linked energy–economy model systems, integrated assessment models (IAMs) seek to combine knowledge from multiple disciplines in an analytic framework to assess the effects of different policy options. The IAM framework typically features broad system linkages and feedbacks, particularly between socio-economic and biophysical processes. For example, within the IMAGE model system (IMAGE-Team, 2001), a macroeconomic model and a population model feed basic information on economic and demographic developments for several world regions into other linked submodels such as a land-cover model (which calculates global land-use and land-cover changes including changes in agricultural land, forests and desertification. Another example is the MIT Integrated Global System Model (IGSM) consisting of a set of coupled submodels of economic development and associated emissions, natural biogeochemical cycles, climate and natural ecosystems (Prinn et al., 1998). There, a macroeconomic model is applied to 'predict' emissions used subsequently as an input in the atmospheric chemistry model and the climate model. To date most of the potential feedbacks between the socio-economic and biophysical systems are not formally modeled owing to uncertainty on concrete causal chains or commensurability problems. Instead, the sub-models use the results of the economic model as exogenous parameters. In other words, there is only a one-way soft link between economic variables and their relationship with biophysical variables.

Hard linkages stand out for the consistent decomposition of a single framework into various model segments. As illustrated initially by Böhringer (1998) in a static stylized macroeconomic model, the detailed representation of certain segments within an otherwise aggregate model is straightforward: practical applications to energy regulation (for example Böhringer and Löschel, 2006b) testify that such hybrid models can enhance the transparency and 'credibility' of simulated technological responses. Recent examples of hard linkages between socio-economic and biophysical model include integrated assessment of the costs and benefits from climate change policies (Böhringer et al., 2006; Böhringer et al., 2007). Similar hard links may substantially improve the applicability of the E3 model family for problem-tailored SIA in various policy fields such as land use, desertification, agriculture or water management.

The objective of SD needs a comprehensive methodology to perform SIA quantitatively. An issue that cannot be clearly measured will be difficult to improve. In this chapter, we have investigated the use of energy–economy–environment (E3) models within the TranSust project for measuring the impacts of policy interference on policy-relevant economic, environmental and social (institutional) indicators: operational versions of E3 models have a good coverage of central economic indicators, whereas environmental indicators with a complex natural science background and – in particular – social indicators are hardly represented. Our cross-model evaluation confirms the need for future modeling activities in the field of integrated assessment that link standard E3 models to theme-specific complementary models with environmental and societal focus.

A final caveat applies: our focus on quantitative analysis should not exaggerate the role numerical approaches can play in SIA. Policy decisions are the outcome of a broader participatory process where stakeholders and other interested parties communicate a wide range of values, perceptions and judgments to policy-makers (Tamborra, 2002). Quantitative analysis – if available at all – can at best strengthen or weaken policy arguments, putting decision-making on a more informed basis.

NOTES

1. This chapter builds to a large extent on a paper entitled 'Computable general equilibrium models for sustainability impact analysis: Status quo and prospects' published in *Ecological Economics* (Böhringer and Löschel, 2006a).
2. IQ.Tools follows the provisions of the EU Commission Impact Assessment Guidelines (EC, 2005) and helps complying with different steps laid out therein.

REFERENCES

Bergman, L. and S. Lundgren (1990), 'General equilibrium approaches to energy policy analysis in Sweden', in L. Bergman, D.W. Jorgenson and E. Zalai (eds), *General Equilibrium Modeling and Economic Policy Analysis*, Oxford: Basil Blackwell, pp. 351–82.

Böhringer, C. (1998), 'The synthesis of bottom-up and top-down in energy policy modeling', *Energy Economics*, **20**(3), 233–48.

Böhringer, C. and A. Löschel (2006a), 'Computable general equilibrium models for sustainability impact analysis: Status quo and prospects', *Ecological Economics*, **60**(1), 49–61.

Böhringer, C. and A. Löschel (2006b), 'Promoting renewable energy in Europe: A hybrid computable general equilibrium approach', *Energy Journal, Hybrid Modelling: New Answers to Old Challenges*, 123–38.

Böhringer, C., A. Löschel and T.F. Rutherford (2006), 'Efficiency gains from "what"-flexibility in climate policy: An integrated CGE assessment', *Energy Journal, Multi-Greenhouse Gas Mitigation and Climate Policy*, 405–24.

Böhringer, C., A. Löschel and T.F. Rutherford (2007), 'Decomposing the integrated assessment of climate change', *Journal of Economic Dynamics and Control*, **31**, 683–702.

Boulanger, P.-M. and T. Bréchet (2005), 'Models for policy-making in sustainable development: The state of the art and perspectives for research', *Ecological Economics*, **55**, 337–50.

EAP (Environmental Action Programme) (1973), 'First environmental action plan, 1973–1977), published in OJ C 112, 20.12.1973.

EC (European Commission) (1999), 'EXTERNE: Externalities of energy', Vols 1–10, Brussels 1995/99, available at http://www.ExternE.info [last accessed May 2008].

EC (European Commission) (2001), 'A sustainable Europe for a better world: A European Union strategy for sustainable development', Commission's proposal to the Gothenburg European Council, COM(2001)264 final, Brussels, 15.5.2001.

EC (European Commission) (2003a), 'Sustainability impact assessment of trade agreements: Making trade sustainable?', Background Paper, DG Trade Seminar, Brussels, 6–7.2.2003.

EC (European Commission) (2003b), 'Structural indicators', Communication from the Commission, COM(2003)585 final, Brussels, 8.10.2003.

EC (European Commission) (2005), 'Impact assessment guidelines', COM(2005)791, Brussels, 15.6.2005.

European Council (2000), 'Presidency Conclusions', Lisbon European Council, 23–24 March 2000, available at http://europa.eu/european_council/conclusions/index_en.htm [last accessed May 2008].

European Council (2001), 'Presidency Conclusions', Göteborg European Council, 15–16

June 2001, http://europa.eu/european_council/conclusions/index_en.htm [last accessed May 2008].

Eurostat (European Commission Eurostat) (2004), 'The EU sustainable development strategy: A framework for indicators', Doc. SDI/TF/30/4 rev. 5 (2004), Brussels.

Friedrich, R. and P. Bickel (eds) (2001), *Environmental External Costs of Transport*, Berlin: Springer.

IMAGE-Team (2001), 'The IMAGE 2.2 implementation of the SRES scenarios. A comprehensive analysis of emissions, climate change and impacts in the 21st. Century', RIVM CD-ROM publication 481508018, National Institute for Public Health and the Environment, Bilthoven, The Netherlands.

Kirkpatrick, C. and N. Lee (1999), 'WTO new round sustainability assessment study', Phase Two Main Report (Manchester Study), Institute for Development Policy and Management and Environmental Impact Assessment Centre, University of Manchester, available at: http://www.idpm.man.ac.uk/sia-trade [last accessed May 2008].

Löschel, A. (2002), 'Technological change in economic models of environmental policy: A survey', *Ecological Economics*, **43**, 105–26.

Otto, V., A. Löschel and R. Dellink (2007), 'Energy biased technical change: A CGE analysis', *Resource and Energy Economics*, **29**(2), 137–58.

Otto, V., A. Löschel and J. Reilly (2006), 'Directed technical change and climate policy', Working Paper, MIT Joint Program on the Science and Policy of Global Change, Massachusetts Institute of Technology, Cambridge, MA.

Parris, T.M. and R.W. Kates (2003), 'Characterizing and measuring sustainable development', *Annual Review of Environment and Resources*, **28**, 559–86.

Prinn, R., H. Jacoby, A. Sokolov, C. Wang, X. Xiao, Z. Yang, R. Eckaus, P. Stone, D. Ellerman, J. Melillo, J. Fitzmaurice, D. Kicklighter, G. Holian and Y. Liu May (1998), 'Integrated global system model for climate policy assessment: Feedbacks and sensitivity studies', *Climatic Change*, **41**(3/4), 469–546.

Schleicher, S.P. and W. Hyll (eds) (2003), 'Model comparison part 1: Model characteristics', TranSust Working Paper 03–01, Graz.

Tamborra, M. (2002), 'Socio-economic tools for sustainability impact assessment: the contribution of EU research to sustainable development', European Communities, Office for Official Publications of the European Communities, Luxembourg.

UN (United Nations) (2001), 'Indicators of Sustainable Development: Guidelines and Methodologies', New York: UN.

UNCED (United Nations Conference on Environment and Development, Earth Summit) (1992a), 'Rio declaration on environment and development', Rio de Janeiro, 3–14 June.

UNCED (United Nations Conference on Environment and Development, Earth Summit) (1992b), 'Agenda 21', Rio de Janeiro, 3–14 June.

WCED (World Commission on Environment and Development, The Brundtland Commission) (1987), *Our Common Future*, Oxford: Oxford University Press.

Young, H.P. (1994), *Equity in Theory and Practice*, Princeton, NJ: Princeton University Press.

5. Interpreting Environmental Policy Cost Measures

Jean-Charles Hourcade and Frédéric Ghersi

5.1 INTRODUCTION

Since the late 1980s, climate policy debates have been making extensive use of modelling results about the costs of meeting climate objectives. To what extent this use succeeded in rationalising discussions is not so obvious. From the Third Conference of the Parties (COP3) (Kyoto) to the semi-failure of COP6 (The Hague), despite the attempts of the second and third reports of the International Panel on Climate Change (IPCC) to clarify what 'good use' could be made of results discrepancies in designing a viable climate regime (Hourcade, 1996; Markandya and Halsnaes, 2001), it did not manage to create a common understanding between the optimists and the pessimists about the costs of Kyoto targets. It did not succeed either in delivering robust and consensual qualitative insights regarding the policy mix most likely to minimise welfare costs. Ultimately, negotiations were conducted under pure diplomatic rhetoric with almost no link to well-grounded, even though controversial, economic analysis.[1]

Reasons for this communication failure between scientific expertise and public decision-making are many, including the diplomatic cycles of the climate affairs, the political resistance to some recommendations, and the lack of convincing power of the modelling state of the art – due to some real weaknesses. However, this chapter starts from the idea that this failure is owed to a great extent to the confusion about the very concept of cost.

The seemingly simple notion of 'cost' is indeed deeply polysemous: there is a significant distance between its meaning for the average consumer keeping an eye on the price of petrol, the industry concerned by its competitive position, and the government in charge of the balance of public budgets. There is yet another hiatus between the point of view of any stakeholder and its significance within the theoretical and empirical constraints of modelling exercises, including those set by incomplete data or computational limits.

In this chapter, we first review the cost concepts used both in public debates and in the modelling community. Secondly, we elaborate on the way the apparently tangible concept of 'abatement expenditures', which conveys technology assumptions, is translated in partial and general equilibrium models. Thirdly, we place some caveats about how to translate the models' information on marginal policy costs into policy signals, at various points in time. A last section focuses on the ways and means of the TranSust models to report costs.

5.2   WHAT COSTS DO WE MEASURE? WHAT COSTS DO WE DISCUSS?

Economic modelling literature circulates costs assessments that are not directly comparable, simply because they measure different realities, in different metrics, and under varying economic, geographic and time aggregations. Combining these three dimensions produces a large number of different cost assessments of the same policy, paving the way to misinterpretations and/or strategic uses of information.

What Type of Cost?

Setting aside the accounting of ancillary benefits,[2] the types of costs commonly used to assess climate policies fit into three broad categories.

Technical costs, or direct abatement expenditures, are the main ingredient of the partial equilibrium models detailing energy production and consumption in a technology-rich manner. They are also the main outcome of these models, through the aggregation of the equipment expenditures emerging from a 'bottom-up' description of energy systems. In bottom-up models, the choice of supply and demand techniques is quite systematically based on a set of energy prices and investment plus operation and maintenance costs. These prices and costs are expressed in some constant currency, that is (implicitly) relative to a constant price index of the non-energy goods and services. Opposed to bottom-up models, the typical 'top-down' macroeconomic models have a limited ability to pinpoint abatement expenditures because of their higher degree of aggregation in the description of energy systems. This level of abstraction is the source of a paramount 'tangibility issue' that will be further addressed below.

Macroeconomic costs relate to evolutions in total output, consumption or revenues (gross domestic product – GDP). In order to be computed they require a comprehensive description of economic flows. Contrary to direct abatement expenditures, they encompass the general equilibrium effects of the energy systems transformation on the rest of the economy.[3] Capturing such interdependences is critical to understanding why the technical cost of a policy action may not indicate the burden it ultimately lays on an economy.

Welfare costs refer to the economic concept of utility losses, and capture the ultimate impact of policies on the well-being of an economy. In a macroeconomic framework they are typically computed for an aggregated household or 'representative consumer', or through the weighted sum of the utilities of various household classes. Expressed in money metric terms, they provide a comprehensive measure of the social costs of climate policies.

The 'costs' of a given policy can refer to any of these three types. The necessary wedge between the three corresponding assessments obviously causes confusion. It is particularly high between technical costs on one side and macroeconomic and welfare costs on the other because of, in a closed economy:

- The structure of the input–output (IO) matrix, or interindustrial relationships, which determines how the direct price increase induced by technical costs spreads throughout the production system and results in a new set of relative prices.
- The impact of this shift of the price vector on the trade-off between factors in production – and the looping of these two first effects to equilibrium.
- The pre-existing tax system, which both distorts carbon price signals, and offers the opportunity to coordinate climate and fiscal policies so as to minimise the marginal welfare losses of a given climate objective – the 'double dividend' issue (Goulder, 1995; Bovenberg, 1999).
- The functioning of the labour market: the degree of wage flexibility determines how policy-induced changes in the relative price of labour affect the level of employment and ultimately real wages. Real wages in turn impact upon the disposable income and households' consumption.
- Public budget constraints: if a policy is revenue-raising (tax, auctioned permits), how is this revenue recycled? If it requires funding (compensating measures, subsidies, guaranteed prices, infrastructure development and so on), how is it financed?
- The costs of redirecting technical change: to some extent, the investment in abatement activities crowds out general investment and has a negative impact on general productivity, unless one allows for fully compensative spillovers (Goulder and Schneider, 1999).

The interplay between these parameters is further complicated by the insertion of economies in international markets, including those for fossil fuels and in some instances carbon itself. The reaction of oil, gas and coal prices to carbon pricing and the general shift in regional relative prices impact upon the terms of trade, with obvious macroeconomic or welfare consequences. Last, but not least, international financial markets constrain the investment decisions to build new energy capacities – they will play an especially important role in decades to come as energy demand will greatly exceed current supply capacities (IEA, 2003).[4]

An ample literature demonstrates that the impact of these national and international factors is such that they can go as far as overruling the direct effect of the policy. They can turn an abatement cost into a macroeconomic gain – the stronger form of 'double dividend' following Goulder's definition (Goulder, 1995) – or, in the opposite direction, exacerbate the social costs of a rather modest policy. Subsequently, the desirability of a policy option can vary widely with the type of cost considered. This probably constituted one of the obstacles to an international agreement in climate affairs: on top of selecting more or less optimistic models to back their positions, advocates and opponents of an active climate policy, even when using the same model, could put the emphasis on the type of cost supporting their stance – and disregard the others.

In What Metric?

Another major interpretation problem regards the economic meaning of the metrics under which cost figures, whatever their type, are delivered. The same type of cost can indeed be expressed in marginal, average or total values,[5] and for each of these values in absolute or relative terms. Some of the underlying issues relate to substantive economic questions. Others are again more rhetorical in nature.

Marginal, average or total cost? The dangers of singling out one indicator

Considering that marginal costs are quite systematically higher than average costs, it is not surprising that the tenants of action against climate change often insist on the latter, while their opponents favour the former. It is obviously possible to limit confusion and provide a sound and policy-relevant assessment by reporting these indicators jointly. Their difference is indeed a good indicator of the convexity of marginal costs around a given abatement target – and consequently of the risk generated by uncertainty: a small (large) wedge between the marginal and average costs means that the marginal cost curve is 'rather straight' ('rather convex') and that, in case of an *ex ante* underestimation of the marginal cost, the extra burden will be low (high).

More generally, there is no scientific conflict behind reporting results in terms of a marginal, an average or a total value. All three metrics matter and should systematically be reported in order to have a precise diagnosis of the impacts of climate policies on an economy. For each of them, it is also important to observe discrepancies in the assessment of the three types of cost introduced above: in most modelling frameworks there is no a priori reason why the measures would match. It may happen, for instance, that the steepness of the marginal abatement expenditures curve is higher than that of the marginal welfare curve, depending on the pre-existing carbon intensity of an economy and on the efficiency of tax recycling. To use this information in public debates would facilitate the understanding of how certain policy packages (various forms of carbon trading with or without safety valve, auctioned permits, carbon taxes, compensating transfers, and so on) hedge against uncertainty, both at an aggregate level and for various social groups.

However, policy-makers tend to insist on marginal costs, interpreting them as the carbon price necessary to meet a given carbon target – our fourth section will question this interpretation. The reason for this insistence is obviously the sensitivity of public opinion to energy prices (for example that of petrol), which constitutes one of the strongest acceptability constraints of environmental policies. But focusing on the price of carbon may be misleading, including in political terms: negative macroeconomic or welfare impacts are the potential indicators of social tensions that can ultimately prove as important. Table 5.1 illustrates this point: for five of the six models reported the ranking of regions from the most to the least impacted,

Table 5.1 *Regional Ranking in Marginal and Macroeconomic Costs of Kyoto Implementation, Six Models*

	Carbon Price in 2010 (1990 USD per ton)			vs	GDP Losses (% BAU 2010 GDP)		
	Highest	Second	Lowest		Highest	Second	Lowest
ABARE-GTEM	Europe (665)	Japan (645)	USA (322)	≠	USA (1.96)	Europe (0.94)	Japan (0.72)
AIM	Japan (234)	Europe (198)	USA (153)	≠	USA (0.45)	Europe (0.31)	Japan (0.25)
G-Cubed	Europe (227)	Japan (97)	USA (76)	=	Europe (1.5)	Japan (0.57)	USA (0.42)
MERGE3	Japan (500)	USA (264)	Europe (218)	≠	USA (1.06)	Europe (0.99)	Japan (0.8)
MS-MRT	Japan (402)	USA (236)	Europe (179)	≠	USA (1.88)	Japan (1.2)	Europe (0.63)
RICE	Japan (251)	Europe (159)	USA (132)	≠	USA (0.94)	Japan (0.78)	Europe (0.55)

Source: Drawn from IPCC (2001), p. 514.

in this example of a 'Kyoto without carbon trading' simulation, widely differs whether one considers the marginal cost (carbon price) or macroeconomic cost (GDP losses). Averaging on the available models depicts the USA facing the lowest marginal cost, a perception which lead many to consider that they should embrace an ambitious target; but at the same time the USA faces the highest macroeconomic costs, and this in turn accounts for its negotiation stance. The contradiction is manifest, and partly explains the consecutive negotiation failure.

In absolute or relative terms? A false but important quarrel
A second dimension of the metric in which literature reports results is the precise unit in which the costs are expressed. Three units are mostly used:

- absolute amounts of some currency;[6]
- relative variations of a macroeconomic indicator (GDP, final consumption, and so on) or welfare at some point in time;
- variation of the annual GDP growth rate between the current year and the year for which the policy is estimated.

The choice between any of these three units – again, theoretically legitimate for any of the cost categories – is very strategic in nature: starting from the same modelling exercise, it may give very different views of the economic and social burden of a given policy. It indeed constituted one of the crucial discussions arising when the IPCC had to summarize the findings of its second assessment report (IPCC, 1996): the same 2 per cent GDP loss at a 20-year horizon can be transformed into a daunting figure of billions of dollars if presented in an absolute value, but into an almost negligible 0.1 per cent decrease in the annual growth rate over 20 years as well.

There is probably no way to circumvent these communication biases. They originate in a more fundamental issue, which is the very meaning of a figure such as a 2 per cent GDP loss at a given date (or its equivalent in the two other units). This issue matters for the costs of mitigation strategies as well as for those of climate change impacts. Macroeconomic assessments of both mitigation and impacts are indeed of the order of a very few GDP percentage points, with variations from one analysis to the other of quite the same order of magnitude. This may lead the reader to conclude that, all in all, the amounts at stake are quite low. Depending upon his pre-existing intuition, he might conclude that action must be undertaken anyway, or that it is useless to be too concerned – or simply that the meaningfulness of climate policy assessments is to be doubted. After all, as reminded by Hogan and Manne (1977) in a striking 'elephant and rabbit' metaphor, costs cannot but be low, simply because energy represents a minor share of total GDP, and a production factor whose cost share is, for most activities, lower than that of labour or many other intermediary inputs. However, nobody would argue that, because energy is a statistical 'rabbit', the energy system is of second-order importance for the stability and pace of economic growth. In fact, a single aggregate figure over a long time period may hide transitional economic costs high enough to induce social and political deadlocks.

To avoid the trap of a quarrel about metrics, the focus should thus be placed on understanding the mechanisms that govern the magnitude of costs, and on the reasons why different policy packages may incur costs separated by a factor of two or three – some of them even changing the very sign of the net outcome in terms of welfare or total income. To debate whether 1 per cent of GDP is too high a cost is far less useful than to understand why this 1 per cent can alternatively be turned into a 2 per cent cost, or indeed a 0.3 per cent gain, by different policy designs.

Under What Aggregation? A Static Aggregation of Sectors, Regions and Households

Paramount policy questions are related to the distributional effects of climate policies on regions, industrial sectors or households. In this regard, the information critical to interpreting the economic meaning of modelling results is the implicit or explicit aggregation principles retained in the models, and the corresponding implicit or explicit compensations. It is very unlikely indeed that climate measures will have evenly distributed effects on regions, individuals or economic sectors: when a 2 per cent loss is reported, this loss is an aggregate measure of variations in income where some may gain and others lose more that 2 per cent. In this respect, a distinction has to be made between the aggregation of sectors and the aggregation of regions and households.

Concerning industry, the higher the level of aggregation, the higher the risk that models overlook how some sectors could suffer from policy-induced shocks too strong to be immediately absorbed in the absence of appropriate accompanying measures. This is a problem of technical limitation rather than one of confusion in the cost concepts or of biased results communication – we will consequently not discuss it further.

Turning to regions and households, the measurement of welfare variations through an aggregate indicator relates to a more fundamental problem. The basic raw materials of welfare assessment (setting aside variations in environmental amenities) are households' income and consumption. But aggregate income or consumption are weak indicators of welfare variations, simply because the utility of a €1 gain or loss is not the same for someone who hardly fulfils their basic needs or for the higher incomes. This difficulty appears whenever one wants to measure the aggregate welfare variation of a group of households or regions from models providing household or regional disaggregations. It is solved by selecting 'weights' to ponder each household category's or each region's welfare.

The first reflex, common for non-economists, is to use the same weights for all household types or regions, as would appear ethically legitimate. But maximising total welfare on such a basis causes a huge movement of income distribution: with the marginal utility of revenue decreasing, minimising the aggregate welfare impact of any environmental policy (in fact of the provision of any public good) results into placing its burden on the richer classes only until per capita incomes are equated. Such a strong egalitarian principle is a matter of ethical and political values; it would be both unrealistic and ethically questionable to adopt it 'in passing', at the occasion of environmental or energy policies Another possibility, retained in optimal control models with several regions, is to resort to Negishi weights, which are roughly inversely correlated to per capita incomes at each point in time (see for example the description of RICE in Nordhaus and Yang, 1996). Doing so imposes a form of 'no redistribution constraint', but at the cost of considering the current and projected distributions of income either as optimal or as unchangeable.

In fact, most general equilibrium models do not directly address distribution issues. Consequently, to avoid misinterpreting an 'x per cent of something' figure, it matters to pay due attention to the fact that this figure is true under two important conditions: the first, rather conservative but politically realistic, is that the individuals and countries forming aggregates are implicitly weighted in function of their revenue (because they represent a higher share of total consumption); the second, more problematic, is that appropriate compensating measures are implemented to moderate the distributive effects. In the absence of such measures, an aggregated figure may mask significant shocks on some portions of the population or of the productive activity, potentially great enough to undermine the political acceptability of climate policies.

A Dynamic Aggregation over Time Periods

Although the costs of climate policies span over years, policy-makers need cost assessments in a form compact enough to be usable in a policy debate. Their need is addressed under two main modalities. The first is a cost at a given point in time, for example a given percentage of GDP loss or a price of carbon in 2012. The second is a discounted sum of costs (whatever their type) over some time period.

The overdominance of these two modalities comes from their apparent simplicity. However, the 'point in time' figures may mislead the comparison of carbon control policies: the policy with the lowest cost at a given date may require a costly acceleration of abatement investments beyond this date. Notwithstanding the long-lasting debates on the appropriate discount rate (see for example Portney and Weyant, 1999; Newell and Pizer, 2001), the 'discounted sum' modality does not present this inconvenience and provides an aggregated indicator, which encompasses all the time periods of the control policy. But the price to pay for this aggregation over time is to lose track of the time profile of costs, making it impossible to detect whether a given policy confronts dramatic peaks in its costs at certain periods. As a striking example, the GDP loss of the First World War for France, with 1.5 million men killed in action (from a population of 40 million) is estimated at only 0.2 per cent of its aggregated 20th century GDP. As long as economic analysis does not provide a convincing evaluation of the difference between the same GDP loss resulting from: (i) a cumulated constant difference between two steady-growth pathways over some extended time-period; and (ii) a 'point' shock on growth concentrated on a short time period, it will be important to supplement the discounted costs assessment by some information on the cost profiles.

Many models are not suited to the in-depth study of such profiles: static general equilibrium models can only report them in a limited way, assuming a smooth and steady transition from the supposed date of the policy implementation to the new equilibrium; recursive models often exogenise the time profile of either the price signal or the emission constraint to derive cost profiles. The models intrinsically suited to studying cost profiles are the optimal control models: their intertemporal decision framework allows them to shift the emission constraint to concentrations or temperature increases – derived from simplified climate modules – thus endogenising both the abatement efforts and the corresponding marginal cost constraints. It is consequently intriguing that they should not be more often applied to richer thought experiments, for example climate policies delayed until some time threshold where new information requires acceleration (Ambrosi et al., 2003).

5.3 THE CRUX OF THE MATTER: CONVEYING TECHNICAL INFORMATION IN AN ECONOMIC ANALYSIS

Among all the measurement issues discussed above, those related to temporality and metrics do not raise any problem that cannot be settled through a careful presentation of results delivering the full set of available indicators. The choice of a type of cost is a much harder nut to crack, as there seems to be a fundamental asymmetry between the tangibility of the notion of 'total abatement expenses', and the theoretical taint of an indicator such as 'total welfare variation'. At a pure scientific level, the core of the matter ultimately hangs on the ability of models to reproduce technical realities, which in turn fundamentally determine the responsiveness of economies to carbon constraints. It is thus important to clarify how technology is described in the various modelling paradigms at hand – this will allow an understanding of why bottom-up analysis does not suffice in providing sound answers in the absence of coupling with general equilibrium analysis.

A first way of representing the techniques that shape the cost of carbon constraints is indeed through the description of explicit detailed equipment stocks in the production and consumption of energy. Such a description is characteristic of bottom-up models, which picture a set of competing equipments identified by their investment, operation and maintenance (O&M) costs, their productivity (in terms of energy services for consumption equipments) and their lifetime. At each period, the scrapping of the existing equipment and the evolution of demand define the need for new capacity. A straightforward cost-efficiency analysis determines which equipment should address this need. Technical progress can be accounted through an evolution of each equipment's characteristics, endogenous or not – some bottom-up models currently feature learning-by-doing (LBD) processes in some way, correlating the investment and O&M costs of an equipment to its market share.

Explicit information about the cost–performance ratio of techniques is thus the 'raw material' of this type of model, from which the most famous types of marginal abatement costs curves (MACCs) are derived. With abatement on the abscissa and marginal cost on the ordinate, these MACCs are generally formed of an ensemble of plateaus, linked by 'stairs' that are rather shallow for low levels of abatement (sometimes with negative costs), become higher as abatement levels increase, and usually end in some form of vertical asymptote: carbon prices tend to the infinite beyond a certain abatement threshold. This engineering-based information is explicit, and easily translated in a very tangible implication: the amount of expenses necessary to a given amount of abatement. However, this should not mask that the MACCs derived from such analysis are also modelling constructs:

- They reflect controversial sets of hypotheses given by technology expertise about negative cost potentials, incremental technical progress and breakthroughs, and so on. These hypotheses interact in more-or-less aggregated technical subsystems that can be highly complex, such as refineries or electric networks.
- Bottom-up analysis still often represents the adoption of technology as 'knife-edge' economic optimisation, in a linear optimization

framework where the shift from one corner solution to another one can be quick. In most models this instability is controlled, but at the cost of modelling artefacts as ad hoc limitations to the penetration rate of techniques. Elements such as market barriers, hidden consumer preferences, the difficulty of economic agents to form long-run expectations in a volatile context, and so on, are yet seldom represented.

- In reality, technical costs are determined by the quantities and prices of intermediary inputs and primary production factors, which are not so easily observable. For instance, in long-run studies the price of bioenergy cannot but depend on the costs of land, labour and transportation and delivery activities, which themselves depend on the scale of production. Bottom-up MACCs are thus conditional upon a set of generally implicit assumptions guaranteeing the precise non-energy price vector considered in their analysis. For the higher carbon constraints, this vector of relative prices may change drastically if compared with that implicitly or explicitly employed, possibly threatening the relevance of bottom-up estimates.

- The carbon price ultimately leading to a certain level of abatement is the price that induces this abatement once all the economic adjustments have operated. As demonstrated by a numerical experiment between IMACLIM and POLES, the wedge between the pre- and post-adjustment prices may be high (Ghersi et al., 2003).

Macroeconomic models address the two latter issues by extending model coverage to all economic flows, at the price of more compact representations of techniques. Thus, they limit the level of detail of the description of technical systems and resort to aggregate production and utility functions as proxies to the real technical flexibilities. The typical multisectoral general equilibrium model thus pictures a number of goods – among them one or several types of energy goods – that compete, to some extent, as: (i) intermediate consumptions in all productions; and (ii) final consumptions for the households. These two competitions are driven by the evolution of the relative prices following substitution elasticities, in more or less complex 'nesting' structures: selected goods compete to form a bundle, which in turn competes with other bundles or goods to form a higher-level aggregate, and so on, up to the output or utility. At each tier of the corresponding tree, different substitution elasticities (possibly nil, under a Leontief assumption) allow enhancement of the match between the model and the realities it is trying to render. As regards production, technical progress typically impacts upon this structure as one or several multipliers applying to some or all factor consumptions; the evolution of these multipliers can be either exogenous or endogenous, with varying specifications in the latter case (LBD, correlation to R&D, to gross investment, and so on). Some models account for another form of exogenous technical progress through the specification of a 'backstop' carbon-free energy technology; the assumptions regarding the cost dynamics of the backstop obviously play a paramount role in the assessment of the higher carbon constraints.

A third option, at the same level of aggregation as the second, submits the dynamics of input–output structure to econometric analysis rather than to production and utility functions. Its main advantage is to relax the constraints imbedded in the functional forms commonly used by macroeconomic models, mechanically enhancing the ability to replicate observed flexibilities. However, econometric specifications are usually estimated on one precise consumption (in economy–energy–environment models, that of energy) and tend to ignore substitution effects.

At the higher aggregation level, optimal control models describe a single-agent ('benevolent planner') economy, in which a production function of primary factors (K, L and possibly but not necessarily some energy goods) approximates all production technologies. Such a high level of stylisation gives the possibility to explore longer terms, over which the basket of technologies cannot be described explicitly – an interesting feature when it comes to carbon policies, considering the inertias involved. On a more pragmatic note, it facilitates calibration, and significantly enhances computation ability, allowing the implementation of intertemporal optimisation over a large number of periods. As a negative consequence, though, its results cannot be linked to an explicit evolution of the energy systems in the short or mid-term; how relevant they are regarding this evolution relies on the specifications governing the decreases in energy or carbon intensity – a representation of technologies by paralipsis.

As is seen from these descriptions, each of the four options to technology description has its pros and cons. To begin with the pros, they all address quite different questions in a satisfactory manner. As for the cons, on the one hand, even the most tangible bottom-up approach, notwithstanding its fundamental partial equilibrium limitations, can be criticized on account of its describing the adoption of new technologies as some cost-efficiency analysis, bypassing the complexity of consumers' preferences as expressed in documented adoption patterns. On the other hand, the more aggregated approaches with implicit technology all suffer, to some extent, from their inability to reproduce technical options and constraints faithfully – a major constraint being the existence of asymptotes to the decreases in energy or carbon intensities, at any given time horizon. Particularly, their treatment of substitution possibilities is inadequate when it comes to households, whose energy-consuming equipment (transportation and residential sectors) is rarely identified, despite its paramount importance in emissions trends.

In a nutshell, there is an obvious need for research devoted to modelling frameworks that allow for an easy back-and-forth reflection from technical realities to integrated price-and-quantities economic analysis. A way out of this deadlock could be hybridisation.

5.4 FROM COSTS TO POLICY SIGNALS: A SOMETIMES TOO HASTY TRANSLATION?

As already hinted, all the nuances brought up in the previous sections are mostly overlooked, not only in the political sphere, but also to some extent in academic circles. Throughout the years, the most successful indicator remained the marginal cost and it is a matter of fact that, whatever the underlying modelling paradigm and the type of cost thus measured, it is often interpreted as the level of price-signal that should be given to agents to achieve a certain environmental objective in a decentralized economy. This rather intuitive interpretation is sometimes correct; but in most cases it should be qualified with some caveats, to say the least.

Let us start with a reminder that, from an economic perspective, any form of marginal carbon cost boils down to the shadow price of some form of carbon constraint, that is, the monetary or welfare costs of strengthening the constraint by one unit. In a dynamic setting, this shadow price exists at any modelling period, from the benchmark year to the projection date. It is explicit in optimisation models, and can theoretically be revealed in any other modelling framework. Starting from there, how far its interpretation can legitimately be stretched in terms of policy signal demands a more in-depth examination.

First, there is no necessary equivalence between the marginal income loss and the marginal value of abatement expenditures (mostly conveyed through a carbon price). To convince oneself of this, suffice it to notice that implementing a carbon constraint in a hypothetical economy without technical flexibility would lead to nil abatement expenditures, but surely to an income loss. On top of this, the body of general equilibrium effects detailed in Section 5.2 determines the wedge at each point in time between the carbon price implied by the required abatement, and the marginal income or welfare losses. The distinction is obvious, if rarely underlined: it is proven by the mere fact that, in the case of a carbon tax, welfare results vary widely with recycling assumptions, as was extensively demonstrated in the exploration of double dividend issues – the following section will exemplify this with the results of the policy runs performed by TranSust modellers during their collaboration. Prominent reviews, though, report both the marginal abatement costs from bottom-up models and the marginal income losses from integrated general equilibrium analyses (IPCC, 1995, 2001). This facilitates the perception that the two notions provide equivalent information about the necessary carbon tax.

Second, the preceding discussion does not incorporate the signalling effect of prices. It is conducted in a static framework, where the abatement cost curve is given, and the carbon price set at the level corresponding to the required abatements. Without entering the difficult discussion of optimal pricing under an induced technical change framework, let us illustrate the point in the case of optimal control models. In such models a wedge may exist between the shadow price of the constraint and the optimal price signal that should be delivered, due to fundamental intertemporal issues. To understand why, let us consider the two time profiles of marginal abatement expenditures and marginal income losses: they are indeed strictly equivalent in models where there is no source of path-dependency between abatement costs at a given date and abatement volumes in the previous periods. But assuming such independency amounts to disregarding the inertia of capital stocks, or learning-by-doing processes – a quite unrealistic stance. Under a more plausible description of technical dynamics, the two profiles do not necessarily match any more: assuming perfect foresight, the 'benevolent planner' considers the entire set of future carbon prices; because of the path-dependency in abatement costs, at each period he decides more abatement expenditures than he would do according to the shadow price of the constraint – variation of the discounted sum of utility along the optimal response pathway up to an infinite horizon. This is due to the fact that, because of inertia in the return of these expenditures in terms of greenhouse gas (GHG) abatement, these expenditures have to be made earlier than they would be in a totally flexible world. Spending more at *t* indeed allows lowering adaptation costs for carbon constraints after *t+n*. The amount of this 'excess expenditure' is directly correlated to the level of inertia in the economy. Now, let us assume the same economy with myopic expectations and the necessity of public signalling to correct this myopia. Should a policy-maker interpreting such results set the time profile of price signals to match that of the marginal abatement expense, or that of the shadow price of the carbon constraint? If he does the latter, myopic agents will under-react. The problem appears dramatically in optimal control models in which heterogeneous sectors are represented; the optimal policy indeed implies spending a far higher amount of expenses on a sector as rigid as the transportation sector in the early periods, when the low level of carbon taxes would imply only marginal departures from the baseline. Conversely, should a carbon tax be set at the shadow price of the carbon constraint, and should the economic agents involved in this sector behave myopically, the transportation sector would under-react, with consequences falling on the entire economy (Lecocq et al., 1998).

There thus appears a policy issue about how to handle 'signalling' deficiencies: is it necessary to set differentiated carbon taxes or carbon taxes complemented by other incentives in the rigid sectors? Is it possible to count on an upgraded credibility of the announcement of carbon prices over the long run, so that economic agents work under perfect expectations in this domain? So far, empirical models have not been much used to explore such debates, although they do incorporate some information to do so.

A final caveat must be placed on another source of gap between the carbon price signal and the marginal social cost at a given point in time: the possibly strong importance of prices other than that of carbon. One simple example is the shadow price of imports: minimising the price of carbon through trading systems, for example by importing tradable emission permits, will induce huge imports that can be a significant political obstacle for some countries (this is one of the arguments of the opponents to Kyoto in the United States). Another example is again related to transportation dynamics. It has been explained why this sector 'should' devote more abatement expenses than those resulting from the shadow prices of carbon during the first decades of a climate policy. However, it is unlikely that any politician will ever take the risk of raising the 'required' levels of carbon taxes on petrol in the early periods; it is also unlikely that decision-makers in this sector will easily internalise the perspective of ever-increasing carbon prices and launch the corresponding adaptation measures (R&D, investment on public transport, switch to oil-free motor fuels, and so on). This should not suggest jumping too quickly to the conclusion that carbon control in the transportation sector is a form of oxymoron. For historical reasons, existing models concentrate on the energy sector and represent transportation as one subdivision of energy demand. The consequence is that they incorporate the price of carbon as the only driver of consumption and technology choices. This is a reasonable simplification for the electricity sector, heating and industrial processing, but in the case of transportation it may be misleading: it is obvious that the demand for mobility, stemming from the location choices of households and firms, is governed not only by transportation costs but also by real estate prices. In other words, when models conclude to the necessity of a certain amount of abatement in the transportation sector, the incentive to reach this amount may be a mix of carbon prices and of policies aimed at controlling the price of the square meter. Carbon prices may thus not be the only signal triggering the appropriate profile of abatement efforts; a far larger set of price signals should be mobilised.

5.5 COST CONCEPTS IN THE TRANSUST MODELS

The TranSust models provide quite a representative sample of the modelling approaches and publication practices of the energy–environment–economy community. The following tables summarize how they represent costs in three broad categories: Tables 5.2, 5.3 and 5.4 respectively echo the two subsections of Section 5.2 and 5.3, by detailing what type of cost, under which temporality, and based on which technology representation, each model is able to deliver.

Table 5.2   Types of Costs Available from the TranSust Models

	Abatement Expenses	Macroeconomic Costs	Welfare Costs
MULTIMAC	.	✓	.
DART	.	✓	✓
DEMETER	.	✓	✓
E3ME	.	✓	.
FEEM-RICE	.	✓	✓
GAIN	✓	✓	.
IMACLIM	✓	✓	.
MARKAL	✓	.	.
MIDE	.	✓	.
PACE	.	✓	✓
W8D	.	✓	.

Note: ✓ Available.

As regards the types of costs reported, the panel of TranSust models expresses the current dominance of the macroeconomic approach to E3 modelling (Table 5.2). A piece of information not appearing in the table: it happens that the models reporting macroeconomic costs are quite evenly divided between macroeconometric models (E3ME, GAIN, MIDE and W8D), and the other approaches. This strongly impacts upon the number of models able to deliver welfare variation estimates, as by definition macro-econometric models do not resort to utility functions to describe household preferences, and hence cannot produce them. MARKAL alone truly belongs to the bottom-up category, which allows it to deliver precise abatement expenses assessments. GAIN and IMACLIM only give elements thereof, either at a quite aggregate level (GAIN), or through a soft-linking

Table 5.3   Costs Temporality in the TranSust Models

	Point-Time Estimate	Discounted Sum	Cost Profile
MULTIMAC	✓	.	.
DART	✓	.	.
DEMETER	✓	✓	.
E3ME	✓	.	.
FEEM-RICE	✓	✓	✓
GAIN	✓	.	.
IMACLIM	✓	.	.
MARKAL	✓	.	.
MIDE	✓	.	.
PACE	✓	✓	.
W8D	✓	.	.

Note: ✓ Available.

with an energy systems model (IMACLIM runs coupled to POLES, a model of prospective energy systems – see Criqui, 2001).

As is the case for cost types, cost temporality is dominated by one of the three distinguished modalities, that of point-time estimates (Table 5.3). Only three models resort to intertemporal optimisation, and thus naturally integrate

Table 5.4   Technology Representation in the TranSust Model

	Explicit Equipment Stocks	Production Functions as Proxies	Econometric Analysis	By Paralipsis
MULTIMAC	.	✓	.	.
DART	.	✓	.	.
DEMETER	.	✓	.	.
E3ME	.	.	✓	.
FEEM-RICE	.	.	.	✓
GAIN	.	.	✓	.
IMACLIM	.	✓	.	.
MARKAL	✓	.	.	.
MIDE	.	.	✓	.
PACE	.	✓	.	.
W8D	.	.	.	✓

Note: ✓ Available.

the discount rates necessary for computing discounted sum estimates. Then, FEEM-RICE alone is able to endogenise (in this instance optimise) cost profiles to attain a given climate target at some horizon. This is partly correlated to the degree of sectoral and regional aggregation, as FEEM-RICE and DEMETER respectively picture a single region and a limited number of commodities, and a single commodity and a limited number of regions. But as regards the point-time–discounted sum distinction this is also a matter of theoretical stance concerning expectations: PACE and DART, typically, are models of a similar structure (CGE) and scope, but respectively consider perfect versus myopic expectations.

Turning to what we described as 'the crux of the matter', Table 5.4 characterizes the representation of technologies in each model, along the four broad categories depicted in Section 5.3 above and their increasing level of abstraction. At one end of the spectrum, MARKAL alone explicitly details concrete equipment stocks that can be characterized according to the particular focus of each analysis. At the other end, FEEM-RICE and W8D, although of a thoroughly different nature, share a similar level of abstraction: they both aggregate all economic activity in a single good, whose production is based on a trade-off between primary factors (capital and labour) only; the link to explicit technologies is thus difficult if not impossible to make. In between those two extremes, the majority of TranSust models disaggregate economic activity in a number of sectors, and resort to either production functions or econometric analysis to describe changes in the corresponding input–output relationships. The 'production function as proxy' paradigm can be argued to be slightly less abstract than its counterpart in the sense that it entails explicit substitution patterns, rather than allowing an independent variation of input volumes.

As another illustration of the preceding sections (namely Section 5.4), the following graphs describe how the marginal costs estimates differ from carbon prices inputs, in the case of the sample runs performed by each modelling team at the occasion of TranSust. For the mere sake of readability, models are grouped according to the only scale of their macroeconomic impact assessment. Figures 5.1 and 5.2 report marginal GDP costs in regard of the carbon taxes corresponding to the five scenarios tested – a general carbon tax linearly increasing from the year 2000 to respectively €10, €20, €30, €50 and €100 per metric tonne of CO_2 in the year 2050. Because of the different time horizons of models, Figure 5.1 presents 2015 estimates, Figure 5.2 presents 2030 ones.

On both graphs, the dotted lines figuring the Identity function $f(x) = x$ make the general point obvious: in most instances the carbon price input, or marginal abatement cost, widely differs from the modelling output of marginal macroeconomic cost. Indeed, for the same model and an identical tax, different recycling options such as through a lump-sum transfer to households (LS), or a decrease in social security contributions (REC, SSC) lead to cost estimates that can go as far as differing in sign.

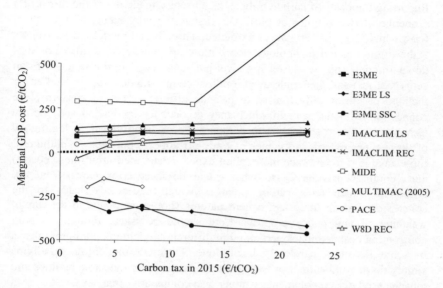

Figure 5.1   Non-Coincidence of Carbon Tax and Marginal Macroeconomic Costs, 2015

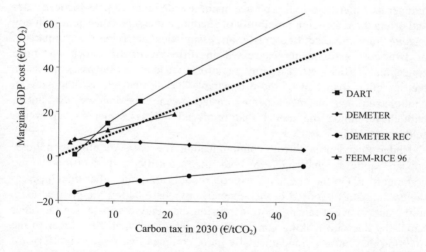

Figure 5.2   Non-Coincidence of Carbon Tax and Marginal Macroeconomic Costs, 2030

5.6   CONCLUSION

Reporting the costs of carbon policies is currently made under the threat of a sequence of two sources of bias. The first is the very nature of the model from which the cost estimate is extracted. Three broad modelling paradigms – the disaggregated technology-rich bottom-up model, the multisector top-down model (be it based on welfare and cost optimisation or on econometrics) and the single-agent optimal control model – are indeed either inclined or intrinsically limited to provide different types of cost, in close connection with the way in which they account for production and end-use technologies. When attempting to compare the meaningfulness or legitimacy of these types of cost, a manner of trade-off appears between 'explicitness' (how easy is it to embrace the explicit expenses summed up in these costs?) and 'comprehensiveness' (to what extent do these costs express the full economic burden of a carbon policy?), which necessarily leads to the conclusion that all three assessment natures should contribute to the careful weighing of any policy proposal. Care should be taken, though, to stop confronting cost estimates pertaining to different modelling paradigms, as has in some instances carelessly been done. Different modelling paradigms simply do not and cannot provide estimates embracing the same realities and must be used in a complementary rather than comparative manner.

A second source of bias lies in the choice of a reporting template, that is in the manner in which modelling results are eventually summed up. The number of dimensions to this choice opens a wide range of possible templates and offers the tantalizing possibility of shaping a message consistent with any *ex ante* conviction, be it optimistic or pessimistic. Clarifying the comparison of two cost assessments expressed in different metrics does not raise conceptual difficulties: it simply requires translating costs assessments in metrics other than that of the original work. The obstacle is pragmatic in nature, as in most instances such a translation cannot be done *ex post*, that is, without rerunning the model that produced the assessment – an option seldom available.

Under this double threat, communicating the costs of climate policies appears quite a challenge, to both the scientific and decision-making communities. On the one hand, experts should bring out rather than hush up the complexities exposed in this chapter, obviously taking the greatest care, in the act, to avoid raising more confusion than they dissipate. On the other hand, the decision-making community should accept that the answer to the question they raise is fundamentally more complex and less straightforward than they would want it to be, on the simple ground, ultimately, that it is manifold in itself.

NOTES

1. A typical example is the European Union maintaining the 'concrete ceiling' proposal as the cornerstone of its diplomatic position, even though economic analysis reveals that this proposal, aimed at forcing the US to undertake diplomatic action, would primarily have penalized Japan and the EU (Hourcade and Ghersi, 2002).
2. Measuring ancillary benefits relates to specific methodological difficulties. But these are not a source of confusion per se because common practice is to present them separately and subtract them from the other policy costs.
3. Another source of misunderstanding, the notion of 'general equilibrium' is often used in referring to a situation in which all markets clear through the adjustment of a price vector, leading to an optimal utilisation of resources. But it is also used in opposition to partial equilibrium, indicating that all markets and their interdependences are accounted for. The question is indeed to capture these interdependences, that is, the propagation of 'policy shocks', regardless of whether the economies under scrutiny are optimal or experience transitional or structural disequilibria.
4. With the notable exception of the G-Cubed model (see for example McKibbin et al., 1999), international financial flows are still dominantly exogenous, determined by the evolution of trade balances.
5. Some models are designed to deliver the average and total costs, others the marginal cost, but all can produce all three indicators. Depending on the type of model from which they are drawn, though, marginal costs ultimately tend to reflect varying realities. This point will be developed in a further section.
6. Welfare variations can be converted to money metrics by computing, alternatively, the equivalent variation in income (the variation in income that would induce the same welfare variation as the policy considered under the initial set of prices), or the compensating variation in income (the variation in income that would maintain welfare at its no-policy level under the policy-induced set of prices).

REFERENCES

Ambrosi, P., J.-C. Hourcade, S. Hallegate, F. Lecocq, P. Dumas and M. Ha-Duong (2003), 'Optimal control models and elicitation of attitudes towards climate change', *Environmental Modeling and Assessment*, **8**(3), 135–47.
Bovenberg, A.L. (1999), 'Green tax reform and the double dividend: An updated reader's guide', *International Tax and Public Finance*, **6**, 421–43.
Criqui, P. (2001). 'POLES: Prospective outlook on long-term energy systems', Institut d'Économie et de Politique de l'Énergie, Grenoble, France.
http://www.upmf-grenoble.fr/iepe/textes/POLES8p_01.pdf [last accessed August 2008].
Ghersi, F., P. Criqui and J.-C. Hourcade (2003), 'Viable responses to the equity–responsibility dilemma: A consequentialist view', *Climate Policy*, **3**(1), 115–33.
Goulder, L.H. (1995), 'Environmental taxation and the double-dividend: A reader's guide', *International Tax and Public Finance*, **2**(2), 157–83.
Goulder, L.H. and S.H. Schneider (1999), 'Induced technological change and the attractiveness of CO_2 abatement policies', *Resource and Energy Economics*, **21**(3–4), 211–53.
Hogan, W.W. and A.S. Manne (1977), 'Energy-economy interactions: The fable of the elephant and the rabbit?', in C.J. Hitch (ed.), *Modeling Energy-Economy Interactions: Five Approaches*, Washington, DC: Resources for the Future, pp. 247–77.
Hourcade, J.-C. (1996), 'Estimating the costs of mitigating greenhouse gases', in

Intergovernmental Panel on Climate Change (IPCC), *Climate Change 1995. Economic and Social Dimensions of Climate Change, Contribution of Working Group III to the Second Assessment Report of the Intergovernmental Panel on Climate Change*, Cambridge: Cambridge University Press, pp. 263–96.

Hourcade, J.-C. and F. Ghersi (2002), 'The economics of a lost deal: Kyoto – The Hague – Marrakesh', *The Energy Journal*, **23**(3), 1–26.

Intergovernmental Panel on Climate Change (IPCC) (1996), *Climate Change 1995: Economic and Social Dimensions of Climate Change, Contribution of Working Group III to the Second Assessment Report of the IPCC*, Cambridge: Cambridge University Press.

Intergovernmental Panel on Climate Change (IPCC) (2001), *Climate Change 2001: Mitigation, Contribution of Working Group III to the Third Assessment Report of the IPCC*, Cambridge: Cambridge University Press.

International Energy Agency (IEA) (2003), *World Energy Investment Outlook 2003 – Insights*, Paris: IEA Books.

Lecocq, F., J.-C. Hourcade and M. Ha-Duong (1998), 'Decision making under uncertainty and inertia constraints: Sectoral implications of the when flexibility', *Energy Economics*, **20**, 539–55.

Markandya, A. and K. Halsnaes (2001), 'Costing methodologies', in Intergovernmental Panel on Climate Change (IPCC), *Climate Change 2001: Mitigation, Contribution of Working Group III to the Third Assessment Report of the Intergovernmental Panel on Climate Change*, Cambridge: Cambridge University Press, pp. 451–98.

McKibbin, W.J., M. Ross, R. Shackelton and P.J. Wilcoxen (1999), 'Emissions trading, capital flows and the Kyoto protocol', in J.P. Weyant and J. Hill (eds), *The Energy Journal*, Special Issue: *The Costs of the Kyoto Protocol: A Multi-Model Evaluation,*, 257–333.

Newell, R. and W. Pizer (2001), 'Discounting the distant future: How much do uncertain rates increase valuations?' Discussion Paper 00–45 (revised version), Resources for the Future, Washington, DC, USA, available at: http://www.rff.org/Documents/RFF-DP-00-45.pdf [last accessed September 2008].

Nordhaus, W.D. and Z. Yang (1996), 'A regional dynamic general equilibrium model of alternative climate change strategies', *The American Economic Review*, **86**, 741–56.

Portney, P.R. and J.P. Weyant (eds) (1999), *Discounting and Intergenerational Equity*, Washington, DC: RFF Press.

6. Technical Progress in TranSust Models

Valentina Bosetti and Marzio Galeotti

6.1 INTRODUCTION

Technological change is a major force in a country's economic growth. Since before the industrial revolution, economies and societies have first relied on wind, water, animal power and wood, then on coal, and finally on natural gas and petroleum. Today, many technologies utilize fossil fuels, which has led to the release of large amounts of carbon to the atmosphere, and the scientific consensus is that these releases will cause the earth's climate to change. Fortunately, however, technology changes over time. Technological innovation is increasingly seen as one of the main practical keys for reconciling the current fundamental conflict between economic activity and the environment.

No one really believes or is ready to accept that the solution of the climate change problem consists of reducing the pace of economic growth. Instead, it is believed that changes in technology will bring about the longed decoupling of economic growth from generation of polluting emissions.

There is a difference in attitude in this respect, though. Some maintain a faithful view that technological change, having a life of its own, will automatically solve the problem. In contrast, others express the conviction that the process of technological change by and large responds to impulses and incentives, and it therefore has to be fostered by appropriate policy actions.

Technological change generally leads to the substitution of obsolete and dirty technologies with cleaner ones. However, technical change is not per se always environment-friendly, as it can lead to the emergence of new sectors and industries with new kinds and degrees of pollution problems, like the generation of new harmful pollutants. Hence, there are no substitutes for policy in directing the innovation efforts toward fostering economic growth and helping the environment at the same time.

All the above remarks are reflected in climate models, the main quantitative tools designed either to depict long-run energy and pollution scenarios or to assist in climate change policy analysis. Climate models have traditionally accounted for the presence of technical change, albeit usually evolving in an exogenous fashion. More recently, however, models have been proposed where the technology changes endogenously and/or its change is induced by deliberate choices of agents and government intervention. We have therefore moved or are moving toward an endogenous and induced formulation of technical change. In particular, both bottom-up and top-down models, a long-standing distinction in energy–economy–environment modeling, have recently been modified in order to accommodate forms of endogenous technical change. As it turns out, the bottom-up approach has mostly experimented with the notion of learning-by-doing (LbD henceforth), while a few top-down models have entertained the notion of a stock of knowledge which accumulates over time via research and development (R&D) spending (see Galeotti and Carraro, 2003 for a survey).

In this chapter we consider what the situation looks like for the various models involved in the TranSust project. The remainder of the chapter is as follows. Section 6.2 briefly reviews the main ways of modeling the process of technological change in economic–climate models. Particular attention is paid to endogenous and induced technical change. There we also consider the key aspects of modeling induced technical change, aspects which the 'ideal' model should incorporate. Section 6.3 assesses the TranSust models from the point of view of technical change (TC) and of induced technical change (ITC). Concluding comments close the chapter.

6.2   LITERATURE OVERVIEW[1]

Dealing with (very) long-run phenomena, every model that purports to describe the essential elements of human economic activities should allow for technological change. Models which describe the interactions between economic activities and the environment – the climate in particular – by necessity incorporate a description of the process of technological change.

From Exogenous to Endogenous Technical Change

In early models used to assess the effects of policies designed to control polluting emissions, technical change had an exogenous representation. This is still true today, even for some celebrated models of integrated assessment, such as Nordhaus and Yang (1996)'s RICE model, where technology does evolve over time, but in an exogenous fashion. And this is also true for most models used in recent assessments of the costs of complying with the Kyoto Protocol (see IPCC, 2001, Chapter 8 for an overview). TC would often take the form of indexes of productivity (labor productivity of Hicks-neutral technical change in production functions) exogenously evolving over time.

Limiting the attention to energy-saving or emission-reducing technical change, one early formulation often exploited in top-down modeling was based on the future adoption of backstop technologies. This is a discrete event which takes place in a given, exogenously determined year and which is assumed to be resource unconstrained. As a prominent example, the GREEN model developed at the Organisation for Economic Co-operation and Development (OECD) (Burniaux et al., 1992) allowed for three backstop options: a carbon-based synthetic fuel, and two carbon-free possibilities. The main hypotheses concerned prices and timing of diffusion: prices are exogenous and the backstop technologies, once they are assumed to come on stream, are available in all regions in unlimited quantities at constant marginal costs.

Subsequently, there followed a number of attempts aimed at endogenizing the linkages between economic variables (policy variables, in particular) and technical progress. The main difficulty faced by modelers was the non-observability of this latter variable. For this reason, earlier models used a deterministic time trend as a proxy of technical change. This was the starting point of some ad hoc attempts to model technical change. For example, in Boone et al. (1992), Carraro and Galeotti (1996) and Dowlatabadi and Oravetz (1997), technical progress was represented by a time variable added to the principal equations of the model. However, this variable was not a deterministic function of time; it was rather a stochastic function of time, in which other economic effects were also accounted for. The problem with these approaches was their ad hoc nature.

Modeling Endogenous and Induced Technical Change

In terms of environmental modeling, the bottom-up approach has mostly appealed to the notion of LbD, while a few top-down models have entertained the notion of a stock of knowledge which accumulates over time via R&D spending.

A number of bottom-up models have integrated endogenous technological change that assumes LbD. Examples are MESSAGE (Messner, 1997) and MARKAL (Barreto and Kypreos, 2002a), dynamic linear programming models of the energy sector that are generally used in tandem with MACRO, a macroeconomic model which provides economic data for the energy sector (Manne, 1981; see also Manne and Barreto, 2004; Seebregts et al., 1999).[2] These models optimize the choice between different technologies using given abatement costs and carbon emission targets. They feature a learning or experience curve describing technological progress as a function of accumulating experience with production (LbD for manufacturers) and with use (learning-by-using – LbU – for consumers) of a technology during its diffusion. Technological learning has been observed historically for many different industries and is a well-established concept.

Recent developments have considered two-factor learning functions in which there is a separate effect, besides cumulative capacity, of R&D expenditures on the costs of specific energy technologies (Criqui et al., 2000; see also Miketa and Schrattenholzer, 2004). Barreto and Kypreos (2004) introduce a knowledge stock function to model a two-factor learning curve in the ERIS model.

In terms of top-down modeling, the focus has been more on R&D-induced technical change than on LbD. Models featuring an endogenous technology belong to either one of two categories: computable general equilibrium (CGE) or optimal growth models. An example of the former group is the multiregion, multisector integrated assessment model called WIAGEM (Kemfert, 2005).

Besides Nordhaus's RICE, which we review below, the other probably most popular climate model is Manne and Richels's (1992) MERGE model. Like RICE, MERGE is an intertemporal growth model in which each of the model's regions maximizes the discounted utility of its consumption subject to an intertemporal budget constraint. A distinguishing feature of the model is that it combines a top-down perspective on the remainder of the economy together with a bottom-up representation of the energy supply sector. A distinction is made between electric and non-electric energy. There are several alternative sources of electricity supply, some of them being in operation in the base year (2000), others due to be available later on. In a very recent version of the model (Manne and Richels, 2004), one of the previous two electric backstop technologies, the low-cost one, is replaced by an LbD process. Its total costs are initially identical to those of the high-cost backstop, but its learning costs decline by 20 percent for every doubling of cumulative experience.

Another recent model which exploits the notion of LbD to endogenize technical change is the DEMETER model proposed by van der Zwaan et al. (2002) (see also Gerlagh and van der Zwaan, 2003; Gerlagh et al., 2004; Gerlagh and van der Zwaan, 2004).[3] A macroeconomic (top-down) model is specified that distinguishes between two different energy technologies, carbon and carbon-free. The costs of the latter are dependent upon the cumulative capacity installed. Thus the model is expanded with learning curves previously used in energy system (bottom-up) models. The model is a global one and cannot address issues such as emission trading.

The RICE model has been used by Nordhaus (2002) to lay out a model of induced innovation brought about by R&D efforts. In particular, technological change displays its effects through changes in the emissions–output ratio. This aspect was actually embedded in the non-regional version of the author's RICE model for climate change policy analysis, called DICE (Nordhaus, 1993). Nordhaus (2002) is often quoted by authors who claim that induced technical change is not very important. More relevant appears to be input substitution away from 'carbon energy', relative to R&D-prompted innovation. The former reduces carbon intensity twice as much as the latter. Nordhaus (2002) compares two versions of DICE, the global counterpart of the RICE model. In one case, output-constrained movements along the production isoquant are considered; in the induced innovation version capital is exogenous, that is, there is no investment and no gross national product (GNP) growth, and a technology with fixed coefficients between carbon energy on the one hand and a capital–labor combination on the other. It remains to be seen how the results change when, more realistically, optimal economic growth is allowed.

This is what Popp (2004) does. As in Nordhaus, R&D is four times more costly than physical investment, to account for the divergent social and private rates of return associated with R&D. The author also admits the possibility of crowding out (at the 50 percent rate). Popp postulates an effective energy input given by a CES combination of purchased energy diminished by an exogenous technical change component and a stock of knowledge based on R&D. There are diminishing returns to R&D when translating into knowledge stock. The author compares a carbon emissions policy scenario under exogenous and endogenous formulations of technical change. A positive effect on welfare results from the induced innovation scenario relative to the exogenous case (on a 1995–2205 horizon), but the impact on the key economic and environmental variables is small. There is a small decrease in emissions under the endogenous model formulation, but no effect on temperature, along with a negligible impact on output.

The conclusions of the study is that technical change is no cure-all for climate change. Technological gains do not occur without a policy signal that R&D is profitable. The welfare gains resulting from induced innovation come from cost savings, but the impact on the environment is minimal. Popp's modified DICE model contains a very careful modeling of the R&D/innovation component and of the way it is embedded in the climate model. A limitation of the model is that it is global and its carefully calibrated parameters typically refer to the US economy. In a very recent variation dubbed ENTICE-BR, Popp (2006) extends the ENTICE model to also include an energy backstop technology.

Another interesting model of knowledge accumulation is proposed by Goulder and Mathai (2000), in which a central planner chooses time paths of abatement and R&D efforts in order to minimize the present value of the costs of abating emissions and of R&D expenditures subject to an emission target. The abatement cost function depends both on abatement and on the stock of knowledge that increases over time via R&D investment. By assuming a central planner, this model sidesteps the problem of explicitly modeling innovation incentives and appropriability. A second formulation studied by the authors assumes that the rate of change of the knowledge stock is governed by abatement efforts themselves. This form of technological change is termed LbD.[4]

Both endogenous and induced technical change are taken into account by Buonanno et al. (2000, 2001, 2002).[5] In particular, it is assumed that R&D investment accumulates into a stock of knowledge that affects both the production technology (endogenous technical change) and the emission–output ratio (induced technical change). Extending Nordhaus and Yang (1996)'s RICE model, it is assumed that the stock of knowledge enters the production function as one of the production factors and, at the same time, affects the emission–output ratio, as originally proposed by Goulder and Mathai (2000) (see also Nordhaus, 2002). Thus, the idea is that more knowledge will help firms increase their productivity and reduce their negative impact on the environment. In this modified version, the central planner in each country chooses the optimal R&D effort that, in turn, increases the stock of technological knowledge. The amount of R&D is therefore a strategic variable.

Using that model, labeled 'ETC-RICE' or 'FEEM-RICE', the policy game played by the six regions in which the world is divided was solved.[6] Each region chooses the optimal level of four instruments: fixed investments, R&D expenditures, rate of emission control and the amount of permits which each country wants to buy or sell. Two versions of the model were considered: in the first one, with endogenous technical change, the choice of the optimal amount of R&D does not affect the emission–output ratio; in the second one, with induced technical change (that is, endogenous environmental technical change), a change in the stock of knowledge also modifies the emission–output ratio. This therefore depends on the optimal R&D chosen by each country, which is in turn dependent on relative prices and hence also on climate policies.

Castelnuovo et al. (2005) use the same model, but further extend it so as to allow for an alternative source of technical change, learning-by-doing (LbD). In particular, the authors use arguments originally made by Arrow (1962) in supposing that the accumulation of knowledge occurs not as a result of deliberate (R&D) efforts, but as a side-effect of conventional economic activity. LbD was first introduced in climate models in the bottom-up approach by Anderson and Bird (1992) and Messner (1997). Central to these dynamic energy simulation models is the notion of a 'learning curve', which reflects the observation that with greater 'experience' (cumulative production), there is a pronounced tendency for a decline in the unit costs of novel technologies (such as photovoltaics and wind power), but there is no obvious decline in the unit costs of more conventional methods (such as supercritical coal and natural gas – combined cycle). The newer technologies tend to be higher in unit costs than the conventional ones. If investors based all their decisions on immediate costs, there would be little tendency to support the newer technologies that are currently more expensive. Their cumulative experience is too small, and they could be 'locked out' permanently. This is the rationale for public intervention in the market. Leaning-by-doing entails the acceptance of high near-term costs in return for an expected lowering of future costs.

In this extension of the RICE model, the authors follow Romer (1996) in modeling LdB in the simplest way, that is by assuming that learning occurs as a side-effect of the accumulation of new physical capital. This entails a production function which exhibits increasing returns to capital. In order to maintain the analogy with the R&D-based version of the model, they also allow for the emission–output ratio to depend upon cumulated capacity, that is, the sum of past physical investment efforts. It should be apparent that these model specifications make explicit reference to the recently developed theory of endogenous growth which emphasizes the role of knowledge, of physical and human capital, R&D activities and LbD.

Technological Spillovers

There is a further dimension of technical change that ought to be incorporated in climate models: new technologies are developed by the most innovative firms and are not immediately available to all. Factors that influence the rate and timing of diffusion are of fundamental importance in assessing the ultimate effectiveness of the innovation.

Modeling this factor is obstructed by certain characteristics of empirical environmental models. In general, top-down models do not provide the degree of sector disaggregation that would be required for an analysis at the level of the firm, while bottom-up studies do not consider strategic market behavior that may delay the diffusion of innovation.

There are however some attempts to model spillovers and diffusion. One such attempt (Buonanno et al., 2002) can be taken directly from the empirical literature on endogenous growth (see, for example, Ciccone, 1996). Here, the production function is specified in order to account for positive R&D externalities. These externalities are the mechanism through which endogenous growth takes place. Recall that in the FEEM-RICE model the agent chooses the optimal R&D effort which increases the stock of technological knowledge. This stock in turn enters the production function as one of the production factors and, at the same time, affects the emission–

output ratio. R&D is thus a strategic variable, the idea being that more knowledge helps to increase a firm's productivity and reduce the negative impact on the environment. In Buonanno et al. (2000, 2002) a further extension of the model has productivity and emission intensity also affected by foreign knowledge, to account for international knowledge spillovers.

Barreto and Kypreos (2002b) embed learning spillovers in their bottom-up multiregional MARKAL model. With these spillovers, emission constraints in a given region, which force the deployment of low-carbon technologies there, affect the technology mix in other regions, even if they do not face emission constraints or have the possibility to trade emission permits with the constrained regions. Spillovers across regions allow the unconstrained regions to benefit from the cost reductions of the learning technologies triggered by the carbon reduction limits fulfilled by the constrained regions. The paper analyzes only the impact of learning in electricity generation technologies and full spillover across regions is considered.

Modeling Induced Technical Change: Key Features and the Ideal Case

Induced TC does not involve the mere passage of time, but it stems out of deliberate research and innovation decisions of economic agents. To be termed 'induced', however, that aspect is not sufficient, as induced TC must respond to policy through a variety of mechanisms that are not limited to the changes in relative prices. In other words, induced TC refers to the idea that policy produces shifts of the production isoquant, and not only shifts along the production isoquant.

As noted by Clarke and Weyant (2002), theoretical work on endogenous TC is comprised essentially of two strands: innovation theory and endogenous growth theory.[7] Innovation theory has a microeconomic focus, looks at individual firms and industries, and stresses the incentives and the inefficiencies that result from the failure to share the benefits of the innovation activity. Endogenous growth theory asks how investment in innovation by private agents can be a source of aggregate economic growth.

Climate change models typically try to combine aspects of both theories: they share the feature of the importance of knowledge being a public good and highlight the importance of spillovers, as the incomplete appropriability of the benefits from innovation by private firms creates positive externalities. Spillovers cause underinvestment in innovation, appropriability causes monopoly behavior. Indeed, theoretical work shows and empirical work confirms that markets do not invest efficiently in innovation and that underinvestment is significant enough to warrant attention by policy-makers. Clarke and Weyant (2002) define this situation as 'innovation market failures', and claim that they are very important and an essential aspect of induced TC modeling. However, these failures are also very complex, so that rigorous modeling is problematic.

It is nonetheless a useful exercise to consider the main ingredients of induced TC and the various aspects of those innovation market failures. Consideration of these elements will provide a sort of checklist that can be used against the numerical climate–economy models incorporating induced TC that have appeared in the literature. We therefore follow and summarize the main modeling implications contained in Clarke and Weyant (2002):

- Because spillovers are a fundamental source of economic growth, they ought to be incorporated in any model aiming to describe the long-term process of TC. A full accounting of spillovers in climate change models is probably asking too much, as they occur within industries, across industries within countries, and across countries. Clearly, however, to account for intersectoral spillovers a model must be sectorally disaggregated, while to account for international spillovers the model must include a regional disaggregation.

- The difference between private and social returns associated with innovation activity ought to be acknowledged. Private returns to R&D tend to be appreciably smaller than social returns, in proportions of 20–30 percent to around 50 percent according to empirical studies.

- Climate models with induced TC must specify the mechanism through which technological change takes place and the way it alters technology. To date two mechanisms have been considered: research and development spending and experience building. An advantage of the LbD approach is its simplicity and its reduced calibration requirements relative to the R&D approach. The latter, on the other hand, allows for more room for policy maneuvering (energy/environmental R&D can be subsidized) and additional control variables to rely on. Clearly, neither approach is a complete picture of what goes on in reality, so that models that are based on one or the other formulation inevitably miss something important. While no model can closely approximate the real world, the question is whether and at what modeling cost it is possible to account for both varieties of induced TC in a satisfactory manner.

- Besides the choice of type of TC – R&D versus experience – it is also important to specify where and how those mechanisms actually bring about a change in technology. One distinction is between the energy and the non-energy sector. In this respect the suggested modeling strategy is to start with induced TC in the energy industry, leaving other TC as exogenous. While, as previously noted, it is true that intersectoral spillovers are important, it would probably be too difficult to include the complex interrelations between energy technologies and other technologies. The resulting model would be too abstract or too cumbersome to be of any use.

- It may be worthwhile to consider two sources of energy-saving or carbon-saving improvements: decarbonization of energy services and reduction in the energy intensity of economic activities. The second source of TC is more complicated to account for since it involves R&D in sectors other than the energy industry. In the light of the previous remark, modelers may consider keeping the evolution of the energy intensity of non-energy technologies as exogenously generated.

- Induced TC is not an all-or-nothing proposition. There are complimentary sources of technological advance. One is public sector R&D: publicly financed research will accompany subsidies to private R&D as a form of TC fostering policies. Another source is intersectoral spillovers, already mentioned before. The final source of TC is major innovations and breakthroughs. What do these complimentary sources tell us about modeling TC? The implication is that ultimately some technological progress must remain exogenous.

- Technological heterogeneity is an important issue. One potential implication is discontinuous TC. Even if innovation is continuous and incremental in individual technologies, the aggregate production function's response to innovation investment may be non-linear and exhibit discontinuities. What do induced TC models miss when they aggregate technologies? Aggregate models are not capable of accounting for the relevance of emerging technologies and the associated notion that the allocation, not only the absolute level, of innovation is important. In this respect, models can in principle entertain heterogeneous technologies. Bottom-up models are best suited for the purpose, whereas top-down models can probably at most distinguish between carbon-intensive and non-carbon-intensive technologies.

- TC is an uncertain process. Uncertainty affects both the rate and direction of TC. Uncertainty characterizes the potential for new technologies, that is the extent to which individual technologies will respond to R&D or experience, and the heterogeneity and discontinuities in technology development. Essentially these are 'parameter' uncertainties, where the parameters refer to the response of technology to innovative effort or R&D. These are important for modeling and the issue can be addressed by basing that response on expected values of uncertain parameter distributions.

- Innovation takes time and is risky. To the extent that markets have different preferences for risk and time than society preferences, markets will invest in innovation differently than would be socially optimal. Risk aversion and discounting start playing a role when we consider technological heterogeneity, and emerging environmental technologies in particular. This aspect can be then best addressed by bottom-up models which are capable of distinguishing between more mature and newer technologies, and between more and less competitive technologies. The deviation of private risk aversion and time preference from socially preferred values can however also be captured, though in an ad hoc fashion, by bottom-up models by arbitrarily increasing the price of R&D resources or adjusting the spillover parameter(s) upward.

- Not all investment activity can be captured by models assuming rational behavior. Entrepreneurial animal spirits can also guide innovation choices. While climate models are likely to face serious difficulties in explicitly accounting for this aspect, they can nevertheless allow for an implication of quasi-rational, or routine-based behavior (as in evolutionary theories): the tendency to undertake research efforts on technologies already in use will bias private sector behavior toward dominant technologies. The effect is therefore similar to the point made in the previous remark.

- The very essence of evolutionary economics and the historical evidence suggest that technological change evolves with a lot of inertia. It is, in other words, characterized by path-dependence. This implies that the rate, and especially the direction, of TC may respond sluggishly to economic stimuli relative to the no-frictions standard neoclassical models. More problematically, it also implies that what we do today affects how the economy will respond in the future: today's actions redirect the future path of TC. Incorporating path-dependence into climate models is probably prohibitively complicated, except perhaps in resorting to adding time lags in the process of technology development.

- A final point refers to technology diffusion as opposed to technology innovation. One obvious way to account for this aspect is the introduction of time lags, as noted above. This strategy does not do justice to the importance and implications of technological diffusion vis-à-vis technology development, but it may represent a reasonable shortcut, an acceptable compromise to make especially in top-down models.

To date the literature includes only few examples of numerical climate–economy models explicitly addressing the problem of incorporating induced TC. A number of them have been mentioned in the previous subsection. Table 6.1 shows the extent to which some of those models address the ideal features of ITC just outlined. With the Clarke and Weyant (2002)'s blueprint we can now turn our attention to the models included in the TranSust project.

Table 6.1   Induced TC Features of Some Climate Models

	R&D	Learning	Technology Spillovers	Private/Social Returns to R&D	ITC in Energy	ITC in Non-Energy	Energy Saving ITC	Carbon Saving ITC	Public R&D/ Complementary Sources of TC	Technological Heterogeneity	Technological Uncertainty	Path Dependence	Diffusion
R&DICE	✓	✗	✗	✓	✓	✗	✗	✓	✓	✓	✗*	✗	✗
ETC-RICE	✓	✓	✓	✗	✗	✓	✗	✓	✓	✗	✗	✗	✗
DEMETER 1	✗	✓	✗	✗	✓	✗	✗	✓	✗	✓	✗	✗	✗
MERGE	✗	✓	✗	✗	✓	✗	✓	✓	✓	✓	✗**	✓	✓
ERIS/MARKAL/MESSAGE	✗	✓	✗	✗	✓	✗	✓	✓	✗	✗	✗	✓	✓
BARRETO KYPREOS	✓	✓	✓	✗	✓	✗	✓	✓	✗	✗	✗	✓	✓
ENTICE	✓	✗	✗	✓	✓	✗	✗	✓	✓	✗	✗	✗	✗
DEMETER 2E	✓	✓	✗	✓	✓	✗	✗	✓	✗	✓	✗	✗	✗
ENTICE-BR	✓	✗	✗	✓	✓	✗	✗	✓	✓	✓	✗	✗	✗
WIAGEM	✓	✗	✓	✓	✓	✓	✓	✗	✓	✓	✗	✗	✗

Notes:
✓   Yes.
✗   No.
*   Uncertainty on technology is however discussed in Nordhaus and Popp (1997).
**   Uncertainty on technology is however discussed in Manne and Richels (2003).

6.3   TREATMENT IN TRANSUST MODELS

Computerized models suitable for addressing climate change issues should be able to describe the dynamics of a few relevant variables. This is because climate change, and more generally sustainability, are (very) long-run phenomena. Key variables appear to be economic growth, population and technology.

Crucially, determining the ability of a model to depict the evolution of technical change over time is the basic structure with respect to the following aspects:

- Intertemporality: is the model optimizing an intertemporal objective?
- Degree of endogenization of other relevant variables, such as population and climate-related variables.
- Degree of sectoral disaggregation.
- Degree of regional disaggregation.
- Degree of technological disaggregation.

These are all aspects which limit the capability of a model to incorporate the 'ideal' features of ITC considered above.

The models involved in the TranSust project belong to quite different groups and they basically cover the whole spectrum of economy–energy modeling. First of all, there is one bottom-up model (MARKAL) while all others are top-down (though it seems that IMACLIM exploits bottom-up information). A second important distinction is between econometrically estimated models (E3ME, MIDE, MULTIMAC, W8D) and calibrated ones (DART, DEMETER, FEEM-RICE, IMACLIM, MARKAL, PACE). Thirdly, there are computable general equilibrium models – one static (IMACLIM) and two recursive dynamic (DART, PACE) – together with growth models (DEMETER and FEEM-RICE).

Looking at the degree of disaggregation, we have single-region models (MARKAL, MIDE, MULTIMAC, W8D) or global models (DEMETER) alongside multiregion models (DART, E3ME, FEEM-RICE, IMACLIM, PACE). Considering the sectoral disaggregation of economic activities, most models are disaggregated with exception of FEEM-RICE, DEMETER and W8D. The disaggregation refers to output production; if, however, we refer to disaggregation of energy sources, only FEEM-RICE is not (indeed, there is no energy source in the model). Multiple technologies are explicitly included in a few models, DEMETER (carbon and non-carbon) and especially MARKAL.

In view of the considerations made in the previous section, it should be clear that the philosophy underlying the construction of each model, its nature, and the degree of disaggregation involved are important ingredients for modeling the process of technical change. Generally speaking, most models in the TranSust project specify technical change either as an exogenous process or as an endogenous phenomenon linked, in a somewhat ad hoc way, to other variables determined within the model itself. Often technical change in production is of the Hicks-neutral variety, so that total factor productivity grows exogenously over time. Sometimes it is labor productivity that grows exogenously over time. As for energy, standard exogenous autonomous energy efficiency improvements (AEEI) are assumed.

The endogenization of technical change is achieved in E3ME by relating a number of endogenous variables (energy demand, imports and import prices, exports and export prices, employment and output production) to variables thought to capture innovation efforts (ITC and non-ITC investment, education as a proxy for human capital, and R&D expenditures). In IMACLIM Hicks-neutral technical change is made a function of equilibrium investment (though the conceptual justification is unclear); there are also spillovers from (energy-oriented) capital accumulation (whatever that means). In the MULTIMAC model the AEEI index is related to specific investments and prices, thus achieving the endogenization of energy technical change.

The two main sources of induced technical change, learning-by-doing and by research, driven by accumulation of knowledge and/or experience, are incorporated in a few TranSust models. In particular, besides E3ME, R&D is featured in the FEEM-RICE model, whereas learning curves are included in DEMETER and in the bottom-up MARKAL model, as well as in an alternative version of FEEM-RICE.

The above information is summarized by the answers to the following questions that are centered upon the notion of ITC, a specialization of the concept of endogenous TC.

Is ITC in the Energy and/or in the Non-Energy Sector Considered in Your Model?

DAEDALUS/MULTIMAC. Partly (in the form of embodied TC).

DART. No.

DEMETER. Yes, for both fossil fuels and renewables a learning curve is included in the model that describes decreasing future energy production costs as experience accumulates.

E3ME. Yes, gross fixed investment, enhanced by R&D expenditure in constant prices, is accumulated to provide a measure of the technological capital stock and technological progress. This measure is introduced into equations for 17 users of aggregate energy and 17 by 4 fuel use equations (for the four energy carriers coal, heavy oil, gas and electricity).

FEEM-RICE. The model is a single-sector model with no energy source. ITC is modeled in the non-energy sector (single good production) and in the relationship linking output directly to emissions.

IMACLIM. In each region of IMACLIM a Hicks-neutral ITC applies to all production sectors. In the energy sector, it cumulates with a change in technologies, implicit in IMACLIM but derived from explicit BU simulations (POLES model).

MARKAL. ITC in the model may be realized through shifts in technology, or by development of technologies themselves. The latter is described primarily as endogenous technological change. At present, this formalism is only applied to technologies in the energy sector. Note, however, that MARKAL is primarily an energy system model, and that therefore the description of sectors other than the energy sector is limited.

MIDE. ITC is neither considered in the energy nor in the non-energy sectors. ITC is a sector on its own related to the other sectors only through sales of inputs. Since technology and technology change is assumed to be exogenous, the only effect of an increase in ITC productivity or production would be an increase in other sectors production.

PACE. The model in its current version does not feature ITC – not least because an appropriate parameterization of a multisector multiregion CGE model based on empirical evidence for ITC poses severe problems of data availability and micro–macro inconsistencies.

W8D. There is only an implicit impact of ITC upon the economy via formation of cumulated TFP, being explicitly included in the model.

Does ITC Affect the Energy Intensity Relationship, or the Carbon Intensity, or Both?

DAEDALUS/MULTIMAC. The energy intensity in heating demand of households and in private transport demand.

DART. No.

DEMETER. The energy intensity will increase when learning makes the future energy supply cheaper. This process is offset by an autonomously assumed increase in energy efficiency of the overall production. Carbon intensity of energy will fall when prices for renewables fall faster than for fossil fuels, due to ITC.

E3ME. ITC affects both energy intensity, through the aggregate energy equations by sector, and carbon intensity, through the mix of aggregate energy demand and use of fuels within each sector. Fuel use equations are estimated for four fuels – coal, heavy oils, gas and electricity – with four sets of equations estimated for the fuel users in each region. These equations are intended to allow substitution between these energy carriers by users on the basis of relative prices, while overall fuel use and the technological progress variables determine the fuel choice mix.

FEEM-RICE. As there is no energy, ITC only affects the carbon intensity of production.

IMACLIM. Both. On the one hand a 'macro' ITC coefficient lowers the amount of primary and secondary factors needed in all production sectors, including the energy consumption. On the other hand the carbon intensity of all consumption (including by households) is based on POLES results, to reflect fuel and/or technology substitutions.

MARKAL. ITC affects either energy intensity or the carbon intensity, depending on which technological options are applied.

MIDE. No.

W8D. There is direct impact of ITC (or rather total factor productivity – TPF) upon the carbon emissions in the equation generating carbon dioxide emission.

What is/are the Driver/s of ITC (R&D Expenditures, Experience Accumulation)?

DAEDALUS/MULTIMAC. Capital accumulation. Different efficiency parameters are linked to different vintages (for houses) and different types (for vehicles) of capital.

DART. n.a.

DEMETER. Experience accumulation.

E3ME. Technological progress is represented by accumulation of investment (learning by doing) and R&D expenditure in key industries producing energy-using equipment and vehicles.

FEEM-RICE. There are two versions of the model. In one ITC is accounted for by learning-by-researching (LbR): it is assumed that innovation is brought about by R&D spending which contributes to the accumulation of the stock of existing knowledge. In another version of the model ITC is accounted for by learning-by-doing (LbD), modeled in terms of installed capacity. This in turn is given by cumulated physical investment. Both LbR and LbD affect the production of the single good and the emission–output relationship.

IMACLIM. ITC is a function of total investment net of abatement expenditures (crowding-out assumption), as a proxy of cumulated investment (IMACLIM is a comparative-static model).

MARKAL. ITC may become available through experience accumulation (in the case of endogenous technological learning) or through (exogenously specified) change in technological options.

MIDE. Since technology and technology change is assumed to be exogenous, the only effect of an increase in ITC productivity or production would be an increase in other sectors' production.

W8D. There are three factors generating accumulation of TFP in the model. Those are: (i) domestic outlays on R&D incurred by state and private agents; (ii) foreign outlays on R&D of the main trading partners of Poland, weighted by the shares of Polish imports from those countries (Germany, the UK, the USA, France, Italy, The Netherlands); (iii) human capital.

Does Your Model Account for Spillover Effects, Either Between Sectors or Between Regions, or Both?

DAEDALUS/MULTIMAC. No.

DART. n.a.

DEMETER. No.

E3ME. There are spillover effects over 41 industrial sectors and 19 EU regions via intermediate demand (modeled through input–output coefficients which change over time to allow for changes in mix and relative prices of different fuels) and through internal and external wage rate and trade (both volume and price) effects.

FEEM-RICE. There is a version of the model with ITC in the form of LbR which allows for international spillover effects of the stock of knowledge.

IMACLIM. Within each region, the extent of spillovers between abatement-specific and general investment is a control variable of the model. No spillover between regions is yet accounted for (the model used for TranSust is a one-region global model anyway).

MARKAL. The model does leave room for spillover effects between sectors on the level of technologies. As it describes the EU-15 as one region, no regional spillover can be modeled.

MIDE. Spillovers between regions are modeled but Spain is divided in only two regions, Andalucia and the rest of Spain.

W8D. The model is a one-sector model and as such it does not account for spillover effects between sectors or regions. However, one may speak about spillover effects between foreign outlays on R&D and the Polish TFP. The latter is made dependent, among other things, upon cumulated outlays on R&D incurred abroad by Poland's main trading partners.

6.4 CONCLUSIONS

In this chapter we have considered and discussed a number of features that the 'ideal' model should possess when tackling the difficult task of specifying the process of induced technical change. Against such a benchmark we have first reviewed the state of the art; we have in other words surveyed the models in the literature that are on the frontier from the point of view of technical change. We have then moved to consider the models included in the TranSust project: they offer a useful sample of tools that are used by researchers and scholars for investigating sustainability issues. Table 6.1 tellingly illustrates our test, the result of contrasting the TranSust models with the ITC 'ideal' model features. The conclusions that can be drawn are, in our opinion, clear. Specifically:

- Many models still portray technical change as an exogenous phenomenon. This is a highly unsatisfactory fact.
- Even those models that endogenize the evolution of technology over time still fail to address a number of ITC-relevant important issues.
- It must be however borne in mind that the basic set-up of the model – say, top-down CGE or bottom-up energy system – significantly constrains the number of ITC-relevant issues that can be incorporated into the model. This fact suggests that the 'ideal', and at the same time 'operational', model is little less than a mirage.
- Nevertheless, the above caveat should not be taken as an excuse for not making the best efforts in the direction of endogenizing the process of technical change in any model addressing sustainability issues.

NOTES

1. Since the TranSust project was completed research on TC modeling has further progressed, in particular in the direction of hybrid models. See for example the 2006 special issue of *The Energy Journal, Endogenous Technological Change and the Economics of Atmospheric Stabilisation* (Edenhofer et al., 2006). The overview of this chapter is chronologically limited to 2006.
2. A version of MARKAL is involved in the TranSust project.
3. DEMETER is part of the TranSust project.
4. The not-so-optimistic results deriving from modeling induced technical change are partly due to the assumption of a single technology, according to Gerlagh and Lise (2005). In their partial equilibrium model of energy supply and demand, these authors consider two energy technologies for the production of a carbon-rich and a carbon-poor input. R&D is combined with LbD: R&D-based knowledge is combined with capital and labor in a technology which produces more and more energy input over time, owing to LbD. Two such energy production processes are combined in a variable elasticity of substitutition aggregator function which allows modeling the transition from one technology to the other. Unlike Goulder and Schneider (1999)'s pessimistic conclusions (they also had a model that includes renewables and fossil fuel-based technologies), those authors obtain a 'factor-five' result: an emission reduction policy (a carbon tax) targeted to concentrations is five times more effective under the induced technical change formulation than in the no-ITC case. The model is partial and global and neglects energy savings as an option to reduce emissions. For that case factor substitution might be more important than ITC.
5. See also Buchner et al. (2002, 2005) and Castelnuovo et al. (2003).
6. The FEEM-RICE model is part of the TranSust project.
7. This is not to say that theorizing in the field of TC reduces to these two areas only. Innovation and endogenous growth are the two areas most directly relevant for modeling induced TC in climate–economy models.

REFERENCES

Anderson, D. and C.D. Bird (1992), 'Carbon accumulations and technical progress: A simulation study of costs', *Oxford Bulletin of Economics and Statistics*, **54**, 1–29.

Barreto, L. and S. Kypreos (2002a), 'Multi-regional technological learning in the energy systems MARKAL model', *International Journal of Global Energy Issues*, **17**, 189–213.

Barreto, L. and S. Kypreos (2002b), 'The role of learning spillovers across regions in 'Bottom-Up' energy-systems models', mimeo, IIASA.

Barreto, L. and S. Kypreos (2004), 'Endogenizing R&D and market experience in the 'Bottom-Up' energy-systems ERIS model', *Technovation*, **24**, 615–29.

Boone, L., Hall, S. and D. Kemball-Cook (1992), 'Endogenous technical progress in fossil fuel demand', mimeo, Center for Economic Forecasting, London Business School.

Buchner, B., C. Carraro and I. Cersosimo (2002), 'Economic consequences of the US withdrawal from the Kyoto/Bonn protocol', *Climate Policy*, **2**, 273–92.

Buchner, B., C. Carraro, I. Cersosimo and C. Marchiori (2005), 'Back to Kyoto? US participation and the linkage between R&D and climate cooperation', in A. Haurie and L. Viguier (eds), *Coupling Climate and Economic Dynamics*, Dordrecht: Kluwer Academic Publishers, pp. 173–204.

Buonanno, P., C. Carraro, E. Castelnuovo and M. Galeotti (2000), 'Efficiency and equity of emission trading with endogenous environmental technical change', in C. Carraro (ed.), *Efficiency and Equity of Climate Change Policy*, Dordrecht: Kluwer Academic Publishers, pp. 121–62.

Buonanno, P., C. Carraro, E. Castelnuovo and M. Galeotti (2001), 'Emission trading restrictions with endogenous environmental technological change', *International Environmental Agreements: Politics, Law and Economics*, **1**(3), 379–95.

Buonanno, P., C. Carraro and M. Galeotti (2002), 'Endogenous induced technical change and the costs of Kyoto', *Resource and Energy Economics*, **25**, 11–34.

Burniaux, J.M, J.P. Martin, G. Nicoletti and J. Oliveira Martins (1992), 'The costs of reducing CO_2 emissions: Evidence from GREEN', OECD Economics and Statistics Department Working Paper no. 115.

Carraro, C. and M. Galeotti (1996), 'WARM: A European model for energy and environmental analysis', *Environmental Modelling and Assessment*, **1**, 171–89.

Castelnuovo, E., M. Moretto and S. Vergalli (2003), 'Global warming, uncertainty and endogenous technical change: Implications for Kyoto', *Environmental Modeling and Assessment*, **8**, 291–301.

Castelnuovo, E., M. Galeotti, G. Gambarelli and S. Vergalli (2005), 'Learning by doing and learning by searching in a model of climate change policy analysis', *Ecological Economics*, **54**, 261–76.

Ciccone, A. (1996), 'Externalities and interdependent growth: Theory and evidence', University Pompeu Fabra, Economics Working Papers no. 194.

Clarke, L.E. and J.P. Weyant (2002), 'Modeling induced technical change: An overview', in A. Grübler, N. Nakicenovic and W.D. Nordhaus (eds), *Technological Change and the Environment*, Washington, DC: Resources for the Future Press, pp. 320–63.

Criqui, P., G. Klaassen and L. Schrattenholzer (2000), 'The efficiency of energy R&D expenditures', paper presented at the Economic Modeling of Environmental Policy and Endogenous Technological Change Workshop, Amsterdam, 16–17 November.

Dowlatabadi, H. and M. Oravetz (1997), 'Is there autonomous energy efficiency improvement?', Department of Engineering and Public Policy, Carnegie Mellon University, mimeo.

Edenhofer, O., C. Carraro, J. Köhler and M. Grubb (2006), 'Endogenous technological change and the economics of atmospheric stabilisation', *The Energy Journal*, Special Issue: *Endogenous Technological Change and the Economics of Atmospheric Stabilisation*.

Galeotti, M. and C. Carraro (2003), 'Traditional environmental instruments, Kyoto mechanisms and the role of technical change', in C. Carraro and C. Egenhofer (eds), *Firms, Governments and Climate Policy: Incentive-Based Policies for Long-Term Climate Change*, Cheltenham, UK and Northampton, MA, USA: Edward Elgar, pp. 222–66.

Gerlagh, R. and W. Lise (2005), 'Carbon taxes: A drop in the ocean, or a drop that erodes the stone? The effect of carbon taxes on technological change', *Ecological Economics*, **54**, 241–60.

Gerlagh, R. and B.C.C. van der Zwaan (2003), 'Gross world product and consumption in a global warming model with endogenous technological change', *Resource and Energy Economics*, **25**, 35–57.

Gerlagh, R., B.C.C. van der Zwaan, M.W. Hofkes and G. Klaassen (2004), 'Impact of CO_2 taxes when there are niche markets and learning-by-doing', *Environmental and Resource Economics*, **28**, 367–94.

Goulder, L.H. and K. Mathai (2000), 'Optimal CO_2 abatement in the presence of induced technological change', *Journal of Environmental Economics and Management*, **39**, 1–38.

Goulder, L.H. and S. Schneider (1999), 'Induced technological change and the attractiveness of CO_2 abatement policies', *Resource and Energy Economics*, **21**, 211–53.

Intergovernmental Panel on Climate Change (IPCC) (2001), *Third Assessment Report: Climate Change in 2001*, Cambridge: Cambridge University Press.

Kemfert, C. (2005), 'Induced technological change in a multi-regional, multi-sectoral trade model', *Ecological Economics*, **54**, 293–305

Manne, A.S. (1981), 'ETA-MACRO: A user's guide', EPRI Report N.EA-1724.

Manne, A.S. and L. Barreto (2004), 'Learn-by-doing and carbon dioxide abatement', *Energy Economics*, **26**, 621–34.

Manne, A.S. and R.G. Richels (1992), *Buying Greenhouse Insurance: The Economic Costs of CO_2 Emission Limits*, Cambridge, MA: MIT Press.

Manne, A.S. and R.G. Richels (2003), 'Stabilizing long-term temperature', Working Paper, Stanford University.

Manne, A.S. and R.G. Richels (2004), 'The impact of learn-by-doing on the timing and costs of CO_2 abatement', *Energy Economics*, **26**, 603–20.

Messner, S. (1997), 'Endogenized technological learning in an energy system model', *Journal of Evolutionary Economics*, **7**, 291–313.

Miketa, A. and L. Schrattenholzer (2004), 'Experiments with a methodology to model the role of R&D expenditures in energy technology learning processes: First results', *Energy Policy*, **32**, 1679–92.

Nordhaus, W.D. (1993), 'Rolling the "DICE": An optimal transition path for controlling greenhouse gases', *Resource and Energy Economics*, **15**, 27–50.

Nordhaus, W.D. (2002), 'Modeling induced innovation in climate-change policy', in A. Grübler, N. Nakicenovic and W.D. Nordhaus (eds), *Technological Change and the Environment*, Washington, DC: Resources for the Future Press, pp. 182–209.

Nordhaus, W.D. and D. Popp (1997), 'What is the value of scientific knowledge? An application to global warming using the PRICE model', *The Energy Journal*, **18**, 1–44.

Nordhaus, W.D. and Z. Yang (1996), 'A regional dynamic general-equilibrium model of alternative climate-change strategies', *American Economic Review*, **4**, 741–65.

Popp, D. (2004), 'ENTICE: Endogenous technological change in the DICE model of global warming', *Journal of Environmental Economics and Management*, **48**, 742–68.

Popp, D. (2006), 'ENTICE-BR: The effects of backstop technology R&D on climate policy models', *Energy Economics*, **28**, 188–222.

Romer, D. (1996), *Advanced Macroeconomics*, New York: McGraw-Hill.

Seebregts, A.J., T. Kram, G.J. Schaeffer, A. Stoffer, S. Kypreos, L. Barreto, S. Messner and L. Schrattenholzer (1999), 'Endogenous technological change in energy system models, synthesis of experience with ERIS, MARKAL and MESSAGE', ECN Report no. ECN-C-99-025.

van der Zwaan, B.C.C., R. Gerlagh, G. Klaassen and L. Schrattenholzer (2002), 'Endogenous technological change in climate change modelling', *Energy Economics*, **24**, 1–19.

7. Revenue Recycling and Labour Markets: Effects on Costs of Policies for Sustainability

Terry Barker, Sebastian De-Ramon and Hector Pollitt

7.1 INTRODUCTION

This chapter considers how the treatment of revenues from environmental taxes and charges affects the results from models that are designed to address economic aspects of sustainability (Barker, 2004), such as mitigation of climate change. Normally, all the models explicitly or implicitly recycle the revenues from taxes or charges. This form of recycling can be by lump-sum transfers to consumers, a form chosen to minimise the theoretical effects of the transfer on the economy (often implicit in the analysis) or by explicit reduction in a burdensome tax or charge, for example employers' social security charges. The chapter identifies the importance of the form of revenue recycling as a factor in reducing the estimated macroeconomic costs of climate change mitigation, using results from published meta-analyses of the costs as published in the literature, and a comparison of TranSust model results.

The chapter begins by reviewing the literature covering more specific econometric and quantified studies of the effects of revenue recycling using large-scale economic models. The treatment of the labour market in the modelling is shown to be important in any study of revenue use because it affects the outcome for employment and inflation, especially if the revenues are recycled by way of reductions in employment taxes. It appears that the use of active revenue recycling in the models (as opposed to lump-sum recycling by default) is one of the most important factors in reducing costs, so the treatment of revenue recycling is also likely to be important in explaining differences in results from the TranSust models.

The chapter then compares the TranSust models in their treatment of revenue recycling and the labour market. The features of the models that are critical to the estimated effects of environmental policies are presented and discussed. Finally the results of the simulations of the effects of carbon taxes on CO_2 emissions and gross domestic product (GDP) are interpreted, taking this treatment into account, including some model scenarios in which the assumption is made that all revenues are used to reduce net government borrowing, that is, there is no revenue recycling.

7.2 THE LITERATURE ON ENVIRONMENTAL TAXATION, THE DOUBLE DIVIDEND AND THE LABOUR MARKET

The literature on the double dividend developed in the 1990s, following government and non-governmental organisation (NGO) interest in environmental tax reform and the potential for a switch in taxation from a burden on employment and other beneficial activities to a disincentive on pollution and other environmentally damaging activities. The two dividends are the environmental dividend from the reduction in pollution and the economic dividend from the improvement in economic efficiency obtained by the use of tax revenues to reduce existing burdensome taxes. The literature is very extensive and there have been several surveys. Three studies in particular have explored the topic. De Mooij (2000) develops the neoclassical model and explains how various departures from optimality permit the emergence of a double dividend. Kratena (2002) is more focused on the treatment of the labour market. Ekins and Barker (2001) discuss the theoretical and empirical aspects of revenue recycling in the context of carbon taxation and emission permit trading. This section briefly summarises the literature based on the last survey.

The neoclassical optimal taxation literature (for example Diamond and Mirrlees, 1971a, 1971b) treats taxes on inputs to the productive process, such as taxes on energy inputs, as distortionary, thereby reducing output and welfare. However, in contrast with this usual tax perspective, an environmental tax wholly or partially corrects a distortion from a pre-existing environmental externality (Bohm, 1997). The adjustments to the new relative prices, and the resulting shift in resource allocation, are not a 'distortion', but a movement towards a higher level of allocative efficiency caused by the internalization of an environmental externality. As Pearce has emphasised:

> While most taxes distort incentives, an environmental tax corrects a distortion, namely the externalities arising from the excessive use of environmental services. (Pearce, 1991, p. 940)

Nevertheless, a loss of marketed output is to be expected from such improvement, unless the instrument of improvement permits the reduction of other, pre-existing, economic inefficiencies, as discussed below.

Importantly, no economy is at a point of non-distortionary equilibrium; there are distortions due to current taxation patterns, market or government failure, or as a result of inefficient government regulation. Depending on the type of model used (for example general equilibrium or otherwise), the macroeconomic effect of an environmental tax will depend on how its introduction, or other associated policy, affects these existing distortions.

Actual economies adjust over time to a complex tax and subsidy structure, designed to raise revenues for the government, redistribute income and penalise or support particular activities. Any changes in the overall fiscal position will have implications for the costs of public funds. The carbon tax, or a scheme of auctioning emission allowances, has the potential to raise substantial funds for governments, so that the use of these revenues becomes important for the macroeconomic effects. If all revenues are used to reduce government borrowing, then the future costs of public funds will be reduced because the governments have lower borrowing and hence lower interest payments. If the revenues are recycled as lump-sum payments to consumers or used to reduce other taxes, then public borrowing will not be affected much, therefore the cost of public funds will be almost unchanged.

Labour taxes, introduced to raise revenues, are seen as distortionary in that they lead to reductions in employment, when this is not their desired effect. Similar taxes to raise revenues may have a similar distortionary effect, typically reducing output and welfare. Hence any new tax introduced for another reason, for example for sustainable development, but which raises revenues, can also have a secondary benefit. The tax revenues can be used to reduce another tax, but one which is seen as distortionary, so reducing apparent inefficiencies in the economy, for a given level of government expenditure. This has been termed 'revenue recycling'. A revenue-recycling dividend is an economic and non-environmental benefit resulting from the revenue-neutral imposition of a tax, that is, all the revenue from the tax is returned to taxpayers by cuts in other taxes or lump-sum rebates, rather than saved or spent by the government. Such a dividend can arise if the revenue recycling improves economic distribution, reduces unemployment or otherwise increases economic efficiency thereby increasing output.

In the neoclassical literature, the theoretical possibility for such a dividend usually depends on the economy being in a non-optimal state to start with: the existing tax structure must be non-optimal in some sense, for example because the tax base is related to employment. In addition, there must be some reason that this departure from optimality is not being corrected by policy, for example because of the need for revenues. Alternatively, there must be existing deficiencies in distribution and market failures in the labour and other markets. Any perception or assumption that the initial condition of the economy is characterised by no externalities, perfectly competitive markets operating in equilibrium, and with taxes imposed on a per capita basis, will a priori rule out the existence or possible achievement of a tax reform with a revenue-recycling dividend which increases economic efficiency.

The key question here, assuming that welfare includes environmental effects, is whether or not the substitution of an environmental tax that corrects a market imperfection for a distortionary tax can reduce the distortions from the tax system as a whole, leading to increased efficiency and output. The focus in this chapter is on substituting an environmental tax for a labour tax in the form of social security contributions paid by employers and comparing the outcome with alternative treatment, principally lump-sum recycling, in models of the economy following different approaches, especially with regard to the fiscal system.

The possible employment effects of introducing a revenue-neutral carbon tax, first without and then with using revenues to reduce employment taxes, can be summarised as follows.[1] The carbon tax is very likely to raise prices of goods and services according to their carbon content, especially if the main producers of carbon-intensive products (for example electricity generated by coal) are operating in unregulated markets. Without any recycling of revenues, the increased prices are expected to lead to increases in wage rates, when the labour market is characterised in terms of the 'real wage bargaining' model with market power on both sides of the labour market, that is, employers and trade unions. With recycling, the main factor determining the extent to which an efficiency dividend would arise is whether or not the reduction of employers' social security taxes combined with the higher wage costs leads to lower or higher overall labour costs per unit of output. The social security component of unit labour costs will fall, but the wage payments to employees per unit of output will rise, because the higher price inflation will lead to higher wage inflation.

The outcome will depend on whether there is an overall increase in real incomes, especially for wage earners. Assuming that there is full employment, but with the possibility of more participation from the labour force, then the implications for employment are ambiguous: being negative because of inflation and macroeconomic deterioration, and being positive through some possible substitution effects in both production and consumption because prices of carbon-intensive products will rise, but prices of some employment-intensive products may fall. Assuming that there are unemployed resources, then the outcome may well be an overall increase in real incomes, especially for wage earners. If there is, then the real wage is increased and the wage inflation pressures will be lower. Employment would unambiguously increase, through both the substitution effects and firms' falling relative labour costs. The higher employment would probably mean that overall labour productivity in the economy was lower.

However, some brief consideration should be given to the so-called erosion and interdependency (or tax interaction) effects.[2] The general conclusions from the literature are that the tax interaction effect in economies with significant pre-existing labour taxes can increase the costs of carbon control, thereby reducing the optimal emission reduction, and that this effect is substantially greater where freely issued permits are the instrument of control, rather than a carbon tax with revenue recycling. However, the result depends on the degree of competitiveness in labour and product markets and on the functional forms chosen, as well as on the precise values of parameters in the models (Kratena, 2002). Different coverage of the economy, functional forms and assumed values of parameters can yield conflicting results, so that the existence of a double dividend is dependent on a specific tax reform in a country or region and the empirical estimation of a model. This chapter reports such empirical results from a variety of models.

7.3 THE LITERATURE ON THE QUANTITATIVE EFFECTS OF REVENUE RECYCLING

Gaskins and Weyant (1993) report the results of the EMF12 comparison of modelling results on the macroeconomic costs of reducing US CO_2 emissions by up to 30 per cent by 2010, compared with 1990 levels. Most of the 14 modelling teams used lump-sum payments to consumers as the means of recycling the carbon tax revenues. However, four of the modellers considered how costs might be reduced by the active use of the revenues to reduce taxes that discourage economic activity. They found that the costs of a 20 per cent reduction in CO_2 for the US by 2010 were in the range 0.9 to 1.7 per cent of GDP with lump-sum recycling. When the revenues were used to reduce taxes in the models these costs were reduced substantially, by 35 per cent to over 100 per cent, particularly if the taxes on capital formation were reduced. Jorgenson and Wilcoxen, using the DGEM model covered by the EMF12 study, state:

Lump-sum recycling is probably not the most likely use of the revenue. ... Using the revenue to reduce a distortionary tax would lower the net cost of a carbon tax by removing inefficiency elsewhere in the economy. (Jorgenson and Wilcoxen, 1993, p. 20)

This is precisely the effect that they find when they reduce distortionary taxes to offset a carbon tax: a 1.7 per cent GDP loss under lump-sum redistribution is converted to a 0.7 per cent loss by reducing labour taxes or to a 1.1 per cent gain by reducing capital taxes (Jorgenson and Wilcoxen, 1993, Table 5, p. 22).

Goulder (1995) has also examined the effects of changing the recycling assumption. The GDP cost as a result of a carbon tax of $25/tC is reduced by 40–55 per cent over the long run when the revenues are recycled via reductions in marginal rates of personal income tax rather than lump-sum payments. The EIA (US EIA, 1998) finds that if the recycling assumption is changed from lump-sum payments so that revenues are used to reduce social security payments by employees and businesses, the costs fall from 4.1 per cent to 1.9 per cent of GDP in 2010 and then to a negligible 0.2 per cent in 2020 (Table ES6). The size of the double dividend has been investigated by other researchers, and they have found that the costs of mitigation have been reduced substantially. Support for the potential benefits of recycling the revenues is given by other researchers (Norland et al., 1998; Parry and Bento, 2000; Sanstad et al., 2000).

The IPCC Third Assessment Report reviewed this and other literature (2001, pp. 514–19) and found many instances of improvement of national welfare associated with reductions in greenhouse gases (GHGs), when tax revenues are recycled through reductions in employment taxes, especially in Europe.

Figure 7.1 helps to place these reductions in costs in context. It shows a scatter plot of observations from six models on the changes in global GDP

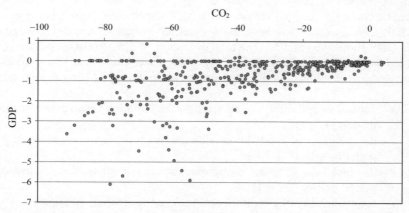

Note: The points shown are results from stabilization scenarios based on six SRES baseline scenarios, six models and many time periods from 2000 to 2100.

Source: Barker et al. (2002).

Figure 7.1 The Effects of Global CO$_2$ Emissions Reductions on GDP to 2100 from Post-SRES Scenarios (% Difference from Baseline Projections)

from baseline associated with the required reductions in CO_2 emissions from baseline, all over the period 2000–2100 and using six contrasting baseline scenarios. The results are strongly clustered, with only a few results outside the range –4 per cent to 0 per cent GDP, with a strong correlation between CO_2 reduction and GDP reduction. Most of the results show that large reductions, up to 80 per cent of CO_2 emissions, are achieved at costs of less than 3 per cent of GDP. This and similar datasets have been analysed by regression techniques to distinguish the effects of different assumptions on the results; this is the so-called meta-analysis of costs reported in the literature. We consider three meta-analyses which have attempted to isolate the effects of revenue recycling.

The first, from the World Resources Institute (WRI) (Repetto and Austin, 1997), reports the results of a quantitative meta-analysis of the GDP costs of mitigation for the US economy. Econometric regression techniques are used to assess the role of assumptions in 162 results from 16 models used to project GDP costs of CO_2 mitigation, including the results from the EMF12 study cited above. Most of the studies used a carbon tax explicitly or as an implicit addition to the price of carbon needed to restrict its use. The regression equation explains the percentage change in US GDP in terms of the CO_2 reduction target, the number of years to meet the target, the assumed use of carbon tax revenues (how the revenues are 'recycled' through the economy) and seven model attributes. It estimates that, as a summary of the results of these models, in the worst case combining these assumptions and attributes, a 30 per cent reduction in US baseline emissions by 2020 would cost about 3 per cent of GDP. The corresponding best case implies an increase of about 2.5 per cent in GDP above the baseline. The total difference of 5.5 percentage points (pp) (that is, 3pp plus 2.5pp) of GDP in lower costs can be attributed to the recycling assumption (1.2pp) and across the other attributes (4.3pp as follows):

- general equilibrium models gave lower costs than macroeconometric models (1.7pp);
- the inclusion of averted non-climate change damages, for example air pollution effects (1.1pp);
- the inclusion of joint implementation and/or international emission permit trading (0.7pp);
- the availability of a constant cost backstop technology (0.5pp);
- the inclusion of averted climate change damage in the model (0.2pp);
- the degree of product substitution in the model (the more the better) (0.1pp);
- the degree of inter-fuel substitution in the model (0.0pp);
- over 70 per cent[3] of the variations in the GDP impacts in the models are explained by these factors and the size of the CO_2 target reductions.

The second meta-analysis, of post-SRES scenarios,[4] was reported by Barker et al. (2002). They carried out a meta-analysis of the literature on the GDP costs of GHG mitigation at the global level to 2100. They analysed the extent to which the post-SRES model results for the global costs of GHG mitigation can be explained by the model characteristics and the assumptions adopted. Use of the set of post-SRES scenarios has the major advantage that all seven models for which suitable data are available have been run using the same, independently defined scenarios. A set of model characteristics (discussed below) is found to be highly significant (1 per cent level), explaining some 70 per cent of the variance. The main conclusion is that all modelling results regarding 'GDP costs of mitigating climate change' should be qualified by a statement setting out the key approaches, model characteristics and assumptions leading to the estimates. These factors can lead to the mitigation being associated with increases in GDP or with reductions.

For these global models revenue recycling was not found to be significant in explaining the differences in GDP costs of mitigation. The reason is simple. The global models do not have a treatment of use of revenues from carbon taxes or permits, so they assume implicit lump-sum revenue recycling. There are no observations to establish the effects in a meta-analysis. When other results from the literature are combined with those from the post-SRES scenarios, recycling effects are found. However, no significant or sizeable recycling effect is evident in the robust regression,[5] although it is significant and sizeable (1 pp) in the OLS results. This may be due partly to the fact that all the post-SRES studies and many of the other studies assume lump-sum recycling, so identification of the effect is problematic.

More recently Barker et al. (2006) carried out a third meta-analysis of the combined dataset from WRI, post-SRES and IMCP models. This research was commissioned by the UK Stern Review into the economics of climate change and identified active revenue recycling as perhaps the most important factor explaining differences in results from the US and global models. The dataset includes results from the Innovation Modelling Comparison Project's 2006 study of the costs of climate stabilisation at 450, 500 and 550 ppmv for CO_2 by 2100 (Edenhofer et al., 2006). The meta-analysis covering some 1500 observations found the major influences on the results for world production and growth (besides the extent of the reduction in CO_2 required) to be assumptions made for the treatment of technological change and the use of revenues from taxes and permit auctions. The active use of revenues within the models brings about some 1 to 2 percentage points improvement in global gross world product by 2030, when the revenues are used to reduce distorting taxes, with perhaps even greater increases if used to provide incentives for low-carbon innovation.

It is worth emphasising that if recycling revenues are to prove beneficial, they must be used to reduce existing burdensome taxes. If the revenues are not used as such, then they may become an opportunity for wasteful government expenditure. There is a controversy in the literature on the attribution of the recycling benefit. Some argue that it is due to reform of the tax system, which should be undertaken in any event and so any benefit from the reform is not attributable to the environmental tax. On other words, if there are taxes that are more burdensome than other taxes, they should be substituted for anyway. Others argue that the new environmental tax gives the opportunity for reform that would not be there otherwise. This controversy surrounding the attribution of the recycling benefit shows that it is best to identify any such benefits separately, as done below.

7.4   THE TREATMENT OF THE LABOUR MARKET IN TRANSUST MODELS

The models reviewed in this section correspond to the ten TranSust models[6] as described in Table 7.1. Table 7.1 classifies the models according to a number of factors or characteristics that are likely to affect the measured costs of environmental policy in any given carbon tax scenario. From the meta-analysis literature, reviewed above, the main factors are: spatial factors; time periods or factors related to the equilibrium reached in the solution; and type of environmental damage considered (climate and no-climate change). In addition, the treatment of the labour market and taxation in each model varies.

The characteristics in Table 7.1 have been derived from the actual TranSust models, bearing in mind their most distinctive features. These items have also been found to be relevant in previous meta-analyses as discussed above. These are:

- Number of countries and/or regions covered as a measure of spatial substitution.
- Time periods covered in the scenarios under scrutiny.
- Time factors such as dynamic behaviour and the adjustment to long-term equilibrium.
- Type of equilibrium reached in the solution or the nature of the model, that is, general equilibrium or macroeconometric.
- Number of products as a measure of product substitution.
- Number of fuels or number of energy sectors as a measure of fuel substitution.
- Technology factors and international cooperation (emission trade, and so on).
- Averted damage: climate change and/or non-climate change damages.

Table 7.1 *Labour Market and Tax Recycling Comparisons*

	E3ME	IMACLIM	MULTIMAC	W8D	MIDE	FEEM-RICE	DART	PACE	MARKAL	DEMETER
Labour market										
Unemployment endogenous	yes	yes	Yes	yes	yes	no	no	no	no	no
Wages endogenous	yes	yes	Yes	yes	yes	yes	yes[a]	no	no	yes[a,b]
Labour types	1	1	3	1	1	0	0	0	0	0
Spatial coverage	W. Europe	World or France	Austria	Poland	Spain	World	World	World	W. Europe	World
Regions or countries	19	1	1	1	1	8	12–16	12	1	1
Time periods	to 2020	2050	2010	1992–2030	to 2025	.	2035	2050	2050	2050
Equilibrium type[c]	RD	S	ID	RD	RD	ID	S	S	ID	ID
Product substitution	40	3	36	1	43	1	11	7	30	1
Fuel substitution	11	2	30	0	.	0	5	5	150	2
Tax-recycled scenario reported	yes	yes	no	yes	.	no	no	no	no	yes
Form of recycling										
Lump sum	yes	yes	.	.	.	.	.	.	.	yes
Social security contribution	yes	yes	.	.	.	.	.	.	.	.
Government expenditure	.	.	.	yes	.	.	.	.	.	.

Notes:
See note 6 for the main model references.
a   DEMETER: Wages are endogenous to ensure equilibrium on the labour market while assuming inelastic labour supply.
b   One of the energy sectors can be considered a backstop, that is, unlimited availability in the long term.
c   RD: Recoursive Dynamic; S: Static; ID: Intertemporal Dynamic.

113

The meta-analysis literature gives a strong indication that the costs of environmental policy measured by GDP in a specific model would be linked to the factors above. In particular, the regional coverage will have a negative impact on costs as separate production variables for various regions will be able to adjust more easily than a single production relationship. The TranSust models range from covering individual countries to covering country clusters such as Western Europe or full global coverage. Some of the models cover only one region, for example national models like MARKAL, MIDE and MULTIMAC, while a maximum of 19 Western Europe regions are covered in version 3 of E3ME, and 12 world regions, including four countries, are covered in PACE.

In any given carbon tax scenario, the larger number of producing sectors enables the adjustment of the model variables through product substitution. In our sample of models, the numbers of producing sectors vary greatly and the country models or models covering one region only are more likely to analyse more products (MIDE for Spain and MULTIMAC for Austria). In addition, both Western Europe models E3ME and MARKAL include a large number of producing sectors.

When it comes to the treatment of the labour market, there are two clear groups of models associated to the way they treat unemployment and the factors that determine employment demand. In the first group, employment and other elements of the labour market are treated more explicitly; in particular the labour market would respond to changes in social security contributions by having an impact on the cost of employment (Barker and Gardiner, 1996; Lee et al., 1990; Lee and Pesaran, 1993). This first group of models includes E3ME, IMACLIM, MULTIMAC, W8D and MIDE; all the econometric models are in this group. In the second group of models, employment is given exogenously and often linked to business-as-usual assumptions about population or labour force growth. In some cases, population, employment and labour force are the same. This group includes ETC-RICE, DART, PACE, MARKAL and DEMETER.

In the first group of models, the labour input necessary to satisfy the demand for a given product (or group of products), in a given geographic unit and/or industry category, responds to variables such as relative labour costs, technological growth and demand for the products. In addition, wages respond to prices and unemployment and normally prices of products will incorporate wages as one of the production costs. Table 7.1 shows the spatial coverage of these models, their treatment of time, and the number of industrial and skill sectors covered. It is clear that the models in this group differ considerably across these features. At the same time some features are common to most models: for example all the models in this group, excluding IMACLIM, are dynamic and all models allow for product substitution, except for W8D and ETC-RICE.

The models in the first group diverge particularly in the way they treat the activities of unions and profit-maximising firms, the market power of each group, labour mobility and the cost of adjustment to long-term outcomes. The second group does not have an explicit treatment of the labour market, so these models cannot easily distinguish different forms of tax recycling that affect labour costs.

The treatment of adjustment over time is also important for the labour market responses. The TranSust models can be readily grouped into those assuming dynamic or static equilibrium. The TranSust dynamic models describe explicitly the year-after-year solution, where economic variables show a gradual transition from one state to another (for example from one level of carbon tax to another) and they often incorporate elements of market disequilibrium. For example, models in this group incorporate market disequilibrium in the product markets (for example E3ME industrial price), and labour markets with involuntary unemployment (for example W8D and MULTIMAC).[7] In the second group a static solution is implemented which corresponds to long-term equilibrium; these models do not describe the year-after-year solution and generally ignore the transition to achieve a new equilibrium.

From Table 7.1 it emerges that recursive dynamic models are associated with an explicit treatment of the labour market with disequilibrium. Static and intertemporal dynamic models, in contrast, are associated with exogenous labour markets, with the exception of IMACLIM, which is static but which treats labour explicitly including involuntary unemployment, and MULTIMAC, which is intertemporal dynamic while it describes employment endogenously.

One distinctive feature of the collection of TranSust models is that there is a negative correlation between the number of regions and the number of products covered by the models. For example, the MULTIMAC, MIDE and MARKAL models cover only one region but about 30 products, while the DART and PACE models cover 12 (or more regions) and 11 and 7 products respectively. In terms of geographical coverage, the TranSust models deal with a variety of world regions ranging from individual European countries and regions of Western Europe to the World. Product substitution is larger in the left-hand side of Table 7.1, which also corresponds to the models treating labour market explicitly. Fuel substitution ranges between two fuels (IMACLIM and DEMETER) and 150 fuels in MARKAL. Finally, the DEMETER, IMACLIM and W8-D models present a low-level substitution across regions, product and fuels. The meta-analysis above implies that the wide range of substitution among the different TranSust models will have an important impact in the scenario results.

Turning to the form of tax recycling and the labour market, it is expected from the analysis above that substantial differences should emerge in any comparison of lump-sum and social security contribution forms of recycling in the estimated cost of CO_2 mitigation. In particular, the social security form of recycling should be less costly in terms of GDP loss. In the TranSust models this comparison is only reported for five of the ten models, mostly the econometric models. Some of the models cannot simulate the different types of revenue recycling because they rely on a limited source of data, in particular the GTAP dataset. Given that the tax representation of GTAP does not include labour taxes or social security explicitly, it is impossible to reassign the revenues from a carbon tax. Lump-sum recycling seems to be the only sensible approach for these models. In other models in this group, the labour market is not represented at all or in sufficient detail, so they cannot model any social security recycling. An option for such models is to run them in combination with a simple macroeconomic model.[8] Another alternative is establishing a soft link with another model that includes labour market and tax-recycling facilities. In DART, by contrast, it is possible to implement different types of revenue recycling, including for example equal-yield tax reforms.

7.5   COSTS OF CO_2 MITIGATION FROM THE TRANSUST MODELS

Each of the models produced six sets of results for each available method of revenue recycling. These were a baseline, and five tax scenarios with different tax rates on carbon emissions. Taxes were increased incrementally every five years in the tax scenarios (allowing comparison of results between static and dynamic models) in the period up to 2050,[9] or the maximum forecast horizon of the model if earlier. In this section, results are shown for the highest tax scenario (see Table 7.2); this should give the clearest distinction between the models. All other exogenous inputs are assumed to remain unchanged.

Table 7.2   Tax Rates (€/tons of CO_2)

Year	2000	2005	2010	2015	2020	2025	2030	2035	2040	2045	2050
Tax	0	10	20	30	40	50	60	70	80	90	100

Given the diversity in model treatment any comparison of costs has to take account of a variety of factors, besides the form of revenue recycling, which may affect the results. From the model comparison above it emerges that the main differences are associated with the forecast period, the spatial dimension and the level of substitution of products, fuels and the regional substitution. Other elements such as international cooperation or technology are not relevant to these scenarios.

Results are presented in Table 7.3 for 2020 (the best year available for a direct comparison) and in Table 7.4 for the end of the forecast period of each individual model.

We begin the comparison by discussing the results for the individual models.

E3ME

E3ME provides results for each year up to and including 2020. In the absence of revenue recycling, E3ME predicts a small fall in GDP of 0.3 per cent. Reductions in carbon emissions are around 7.4 per cent in comparison to the baseline, a small reduction when compared to the other models. Energy intensity is reduced by around 5.4 per cent when compared to the baseline case.

When the tax revenue is recycled through either a lump-sum payment or social security contributions, E3ME predicts a small increase in GDP of about 0.5 per cent to 1 per cent. Emission reductions (and energy intensity) are by and large similar to the scenarios with no revenue recycling, as industries find more energy-efficient ways of producing the extra output. Reducing social security contributions is a marginally better way of recycling the tax revenues, because of the increase in efficiency resulting from reducing the distortionary effects of employment taxes.

E3ME is not an optimizing model in the sense of assuming that there is a social planner, who maximizes social welfare. The results suggest that GDP could be increased further by even higher carbon taxes and more recycling. This is not necessarily so because eventually the unemployed resources in the baseline will all be used, so that further reductions in labour taxes will result in wage inflation, with little extra employment. The outcome will depend on assumptions about monetary and fiscal policy. With higher inflation, the role of the central bank and the treatment of trade and the exchange rate become important. At fixed exchange rates, the loss of price competitiveness will lead to a loss of net trade and reductions in GDP. If exchange rates are flexible, inflation will be accelerated and the central bank will respond by raising interest rates.

IMACLIM

IMACLIM predicts that the carbon tax would reduce GDP by 2 per cent to 3

Table 7.3   Summary Results of Scenario Cost of Tax by Form of Recycling – 2020 or Nearest Year

	E3ME	IMACLIM	MULTI-MAC	W8D	MIDE	ETC-RICE	DART	PACE	MARKAL	DEMETER
Year	2020	2020	2010	2020	2020		2020	2020	2020	2020
Geographical coverage	W. Europe	World	Austria	Poland	Spain	World	World	World	W. Europe	World
Social security contribution recycling										
GDP	+0.90	−2.3	+0.47	.	.	.	.	.	.	+0.27
CO$_2$	−7.50	−29.2	−8.70	.	.	.	.	.	.	−37.8
Energy Intensity	−6.60	−16.8	.	.	.	.	.	.	.	−14.0
Lump sum recycling										
GDP	+0.76	−2.9	.	.	−0.47	.	−0.40	−2.20	.	.
CO$_2$	−6.90	−29.0	.	.	−2.10	.	−27.1	−42.2	.	.
Energy Intensity	−6.00	−16.5	.	.	−11.4	.	−25.6	−27.0	.	.
Other (increased budget expenditure)										
GDP	.	.	.	−2.60	.	.	.	.	.	.
CO$_2$	.	.	.	−29.0	.	.	.	.	.	.
Energy Intensity	.	.	.	.	.	.	.	.	.	.
No recycling										
GDP	−0.30	.	.	−4.50	.	.	−0.70	.	−0.10	−0.12
CO$_2$	−7.40	.	.	−29.9	.	.	−27.2	.	−37.5	−19.8
Energy Intensity	−5.60	.	.	.	.	.	−25.4	.	−4.80	−13.7

Note: See Table 7.1 notes.

118

Table 7.4 Summary Results of Scenario Cost of Tax by Form of Recycling – Maximum Forecast Horizon

	E3ME	IMACLIM	MULTI-MAC	W8D	MIDE	ETC-RICE	DART	PACE	MARKAL	DEMETER
Year	2020	2050	2010	2030	2025		2035	2050	2050	2050
Geographical coverage	W. Europe	World	Austria	Poland	Spain	World	World	World	W. Europe	World
Social security contribution recycling										
GDP	+0.90	−3.10	+0.47	.	.	.	.	.	.	.
CO_2	−7.50	−49.9	−8.70	.	.	.	.	.	.	.
Energy Intensity	−6.60	−19.9	.	.	.	.	.	.	.	.
Lump sum recycling										
GDP	+0.76	−4.00	.	.	.	.	−0.70	−2.40	.	+0.36
CO_2	−6.90	−49.3	.	.	.	.	−33.9	−62.6	.	−70.8
Energy Intensity	−6.00	−19.4	.	.	.	.	−33.2	−51.7	.	−27.1
Other (increase budget expenditure)										
GDP	.	.	.	−5.50	−0.74	.	.	.	.	.
CO_2	.	.	.	−34.1	−3.30	.	.	.	.	.
Energy Intensity	.	.	.	.	−15.1	.	.	.	.	.
No recycling										
GDP	−0.30	.	.	−7.06	.	.	−1.30	.	−0.37	−0.07
CO_2	−7.40	.	.	−34.7	.	.	−33.9	.	−66.1	−53.0
Energy Intensity	−5.60	.	.	.	.	.	−32.8	.	−7.4	−24.8

Note: See Table 7.1 notes.

119

per cent in 2020, and 3 per cent to 4 per cent in 2050. However, a much larger fall in emissions is predicted, of 30 per cent in 2020, rising to 50 per cent in 2050. Clearly, the carbon tax is predicted to have a much larger effect, and there is major economic restructuring (energy intensity also falls by 20 per cent).

Much of the difference can be explained by the fact that IMACLIM is the only global labour-market model in the group. It is the only model to include developing nations, where CO_2 emissions are predicted to grow fastest. Naturally a tax of €100/tonne of CO_2 will have a relatively larger effect in a poorer economy. However, GDP declines substantially compared to the results from other world models. The fall of 3 to 4 per cent for a 50 per cent fall in CO_2 seems to be at the high end of costs compared to results in the post-SRES stabilisation scenarios analysed in Barker et al. (2002).

IMACLIM also finds reductions in social security contributions to be the better method of recycling the tax revenues. The difference between the lump-sum and social security contribution scenarios is 0.6 percentage points of GDP in 2020.

MULTIMAC

MULTIMAC only provides results for one revenue-recycling scenario: reductions in social security contributions. The forecast period only goes to 2010, so it is difficult to compare results directly with the other models. However, a small predicted increase in GDP of 0.5 per cent is very similar to the pan-European results from E3ME (which otherwise has a similar structure) for that year. Predicted falls in emissions are much higher, though: around 8.7 per cent when compared to the baseline scenario (E3ME shows a 4.2 per cent reduction).

W8D

With no revenue recycling, W8D predicts a very large fall in GDP of 4.5 per cent in 2020 when comparing the high tax scenario to the baseline. However, this is coupled with a large fall in emissions, around 30 per cent of CO_2 compared to the baseline. This is apparently because supplies in the model are derived from demands as in traditional Keynesian demand-side models. The increase in taxation removes effective demand, and output is reduced. When this revenue is recycled (through increases in government expenditure), the fall in GDP is less, around 2.6 per cent in 2020. Emission reductions are similar with or without revenue recycling, as industries adapt to find more efficient ways of producing the extra output.

There is similarity between results for W8D and IMACLIM in 2020. W8D models the economy of Poland, where average incomes are lower than the other European regions covered by the other models, and so the carbon tax has a much greater effect.

MIDE

In 2020, MIDE predicts a small fall in GDP of around 0.5 per cent compared to the baseline, when the tax revenues are recycled through a lump-sum payment to all adults. This is after a small increase in predicted output over the period 2005–15. Predicted falls in carbon emissions are very small (around 2 per cent), much less than the other models. There is a reduction in energy intensity of more than 11 per cent.

This may seem odd, but is explained by the fact that energy is measured as the output of the energy sectors rather than an input to other sectors. As the energy sectors have higher emission rates, output (and emissions) falls more in these sectors than in the other sectors. Therefore it appears that energy use falls more than output and emissions from other sectors, and the economy as a whole.

In addition, the lack of any substitution effects between energy inputs and the exogenous technology changes negate the possibility of producing more energy while reducing emissions.

Models Which Do Not Include a Labour Market

As these models by definition cannot simulate scenarios where tax revenues are recycled through social security contributions, we can only make comparisons for the scenarios with no revenue recycling and the scenarios with lump-sum revenue recycling.

Effects on GDP are generally much smaller amongst these models, usually there is less than 1 per cent difference in output between the high tax scenario and the baseline. The exception to this is the PACE model which predicts a 2.2 per cent fall in GDP in 2020, even with revenue recycling.

Effects on emissions are much greater, however. All of the models which reported results predict falls in CO_2 emissions of 20 per cent to 42 per cent in 2020, and 53 per cent to 71 per cent in 2050. While this does to some extent represent the global coverage of these models, it is also because the models are reporting for a later date, 2050. Reported results for energy intensity also vary between these models, but differences are generally greater than in the labour market models.

7.6   A COMPARISON OF THE EFFECTS ON EMPLOYMENT

In most cases the direction of employment and output changes match: if output goes up, so does employment. It is more interesting to look at the difference between employment results according to the revenue recycling method represented.[10] This demonstrates a key advantage of including a fully functional labour market in the model and is illustrated in the E3ME results in Table 7.5. Given that the differences in output between the lump-sum and social security contribution methods were quite small (output in the social security contributions scenarios was less than 0.2 per cent higher in 2020), there is a substantial increase in employment when the revenue is recycled directly through the labour market rather than the general economy. This has its own implications for changes in overall welfare because more participation in the labour market is associated with more happiness (Layard, 2005).

Table 7.5   E3ME Percentage Difference in Employment from Baseline, High Tax Scenarios

Revenue Recycling Method	2000	2005	2010	2015	2020
None	0.00	−0.02	−0.10	−0.15	−0.16
Lump sum	0.00	0.05	0.04	0.06	0.09
Social security contributions	0.00	0.08	0.24	0.40	0.53

MULTIMAC reports an even larger increase in employment of 0.7 per cent in 2010 (compared to the baseline) when tax revenues are recycled through reductions in social security contributions (output increase 0.4 per cent). This is attributed to the fact that employment becomes relatively cheaper while energy becomes more expensive, leading to a substitution effect between energy and labour.

IMACLIM also reports significant differences in the labour market when using these two forms of revenue recycling. Global unemployment rates are virtually unchanged in scenarios featuring payroll tax recycling (largest increase from 10 per cent to 10.12 per cent in 2050), but there is a much larger increase in the scenarios with lump-sum revenue recycling, with unemployment reaching 10.7 per cent in the highest tax scenario.

7.7 CONCLUSIONS

The main research conclusions from this literature review and comparison of TranSust model results are as follows. First, meta-analyses of published results from many modelling studies indicate that the use of revenue recycling is an important factor in reducing the costs of mitigation in carbon tax scenarios. This is confirmed by the discussion of the individual model studies that have been used to explore the issue in the literature. However many models in the TranSust project do not include the labour market explicitly, so cannot address the issue of revenue recycling through reductions in employment taxes and charges, such as employers' social security contributions. It is the case that those models that do treat the labour market explicitly are also associated with higher product substitution and the econometric modelling of dynamic behaviour of economies, but these factors affect the overall costs of mitigation rather than the comparison between costs associated with the different forms of revenue recycling. The results from the TranSust models are found to confirm those from earlier studies on recycling. From the scenario results, we see that the form of recycling (social security or lump-sum) has a major impact on the cost of a carbon tax as measured by loss of GDP. The social security recycling produces the extra benefit of stimulating the labour market, thereby improving overall efficiency, providing examples of a small double dividend in two of the model studies (E3ME and MULTIMAC).

NOTES

1. This account follows the treatment in the multisectoral E3ME model (see http://www.e3me.com), which assumes differing degrees of competition in each industry, varying returns to scale, irreversibilities and a dynamic solution (Barker, 2004). Barker and Gardiner (1996) discuss the empirical modelling of environmental tax reform for the EU using E3ME and discussing in detail the responses in the labour market. The model manual is available at http://www.camecon-e3memanual.com/cgi-bin/EPW_CGI. For a neoclassical approach see de Mooij (2000).
2. See de Mooij (2000) for a discussion of the neoclassical analysis of the tax interaction effect.
3. Repetto and Austin (1997) report goodness of fit of 0.8, but this value can only be reproduced by omission of the constant term in the regression. See Barker et al. (2002).
4. SRES: IPCC Special Report on Emissions Scenarios (Nakicenovic et al., 2000). The modelling teams involved with the SRES have run their models to achieve a series of different levels of stabilisation of GHG concentrations in the atmosphere: these are referred to as the post-SRES scenarios. Morita et al. (2000) present and discuss these scenarios.
5. Robust regressions are a technique for allowing for multiple results generated from individual models, where the errors may be hetrogeneous or otherwise non-normal (see Judge et al., 1988, Chapter 22).
6. Main model references are in this book, with more information in: E3ME by Cambridge Econometrics (CE), Barker (1998), www.e3me.com; IMACLIM by Centre International de

Recherche sur l'Environnement et le Developpement (CIRED), Ghersi et al. (2003); MULTIMAC by Österreichsches Institut für Wirtschaftsforschung (WIFO), Kratena and Zakarias (2001); W8-D Lodz Institute for Forecasting and Economic Analyses (LIFEA), Welfe el al. (2001); MIDE by Centro de Estudios Económicos Tomillo (CEET); ETC-RICE by Fondazione Eni Enrico Mattei (FEEM); DART by Kiel Institute of World Economics (IfW), Klepper and Peterson (2004); PACE by Centre for European Economic Research (ZEW); MARKAL by Energy Research Centre of the Netherlands (ECN), Seebregts et al. (2001); DEMETER by Institute for Environmental Studies, Free University of Amsterdam (IVM).

7.   In addition, the E3ME wage-setting equations incorporate the workers' union activities.
8.   For example, MARKAL can be run in combination with a macro model, the MARKAL-MACRO version of the model. However, this version does not include a tax-recycling facility; therefore running this scenario with MARKAL-MACRO would require additional model extensions.
9.   For E3ME we interpolated these five-year increases into annual tax increases.
10. US EIA (1998), Goulder (1995) and Jorgenson and Wilcoxen (1993) using models of the US economy indicate large differences between scenarios that use lump-sum recycling and social security recycling. The TranSust scenarios (that is, E3ME and IMACLIM) show much smaller differences.

REFERENCES

Barker, T. (1998), 'Large-scale energy–environment–economy modelling of the European Union', in I. Begg and B. Henry (eds), *Applied Economics and Public Policy*, Cambridge, MA: Cambridge University Press, pp. 15–20.

Barker, T. (2004), 'Economic theory and the transition to sustainability: A comparison of general equilibrium and space-time-economics approaches', Tyndall Working Paper, 62, Tyndall Centre, University of East Anglia.

Barker, T. and B. Gardiner (1996), 'Employment, wage formation and pricing in the European Union: empirical modelling of environmental tax reform', in C. Carraro and D. Siniscalco (eds), *Environmental Fiscal Reform and Unemployment*, Dordrecht: Kluwer Academic Publishers, pp. 229–72

Barker, T., J. Koehler and M. Villena (2002), 'The costs of greenhouse gas abatement: A meta-analysis of post-SRES mitigation scenarios', *Environmental Economics and Policy Studies*, **5**, 135–66.

Barker, T., M.S. Qureshi and J. Köhler (2006), 'The costs of greenhouse gas mitigation with induced technological change: A meta-analysis of estimates in the literature', Tyndall Working Paper 89, Tyndall Centre, University of East Anglia, July.

Bohm, P. (1997), 'Environmental taxation and the double dividend: Fact or fallacy', in T. O'Riordan (ed.), *Ecotaxation*, London: Earthscan, pp. 106–24.

De Mooij, R.A. (2000), *Environmental Taxation and the Double Dividend*, Amsterdam, New York and Oxford: Elsevier Science, North-Holland.

Diamond, P. and J. Mirrlees (1971a), 'Optimal taxation and public production I: Production efficiency', *American Economic Review*, **61**(1), 8–27.

Diamond, P. and J. Mirrlees (1971b), 'Optimal taxation and public production II: Tax rules', *American Economic Review*, **61**(3), 261–78.

Edenhofer, O., K. Lessman, C. Kemfert, M. Grubb and J. Köhler (2006), 'Induced technological change: Exploring its implications for the economics of atmospheric stabilisation', *Energy Journal*, Special Issue: *Endogenous Technological Change and the Economics of Atmospheric Stabilisation*, **27**, 1–51.

Ekins, P. and T. Barker (2001), 'Carbon taxes and carbon emissions trading', *Journal of Economic Surveys*, Special Issue, **15**(3), 325–76, also published in N. Hanley and C. Roberts (eds) (2002), *Issues in Environmental Economics*, Oxford: Blackwell, pp. 75–126.

Gaskins, D.W. Jr. and J.P. Weyant (1993), 'Model comparisons of the costs of reducing CO_2 emissions', *American Economic Review Papers and Proceedings*, **83**, 318–23.

Ghersi, F., J.-C. Hourcade and P. Criqui (2003), 'Viable responses to the equity-responsibility dilemma: A consequentialist view', *Climate Policy*, **3**(1), 115–33.

Goulder, L.H. (1995), 'Effects of carbon taxes in an economy with prior tax distortions: An intertemporal general equilibrium analysis', *Journal of Environmental Economics and Management*, **29**, 271–97.

IPCC (Intergovernmental Panel on Climate Change) (2001), *Third Assessment Report: Climate Change, 2001, Mitigation*, Cambridge, MA: Cambridge University Press.

Jorgenson, D. and P. Wilcoxen (1993), 'Reducing US carbon emissions: An econometric general equilibrium assessment', *Resource and Energy Economics*, **15**(1), 7–25.

Judge, G., R.C. Hill, W.E. Griffiths, H. Lütkepohl and T.-C. Lee (1988), *Introduction to the Theory and Practice of Econometrics*, New York: John Wiley & Sons .

Klepper, G. and S. Peterson (2004), 'DART: A non-technical model description', mimeo, Kiel Institute for World Economics.

Kratena, K. (2002), *Environmental Tax Reform and the Labour Market: The Double Dividend in Different Labour Market Regimes*, Cheltenham, UK and Northampton, MA, USA: Edward Elgar.

Kratena, K. and G. Zakarias (2001), 'Multimac IV: A disaggregated econometric model of the Austrian economy', WIFO Working Paper, Heft 160/2001.

Layard, R. (2005), *Happiness: Lessons from a New Science*, London: Allen Lane.

Lee, K.C. and M.H. Pesaran (1993), 'The role of sectoral interactions in wage determination in the UK economy', *Economic Journal*, **103**(416), 21–55.

Lee, K., M.H. Pesaran and R.G. Pierse (1990), 'Aggregation bias in labour demand equations for the UK economy', in T. Barker and M.H. Pesaran (eds), *Disaggregation in Econometric Modelling*, London: Routledge, pp.113–36.

Morita, T., N. Nakicenovic and J. Robinson (2000), 'Overview of mitigation scenarios for global climate stabilization based on new IPCC emission scenarios (SRES)', *Special Issue of Environmental and Economics and Policy Studies*, **3**(1), 65–88.

Nakicenovic, N., J. Alcamo, G. Davis, B. de Vries, J. Fenhann, S. Gaffin, K. Gregory, A. Grübler, T.Y. Jung, T. Kram, E.L. La Rovere, L. Michaelis, S. Mori, T. Morita, W. Pepper, H. Pitcher, L. Price, K. Raihi, A. Roehrl, H-H. Rogner, A. Sankovski, M. Schlesinger, P. Shukla, S. Smith, R. Swart, S. van Rooijen, N. Victor and Z. Dadi (2000), *Emissions Scenarios: Special report of Working Group III of the Intergovernmental Panel on Climate Change*, Cambridge: Cambridge University Press.

Norland, D., K.Y. Ninassi and D.W. Jorgenson (1998), 'Price it right: Energy pricing and fundamental tax reform', Alliance to Save Energy, Washington, DC.

Parry, I.W.H. and A. Bento (2000), 'Tax deductions, environmental policy, and the "double dividend" hypothesis', *Journal of Environmental Economics and Management*, **39**(1), 67–96.

Pearce, D. (1991), 'The role of carbon taxes in adjusting to global warming', *Economic Journal*, **101**(407), 938–48.

Repetto, R. and D. Austin (1997), 'The costs of climate protection: A guide for the perplexed', World Resources Institute, Washington, DC.

Sanstad, A.H., S.J. De Canio, G.A. Boyd (2000), 'Estimating bounds on the macroeconomic effects of the CEF policy scenarios', Appendix E-4 in Interlaboratory Working Group, *Scenarios for a Clean Energy Future* (Oak Ridge, TN: Oak Ridge National Laboratory and Berkeley, CA: Lawrence Berkeley National Laboratory), ORNL/CON-476 and LBNL-44029.

Seebregts, A.J., G.A. Goldstein and K.E.L. Smekens (2001), 'Energy/environmental modeling with the MARKAL family of models', Mimeo ECN, available at: http://www.ecn.nl/docs/library/report/2001/rx01039.pdf [last accessed August 2008].

US Energy Information Administration (EIA) (1998), 'Impacts of the Kyoto Protocol on US Energy Markets and Economic Activity', Washington, DC.

Welfe, W., W. Florczak and L. Sabanty (2001), 'Ekonometryczne modelowanie postępu technicznego, jego efektów oraz źródeł', in W. Welfe (ed.), *Ekonometryczny model wzrostu gospodarczego*, Łódź: ydawnictwo Uniwersytetu Łódzkiego, pp. 124–8.

8. Carbon Dioxide Capture and Storage Supporting Sustainable Energy Systems

Bob van der Zwaan

8.1 INTRODUCTION

Today, overwhelming evidence exists that mankind's energy use is provoking an increase of the average global atmospheric temperature and the associated detrimental effects of regional and local climate change (IPCC, 2001, 2007). In order to minimise the risks induced by substantial climate change, carbon dioxide concentrations should be stabilised, preferably during the 21st century and probably at a level not exceeding more than twice the pre-industrial level (see for example UNFCCC, 1992; IPCC, 1996, 2001, 2007). Therefore, emissions of anthropogenic greenhouse gases, in particular carbon dioxide, should be reduced substantially below the levels that would be implied by a 'business-as-usual' scenario.

This challenge, however large, can be met. Many different measures will need to be exploited simultaneously to deviate significantly from the expected business-as-usual carbon dioxide emissions scenario. Predominant among these is decreasing the intensity of these emissions per unit of energy consumption. Whatever specific means may contribute to alleviating the problem of global climate change, decreasing the overall carbon intensity of energy consumption is indispensable. Clearly no single silver bullet or panacea exists for this 'decarbonisation' conundrum. Hence, it seems prudent to let as many non-carbon dioxide emitting technologies as possible, for the moment at least, contribute to decarbonising our energy system and be part of a widely diversified energy mix. The set of employed energy options could include both conventional and more advanced technologies, and cover diverse options from hydropower and renewables to nuclear energy and decarbonised fossil fuels (see for example UNDP, 2000). While these alternatives are all essentially 'carbon-free', each of them also involves certain environmental drawbacks that impede their expandability. The use of hydropower, for example, may negatively affect water supply and generate changes in agriculture and natural ecosystems, while in many parts of the world its full potential has been exploited already, so that it seems unrealistic for hydropower to maintain a constant supply share under a rapidly increasing demand for energy worldwide (IEA, 2006). Renewables (such as wind, solar and biomass energy) seem promising in many respects, but when and to what extent they can significantly contribute to global energy supply remains to be seen, impeded for the moment by relatively high costs and/or large land-use or resource requirements, and because it is unresolved whether renewables can be effective in ascertaining energy supply security (see for example Turner, 1999). Irrespective of its multiple merits, nuclear energy's future remains unclear, since it faces a variety of intricate problems related to notably radioactive waste, reactor accidents, nuclear proliferation, economic competition and public perception (Sailor et al., 2000; van der Zwaan, 2008). Given the limitations of each of these carbon-free alternatives, expanding the gradual decarbonisation of fossil fuels to options beyond a transition from carbon-intensive fossil fuels (coal and oil) to carbon-poor ones (natural gas) is currently receiving enhanced attention. One of the most promising decarbonisation methods today is probably carbon dioxide capture and storage (CCS) technology (see notably IEA, 2004; IPCC, 2005).

Since CCS became the subject of serious analysis as a potential large-scale application in the energy sector in the 1990s, it has quickly become one of the promising concrete options to contribute to reducing carbon dioxide emissions in the short term. At present it is high on the agendas of scientists, energy analysts and policy-makers. As CCS technology may constitute one of the main means to decarbonise our energy system during this century, it is natural to include CCS in models dedicated to analysing possible transitions towards a carbon-extensive energy economy and sustainable development: it is therefore the main subject of this cross-cutting chapter. This chapter briefly describes some of the main features of CCS, concisely explains how it is represented in a few models of the TranSust project, and how modelling work in this field could be advanced. While CCS constitutes the main topic of this chapter, considerable attention will also be paid to renewables, first because the modelling experience obtained over the years in simulating renewables in energy–economy–environment (EEE) models can be instrumental for the model-implementation of CCS, and second because under climate change constraints sizeable interaction may exist between policies stimulating CCS and those benefiting renewables, so that renewables cannot be left unmentioned in this context. Given the optimistic prospects for their future deployment, mistaken policy advice may follow from models without CCS or renewables. Hence, this chapter is dedicated to the question of how they can be included and simulated in EEE models.

While today only a few of the 11 TranSust models explicitly simulate CCS technology, and only a couple more also reflect renewable energy resources, this subset provides valuable insight to the potential long-term significance of CCS and renewable technologies in energy and climate change scenarios. This chapter provides a comparison, on the basis of answers given to a questionnaire distributed among TranSust project partners, of how this subset of TranSust models simulates CCS and renewable energy technologies. In particular, Section 8.2 of this chapter explains some of the main characteristics of CCS technology and lists, non-exhaustively, some of the relevant literature in this field. Given that many of its features and potentials are already relatively well known today, it mostly provides some critical comments and points out topics that remain open for further research, notably regarding the potential risks involved with geological carbon dioxide storage. Section 8.3 describes which of the TranSust models simulate CCS and/or renewable energy technologies, with what technical detail these models investigate CCS and renewables, and what the respective cost assumptions are for these technologies. Section 8.4 describes the specific lessons learned in the TranSust project, and gives some overall conclusions and recommendations, as well as directions for future model development regarding CCS and renewables.

8.2 LITERATURE OVERVIEW

The decarbonisation of fossil fuels through carbon dioxide capture and storage deep underground or in the ocean could significantly contribute to reducing anthropogenic greenhouse gas emissions (IEA, 2004; IPCC, 2005). Technologies for both pre- and post-combustion carbon dioxide capture in power stations, as well as pre-combustion capture fuel cell applications, are available and have already been demonstrated, notably through their use for a number of other industrial purposes (see for example Hendriks, 1994; Williams, 1998). Technologies for carbon dioxide transport, via pipelines or with tankers, and for its compression or solidification, needed for storage, are all known in principle (IEA-GHG, 2006; IPCC, 2005). Whereas deep-ocean storage is still at a relatively early stage of development and is likely to remain controversial, it has been shown that geological carbon dioxide storage is feasible and probably acceptable today (for example Herzog et al., 2000; Parson and Keith, 1998). The Earth's geological storage capacity, in depleted natural gas and oil fields, aquifers and coal-beds, is likely to be large, and since price increases for CCS application to fossil-based electricity generation lie typically in the range of 25–50 per cent, CCS is probably competitive with respect to many other non-carbon energy technologies (for example Hendriks et al., 2003; IPCC, 2005). Given that CCS might, already in the short term and especially when through learning processes cost reductions are achieved, play an important role in reducing carbon dioxide emissions and thus protecting mankind against the detrimental local effects of global climate change, energy analysts have recently started to include CCS technologies in integrated assessment studies of carbon dioxide abatement scenarios.

Whereas the prospective benefits of carbon dioxide storage are great, also because it possesses the potential to catalyse a transition to the widespread use of hydrogen as fuel – seen by many as the ultimate energy carrier in a sustainable energy economy – a number of important questions related to environmental hazards and safety risks remain. A qualitative taxonomy of the various risks and potential environmental impacts involved with geological carbon dioxide storage is available, and quantitative data are accumulated regarding the potential external effects of CCS (see for example Wilson et al., 2003). In both scientific and policy-making communities, a closer inspection of these external impacts of CCS is now gathering momentum. Such impacts have recently also been included in exercises of long-term integrated assessment modelling (Smekens and van der Zwaan, 2006; van der Zwaan and Smekens, 2009). Still, especially detailed quantitative information about the potentially detrimental external environmental effects of geological carbon dioxide storage is at present far from complete. Uncertainties associated with negative underground carbon dioxide storage impacts – that ideally ought to be addressed before carbon dioxide storage is employed on a large scale – abound, and their precise nature and extent are for the moment insufficiently understood.

Geological carbon dioxide storage can acidify water present at great depths underground. While natural gas and oil fields have a proven containment integrity record for millions of years, storing carbon dioxide in such fields (once depleted, or while depleting) could have an acidification impact on underground water pockets. In a similar way, water in deep underground aquifers could undergo acidifying effects by carbon dioxide injection (Chen et al., 1999). In both cases, groundwater pollution of nearby freshwater aquifers may result, if the containment of the reservoirs into which carbon dioxide (CO_2) is injected is breached. This could affect the quality of drinking water, if the latter is obtained from sources fed by the polluted groundwater. Enhanced coal bed methane (ECBM) recovery and enhanced oil recovery (EOR) CO_2 storage can in principle pose similar groundwater pollution effects (see for example Liu et al., 1999; Wong et al., 1999). A related problem is that the process of reservoir fluid or gas displacement by CO_2 injection, possibly resulting in a modification of the hydrodynamic properties of the geological layers concerned, can have a negative impact on the water extraction potential of certain sources. Also, as a result of CO_2 injection into geological layers, their integrity could be disturbed. In the case of aquifers this could lead to the brine they contain migrating to other layers and coming into contact with freshwater aquifers that serve as sources for drinking water.

As a result of underground CO_2 storage, structural changes could occur in geological formations, as well as modifications of the thermodynamic properties – and even dissolution – of underground geological layers. Such geological changes and the CO_2 injection process itself could involve seismic activity and soil depressions or cave-ins, with uncertain above-ground impacts, depending both on site and option chosen.[1] Altered chemical properties of geological formations as a consequence of CO_2 storage, or the build-up of localized high pressures, could affect the stability of the geological layers above. Resulting from a large range of possible geochemical reactions of CO_2 with underground geological structures, cocktails of gases can be formed, the bearings of which to either the underground or above-ground environment (including plants, animals and humans) are largely unknown today. All these matters can affect or have pervasive consequences for natural habitat conditions.

It is not improbable that CO_2 gas could gradually – and without being noticed – migrate and slowly leak from where it is stored (Ha-Duong and Keith, 2003). This threat ranks high among the potential risks of geological CO_2 storage, since it could seriously hamper its suitability as a global climate change mitigation alternative. Since natural gas has long been stored in geological formations, one could draw a parallel and conclude that long-term secure storage of CO_2 should also be feasible. Given that the physical and chemical properties of CO_2 are different from those of CH_4, however, it may not be guaranteed that its artificial storage underground retains integrity forever. Especially regarding options other than depleted gas and oil fields, such as aquifers and coal beds, long-term storage effectiveness aspects remain, for the moment at least, uncertain. Migration times will probably vary according to the storage option chosen, and depend on the characteristics of the geological formation of the site specified (see for example NITG, 2006). The leakage time frame that typifies an option and site, and the compatibility of that time frame with global climate management efforts and features of the natural carbon cycle, is fundamental for the option's suitability to preclude or postpone presumed climate change effects.

Probabilities for catastrophic well blowouts (for example during injection) may be exceedingly small and the associated risks negligible in comparison to those involved with carbon seeps, but the eventuality that artificially stored CO_2 gas escapes rapidly, in large amounts at once, may not be left unmentioned. Sudden CO_2 releases could in principle have global climate change effects – if large enough – as well as involve severe accidents with human casualties. Although most blowout hazards are likely to be only local and temporary, they could be pervasive. A frightening example is the natural disaster that occurred in Cameroon in August 1986. Carbon dioxide welled up from deep in Lake Nyos, and was responsible for killing, by asphyxiation, 1700 people and their livestock (Holloway, 2000). This concerned a unique and unfortunate case, different in many ways from CO_2 artificially stored underground, so that a comparison between artificially stored CO_2 through CCS and amounts built up in some natural cases may seem inappropriate. Still, this example suggests that unexpected blowout risks cannot be fully excluded, and should thus be kept in mind when considering the application of CCS for climate control purposes.[2]

Accidental releases of CO_2 should also be considered concerning high-pressure CO_2 transportation, which would become part of the CO_2 storage solution. CO_2 pipelines exist already, and specialists ascertain that their safety record can be considered better than that of natural gas pipelines. Multiple safety devices are built in the various stages of CO_2 transportation methods, but risks for personal accidents as a result of pipeline defaults and sudden CO_2 releases, for example for workers involved in network maintenance or for people living in the vicinity of pipelines or CO_2 compression installations, are not zero. If CO_2 transportation via pipelines is operationalised on a large scale, such risks will in principle augment accordingly. Land-use issues may then also play a role of increasing significance.

8.3   TREATMENT IN TRANSUST MODELS

At the start of the TranSust project, six of the 11 TranSust models simulated CCS or renewable energy technologies, either explicitly or implicitly. Only one model explicitly simulated both CCS and renewables. Below, it is summarised: (i) which of the TranSust models simulate CCS and/or renewable energy technologies; (ii) what is the nature of the simulated CCS and renewables energy technologies; and (iii) how the costs of these technologies are modelled.

Simulation of CCS and Renewable Energy Technologies

Top-down EEE models have so far usually not explicitly simulated CCS technologies or renewable energy resources. For bottom-up models, on the other hand, the explicit modelling of these technologies and energy options is now common. The inclusion of CCS technologies in integrated assessment models, whether top-down or bottom-up, is more recent than the incorporation of renewable alternatives. The main reason is that renewables gained interest much earlier, especially since the oil crises of the 1970s, while

CCS only started to receive serious attention as a potential climate change mitigation option since the 1990s. Consequently, renewables also entered the EEE modelling scene about two decades earlier than CCS. When the TranSust project started, CCS was modelled by three of the 11 models: IMACLIM, MARKAL and PACE (see Table 8.1). Renewables were modelled by five of the 11 models: DART, DEMETER, GAIN, IMACLIM and MARKAL (see also Table 8.1).

Table 8.1   The Simulation of Carbon Dioxide Capture and Storage (CCS), Renewables (R) and Endogenous Technological Change (ETC) for CCS and R, in the 11 TranSust Models

Model	Institute	CCS	R	ETC
MULTIMAC	WIFO	✕	✕	✕
DART	IfW	✕	Implicitly	✕
DEMETER	IVM /ECN	✓	✓	Learning curves
E3ME	CE	✕	✕	✕
FEEM-RICE	FEEM	✕	✕	✕
GAIN	WIFO	✕	✓	Learning curves
IMACLIM	CIRED	Implicitly	Implicitly	✕
MARKAL	ECN	✓	✓	Learning curves
MIDE	CEET	✕	✕	✕
PACE	ZEW	✓	✕	✕
W8D	LIFEA	✕	✕	✕

Note: ✓ Yes; ✕ No.

In IMACLIM, CCS technology is only implicitly accounted for, as CCS is simulated through the POLES model that serves as its energy sector input source. The output of POLES, in terms of energy demand and supply curves derived from assumptions on price ratio evolutions, is employed as feed-in for IMACLIM. By reintroducing the price ratio data computed by IMACLIM into POLES, one can determine quantitatively variations in the contribution to total energy use of any given energy technology. Among the TranSust models, MARKAL provides the most explicit and detailed description of CCS technologies (see for example Smekens and van der Zwaan, 2006). For the capture of CO_2 from large point sources, in total 21 technologies are modelled: 10 in the electricity sector (coal, oil, natural gas and biomass based), 6 in industry (mainly in ammonia, iron and steel production) and 5 in the fuel conversion sector (for the production of for example hydrogen from fossil fuels). MARKAL distinguishes six geological CO_2 storage options: aquifers, enhanced oil recovery (EOR), enhanced coal bed methane (ECBM) recovery (two different options, at different depths) and depleted oil and gas fields (two options: onshore and offshore). PACE models a low- and high-cost carbon-free backstop technology (see Böhringer, 1998). The carbon-free backstop technology can be interpreted as representing CCS activity, which requires input of non-energy goods. Unlike MARKAL, PACE is a highly aggregated model with only a stylistic expression of different energy options. PACE has thereby several features in common with DEMETER, but unlike the latter simulates more explicitly fuel resource availability, including an upper bound on world fossil fuel prices. During the TranSust project DEMETER has also been extended to include a simulation of CCS technology (Gerlagh and van der Zwaan, 2006).

Since renewables have been modelled longer than CCS technology, and more TranSust models simulate renewables than represent CCS, more experience has been accumulated with introducing the former than with the latter. DART does not explicitly model renewable energy resources, but some renewable options in the electricity sector are implicitly represented. DEMETER simulates a generic renewable energy resource that stylistically represents an aggregate of non-carbon-emitting energy alternatives (excluding the more conventional nuclear energy and hydropower; see van der Zwaan et al., 2002). GAIN simulates renewable energy with some disaggregated detail, as it explicitly distinguishes between hydropower, biomass and other renewables. IMACLIM implicitly accounts for renewables in the way it does for CCS, that is, through a soft link with POLES, in which the simulation of renewables delivers the energy demand and supply input for IMACLIM. Of all TranSust models, MARKAL yields the most explicit and detailed description of renewable energy technologies. The database linked to MARKAL contains about 70 energy demand categories at the end-use side, and more than 900 energy technologies at the supply side, including scores of renewable energy options. This rich energy system simulation allows for a detailed inspection of the mutual behaviour of renewable energy technologies. MIDE does not simulate CCS or renewables at present, but, since agriculture and forestry are included as separate productive sectors, a relatively straightforward extension can be realised by adding a proxy for the quantity of CO_2 absorbed by these sectors.

Nature of Simulated CCS and Renewable Energy Technologies

Both CCS and renewable energy technologies can be modelled in several different ways. For CCS, for example, various options are available depending on which capture technology is employed and what medium is used to store the captured CO_2. As for the former, one can choose from a range of different alternatives among the main categories of pre-, post- and oxy-combustion capture methods. For the latter, the main options are geological storage, ocean storage and chemical fixation through industrial processes. Some models allow for biological methods for CO_2 storage. Under the currently prevailing terminology, CCS usually only involves physical and chemical approaches towards CO_2 storage, and excludes biological options (for which the term CO_2 sequestration is used; see IPCC, 2005). For renewables flexibility exists regarding the type of energy resources that are modelled and the technological detail with which they are simulated. Among the main renewable energy categories are notably wind, solar and biomass energy. The technological detail with which one simulates these various CCS and renewable energy technologies much depends on whether one models in a top-down or bottom-up setting. In other words, differences exist as to how stylistic the modelling of these technologies may be. While some (top-down) models employ only generic representations of CCS or renewable energy options, other (bottom-up) models simulate them explicitly and in great technical detail. Of the 11 TranSust models, CCS is now modelled explicitly by DEMETER, MARKAL and PACE, and implicitly by IMACLIM (see Table 8.1). Among the TranSust models, renewables are modelled explicitly by DEMETER, GAIN and MARKAL, and implicitly by DART and IMACLIM (see also Table 8.1).

When ranking these models by their level of technical detail, PACE and DEMETER are to be listed first, at the lowest degree of technological specification, as both simulate their additional backstop energy technology (interpreted as CCS for PACE, and as renewables for DEMETER) in a highly stylistic way. For example, the generic renewable resource in DEMETER is produced using capital and labour inputs only, and DEMETER simulates no further detail for this non-carbon energy resource other than an approximate but realistic representation of its costs and the future evolution of these costs. Biological processes or physical limitations are not modelled in DEMETER. In the new version of the model (available for the follow-up TranSust.Scan project), CCS is modelled in a way similar to that of the renewable energy technology, as an activity that has capital and labour as inputs and a reduced fossil-fuel emission intensity as output. The simulation of the renewable energy resource in DART is also very stylistic, and constitutes only an implicit representation of renewable technology that lacks any technical detail. GAIN extends in technological detail by simulating various renewable energy resources, among which are cogeneration with biomass, hydropower at various scales, wind energy, geothermal energy, thermal solar energy and photovoltaic electricity. POLES, generating the input necessary for running

IMACLIM, describes a somewhat richer set of renewable technologies by simulating 1 technology for cogeneration, 1 for hydropower, 1 for wind power, 4 for solar energy including thermal and photovoltaic technologies, 2 for biomass energy for the transport and power sector, and 3 (proton exchange membrane and solid oxide) fuel cell technologies including stationary and mobile applications. The capture part of CCS in POLES is a post-combustion process, modelled as an optional feature for fossil-based electricity production. Depending on the prevailing CO_2 penalty, CCS technologies applied to existing electricity generation options gain market share. The storage part of CCS in POLES is treated only stylistically. For both renewables and CCS, IMACLIM only proffers implicit simulations, as the true modelling of these technologies occurs in POLES. The richest technological detail among the TranSust models can be found in MARKAL. Pre-combustion CO_2 capture technologies are modelled for power stations using coal and biomass in gasification processes, while post-combustion CO_2 capture is modelled for both coal- and gas-based power stations. Three of the six CO_2 storage options (aquifers and off- and onshore depleted oil and gas fields) do not imply the recovery of new energy resources, that is, oil or natural gas, and hence do not involve economic benefits. The other three options (EOR and shallow or deep ECBM) are simulated in such a way as to also reflect the value of energy recovery, which has an important impact on the modelling outcome. While CO_2 storage in biomass (that is, CO_2 sequestration) is also simulated in MARKAL, in the form of biological sinks, storage in oceans is not. As for renewable energy systems, MARKAL describes in detail 6 water-related technologies, 3 partially renewable municipal waste technologies, 1 technology for geothermal energy, 8 for wind power, 8 for solar energy and 19 for biomass energy. While MIDE in principle models neither CCS nor renewables, it allows for the simulation of biological approaches towards CO_2 storage. Since it simulates the land devoted to forests and crops, it can also model the amount of CO_2 the corresponding area can absorb.

Costs of Simulated CCS and Renewable Energy Technologies

Probably most determinant for the outcomes of modelling exercises and scenario calculations is the way in which costs are simulated. Energy technology costs can be modelled in several different ways, especially regarding how future cost evolutions and expected cost reductions are thought to materialise. Technological change, in particular regarding CCS and renewable technologies, can be simulated either endogenously or exogenously. The former approach renders cost changes dynamic within the model and dependent on other modelling variables, while the latter approach involves cost evolution processes that are determined *ex ante* and are independent of other variables. One of the methods to model CCS and renewable technologies endogenously is through the introduction of learning-by-doing, or learning curves. Employing learning curves necessitates making choices regarding the value of the corresponding learning rates. Another method to endogenise technological change is to allow for investments in research and development (R&D), as a result of which cost reductions may be achieved. Only three of the 11 models include endogenous technological change for CCS or renewables: DEMETER, GAIN and MARKAL (see Table 8.1). Of course, specific modelling features other than costs matter too, such as capacity or resource constraints that apply on the employment of, in this case, CCS and renewables. These may also significantly affect the potential role that CCS and renewables are expected to play in energy and climate change scenarios.

In DEMETER endogenous technological change has been introduced through the application of learning curves. DEMETER simulates learning curves, for both the fossil and non-fossil energy resources, with a 20 per cent learning rate representing decreasing energy costs when experience accumulates. With a 20 per cent learning rate, costs decrease by 20 per cent with every doubling of installed capacity of the technology under consideration. The new DEMETER version applies a 10 per cent learning rate to CCS costs development. The investment and operating costs used in GAIN are estimated based on our knowledge of currently available technologies as well as anticipated learning curves. Along with the modelling of various energy technologies, the impact of technological change in terms of learning processes – and the potential fuel shifts that may take place as a result of the corresponding cost reductions – on the evolution of the energy system and overall economy can thus be simulated. Energy technologies simulated in MARKAL are also subject to endogenous learning. For many technologies, the concept of 'cluster learning' is applied. For renewable energy technologies, related to for example hydropower, wind or solar energy, a cluster involves a group of technologies that have one or more key components in common experiencing the same cost reduction process through learning. For biomass energy, for example, spillovers are assumed from conventional technologies, that is, biomass technology is supposed to belong to a cluster in which fossil fuel gasifiers are included, so that learning taking place with regard to gasifying for example coal also translates into cost reductions for gasifying biomass. The learning rates employed in MARKAL are given in Table 8.2. They are centred around a value of 10 per cent (corresponding to a progress ratio of 0.9), since learning rates usually lie within a range between 0 and 20 per cent (that is, a progress ratio between 1 and 0.8). Because for many technologies the available statistics are at the moment too poor to guarantee a reliable determination of the learning rate, fairly large uncertainty ranges apply to the figures of Table 8.2. Correspondingly, the results obtained with MARKAL on the basis of these learning rates should also be carefully interpreted. In MARKAL, both renewable options and CCS technologies are subject to capacity bounds. These bounds are based on estimated values for technical potential as well as political limits, as in the case of for example hydropower and wind energy. Obviously, such constraints also significantly affect the actual technology implementation level.

Table 8.2   Estimates for Learning Rates as Presently Implemented in MARKAL

Key component	Progress ratio (%)
CO_2 capture, flue gas, coal	0.9
CO_2 capture, input gas, coal and biomass	0.9
CO_2 injection	0.9
Hydro	0.997
Solar PV	0.82
Wind	0.9

Notes: This table provides estimates for learning rates as presently implemented in the MARKAL model.
Some of the rates should be considered as theoretical values, as for example for CCS-related technologies the statistics are still too poor to determine learning curves.

While not modelling endogenous technological change, some of the other models deserve further specification in terms of their features with regards to technology costs. In DAEDALUS/MULTIMAC, renewable energy demand is exogenously modelled by sector. Different scenarios reflect varying paths for possible technology diffusion, leading to cost reductions consistent with higher renewables deployment. Since the specification of energy supply and demand in IMACLIM is based on a partial-equilibrium assessment using POLES, IMACLIM implicitly benefits from a significant level of detail that could not be encompassed in a regular computable general equilibrium model. While IMACLIM itself possesses no endogenous technological change features, the prices of for example oil, natural gas and coal are endogenous in POLES. Also the POLES investment costs of energy technologies, including CCS and renewables, evolve according to globalised technology-specific learning curves, while cost elasticity is modelled with respect to exogenous R&D as the control variable of the model. Operation and maintenance costs are either fixed, expressed as a proportion of the original investment costs, or correlated to the evolution of investment costs. All technologies have a fixed maximum capacity over the range of projection. In MIDE, overall and energy-specific prices are exogenous, as is technical change in the energy and non-energy sectors. Since MIDE is basically a dynamic input–output model, different energy price paths can be simulated, but the model as such is not conceived to allow studying endogenous technical change in the use of for example renewables or CCS. In the W8D model, energy costs are not explicitly accounted for. A simulation of the influence of CO_2 taxes, however, on the general price level is incorporated. Via the modelling of a set of different feedback mechanisms, W8D allows for assessing the macroeconomic consequences of levying taxes on CO_2 emissions.

8.4 CONCLUSIONS

After a brief description of some of the main characteristics of CCS technology – the main subject of this cross-cutting chapter – as well as a concise listing of some of the potential risks involved with geological carbon dioxide storage, this chapter has given an overview of how and which of the TranSust models simulate CCS technologies. The first conclusion is that CCS has been successfully introduced in some of these models. Still, so far only a few of the TranSust models adequately simulate CCS technology, explicitly or implicitly. Given the important role most analysts think CCS is soon going to play, especially in a climate-constrained energy system, irrespective of its potential risks, and in view of the ongoing TranSust work on expanding the sustainability features of a representative set of existing EEE models, one of the main recommendations is to adapt those models that do not yet include CCS in order to account appropriately for this technology. Of course, there may be practical or programmatic limitations to the extent to which CCS technology may actually be incorporated in these models. Since the availability and widespread development of CCS technology may significantly alter the way in which energy services will fuel the world economy, however, it would in that case at least be useful indirectly or through a proxy to account for CCS. The introduction into each of the TranSust models of some form of CCS technology would render them significantly more realistic, and thereby benefit the ongoing work of the TranSust project. As has been demonstrated in this chapter, the degree of freedom regarding the technological detail with which each of the models can be expanded in this respect is large.

A second concluding observation is that over the past few decades significant experience has been obtained with the simulation of renewable energy technologies in EEE models, and in recent years in particular in TranSust models. As another set of technologies capable of providing alternatives for the current large-scale combustion of fossil fuels, renewable technologies, while of course very different in nature from the application of CCS, have several modelling and programmatic features in common with CCS technology. For example, cost assumptions and especially dependencies of these costs on time and place are typically reflected in similar ways in the TranSust type of models for renewable and CCS technologies. The lessons learned with regards to the modelling of renewable energy technologies may thus be instrumental for the introduction and simulation of CCS technology in these models. Hence, this chapter has also described how about half of the TranSust models have in some form or another accounted for a simulation of renewable technologies.

Another reason for having presented CCS technology and its simulation in TranSust models in conjunction with that of renewable energy technologies is their mutual policy relevance. Focused policies may be designed to be specifically directed towards either of these sets of techniques or resources, but the majority of climate control policies are likely to be more generic in nature and stimulate both options at once, such as the levying of CO_2 taxes. In that case, it will a priori not be evident which of these two sets of technologies will receive more impetus. Concern has been expressed that the large-scale introduction of CCS technology may outsource the expansion of the use of renewable energy. With models conjointly able to study the behaviour of CCS and renewables, the interaction between these two options and the evolution of each of them in tandem, under policies designed and dedicated to mitigate global climate change, can be studied simultaneously.

The third conclusion is thus that TranSust models should ideally be expanded with respect to their simulation of both CCS and renewable technology so as to allow the study of their mutual behaviour under a diverse set of environmental policies. It has been shown that a comprehensive introduction of the capture and storage of carbon dioxide reduces the costs of complying with stringent climate change goals, but does not obviate the need for renewables, given the size of the climate management challenge (see for example Gerlagh and van der Zwaan, 2006; Smekens and van der Zwaan, 2006). A great deal of research is still to be performed as to how the deployment of CCS technology interplays with that of renewable energy resources, and also with that of nuclear energy. Important questions remain as well regarding how policies designed to stimulate these respective carbon emission-reducing options interact with each other. These topics are among the valuable subjects for further study.

The above is certainly not to say that for the TranSust models already incorporating CCS and renewables no new interesting work can be done. Plenty of research fields remain and many opportunities exist for further analysis with the TranSust models, in terms of their refinement and improvement, notably regarding the simulation of CCS and renewable technologies. An example for further study concerns the external environmental effects of CO_2 storage, among which is the risk of carbon dioxide leakage, about which today our knowledge is incomplete. Attempting to include such effects in the present generation of integrated assessment models, notably those of TranSust, may provide essential insight regarding the employability of CCS. Another issue is that the nature of simulated CCS and renewable energy technologies, as demonstrated above, may vary significantly over different models. A great deal of comparative work remains to be performed in terms of describing the various possible modelling methods and attempting to explain the resulting differences in simulation results. Valuable insight could be obtained if different modelling groups adopt and learn from each others' modelling techniques, as well as comparing their results obtained under different modelling methods. For the moment, for example, whenever in TranSust models CCS and renewable energy resources are modelled endogenously, the chosen simulation method is that of learning curves, rather than through R&D. Among the possible model extensions could be the introduction of an option that allows for switching between these two channels for representing endogenous technological change. Endogenising technological change is not necessarily an easy task, as it typically generates non-convexities, implying that the appropriate solver needs to be employed to run the programme. Of course, whatever method is used to model CCS technology, as well as its costs, and whether these costs develop endogenously or exogenously, one should not forget that every model intrinsically possesses limitations. Especially regarding technology costs, the real economy is always far much richer and has many more dimensions than can ever be reflected in an EEE model, irrespective of its technological detail. To give just one example related to CCS, limitations may exist dictated by the number of locations where it is practically possible to store CO_2 underground. Transportation costs will typically not much exceed the 10 per cent level of total CCS costs when CO_2 transportation distances remain around hundreds of kilometres. If, on the other hand, CO_2 is captured at for example power plants thousands of kilometres away from where it can effectively be stored, this picture may fundamentally change. Since most TranSust models are of the top-down kind, it will not be trivial to model these sorts of effects, which may yet significantly affect the overall costs of CCS deployment.

TranSust models have evolved over the past few years, and recently progress has been achieved regarding in particular the simulation of CCS and renewables. More model extensions are planned for the years to come. For example, there is no explicit representation of renewable energy technologies in the present version of PACE. In its next version a link will be made to an energy system submodule such that renewable technology options are explicitly represented. POLES as input-generator for IMACLIM today does not simulate biological carbon sequestration, but the coupling with an extensive carbon cycle model is in progress. DEMETER did not include CCS in its version at the start of the TranSust project, but meanwhile the initial two stylistic energy resources have been complemented with CO_2 capture and storage. Similar expansions with respect to the generic renewable energy resource are feasible in the future. Likewise, all TranSust models may be subjected to expansion, in terms of sustainability, and regarding CCS and renewables in particular. For all these models, pursuing the modelling expansions and refinements as suggested above will improve our understanding of how to model transitions to sustainable development.

NOTES

1. Inversely, CO_2 storage could be employed to restore (repressurise) natural or artificial surface soil depressions, for example resulting from pressure decreases generated by fossil fuel extraction.
2. In the case of Lake Nyos, CO_2 rises up from deep volcanic activity and via groundwater beneath the lake dissolves in the lake's lower water layers. Lake Nyos does not turn over, however, so that CO_2 gas saturates the bottom water until some trigger (for example a storm or earthquake) provokes the deep water to move suddenly upward. This resulted in 1986 in CO_2 coming out of solution in large quantities, and erupting, like champagne uncorked, into an 80 m high jet of water and CO_2. The resulting CO_2 cloud, heavier than air, filled a nearby valley, asphyxiating everything it encountered.

REFERENCES

Böhringer, C. (1998), 'The synthesis of bottom-up and top-down in energy policy modeling', *Energy Economics*, **20**(3), 233–48.

Chen, Z., G.H. Huang, A. Chakma and P. Tontiwachwuthikul (1999), 'Environmental risk assessment for aquifer disposal of carbon dioxide', in P. Riemer, B. Eliasson and A. Wokaun (eds), *Greenhouse Gas Control Technologies*, Kidlington: Elsevier.

Gerlagh, R. and B.C.C. van der Zwaan (2006), 'Options and instruments for a deep cut in CO_2 emissions: Carbon capture or renewables, taxes or subsidies?', *The Energy Journal*, **27**(3), 25–48.

Ha-Duong, M. and D.W. Keith (2003), 'Carbon storage: The economic efficiency of storing CO_2 in leaky reservoirs', *Clean Technologies and Environmental Policy*, **5**, 181–9.

Hendriks, C.A. (1994), 'Carbon dioxide removal from coal-fired power plants', PhD Thesis, Utrecht University, Department of Science, Technology and Society, Utrecht, The Netherlands.

Hendriks, C., T. Wildenborg, P. Feron, W. Graus and R. Brandsma (2003), 'EC-CASE carbon dioxide sequestration', M70066, Ecofys / TNO, Utrecht, The Netherlands.

Herzog, H., B. Eliasson and O. Kaarstad (2000), 'Capturing greenhouse gases', *Scientific American*, **282**(2), 1–8.

Holloway, M. (2000), 'The killing lakes', *Scientific American*, **283**, 92–102.

IEA (2004), *Prospects for CO₂ Capture and Storage*, OECD: Paris.

IEA (2006), *Energy Technology Perspectives 2006*, OECD: Paris.

IEA-GHG (2006), 'IEA greenhouse gases R&D programme', Cheltenham, http://www.ieagreen.org.uk [last accessed July 2008].

IPCC (Intergovernmental Panel on Climate Change) (1996), 'Technical summary', in IPCC, *Climate Change 1995*, Cambridge: Cambridge University Press.

IPCC (Intergovernmental Panel on Climate Change) (2001), Workgroup III, *Third Assessment Report*, Cambridge: Cambridge University Press.

IPCC (Intergovernmental Panel on Climate Change) (2005), Working Group III, *Special Report on Carbon Dioxide Capture and Storage*, Cambridge: Cambridge University Press.

IPCC (Intergovernmental Panel on Climate Change) (2007), *Fourth Assessment Report*, Cambridge: Cambridge University Press.

Liu, L., H. Huang and A. Chakma (1999), 'Environmental impacts and risks of CO_2 injection for enhanced oil recovery in western Canada', in P. Riemer, B. Eliasson and A. Wokaun (eds), *Greenhouse Gas Control Technologies*, Amsterdam: Elsevier.

NITG (Netherlands Institute of Applied Geoscience) (2006), 'TNO', http://www.nitg.tno.nl /eng /projects /6_stor /index.shtml [last accessed July 2008].

Parson, E.A. and D.W. Keith (1998), 'Fossil fuels without CO_2 emissions', *Science*, **282**, 1053–4.

Sailor, W.C., D. Bodansky, C. Braun, S. Fetter and B.C.C. van der Zwaan (2000), 'A nuclear solution to climate change?', *Science*, **288**, 1177–8.

Smekens, K. and B.C.C. van der Zwaan (2006), 'Atmospheric and geological CO_2 damage costs in energy scenarios', *Environmental Science and Policy*, **9**, 217–27.

Turner, J.A. (1999), 'A realizable renewable energy future', *Science*, **285**, 687–9.

UNDP (United Nations Development Programme), United Nations Department of Economic and Social Affairs, World Energy Council (2000), *World Energy Assessment: Energy and the Challenge of Sustainability*, New York: UNDP.

UNFCCC (United Nations Framework Convention on Climate Change) (1992), http://www.unfccc.de [last accessed July 2008].

van der Zwaan, B.C.C. (2008), 'Prospects for nuclear energy in Europe', *International Journal of Global Energy*, **30**(1/2/3/4), 102–21.

van der Zwaan, B.C.C., R. Gerlagh, G. Klaassen and L. Schrattenholzer (2002), 'Endogenous technological change in climate change modelling', *Energy Economics*, **24**(1), 1–19.

van der Zwaan, B.C.C. and K. Smekens (2009), 'CO_2 capture and storage with leakage in an energy–climate model', *Environmental Modeling and Assessment*, **14**(2), 135–48.

Williams, R.H. (1998), 'Fuel decarbonization for fuel cell applications and sequestration of the separated CO_2', in R.U. Ayres (ed.), *Ecorestructuring*, EN-98-04, Tokyo: UN University Press.

Wilson, E.J., T.L. Johnson and D.W. Keith (2003), 'Regulating the ultimate sink: managing the risks of geologic CO_2 storage', *Environmental Science and Technology*, **37**(16), 3476–83.

Wong, S., C. Foy, B. Gunter and T. Jack (1999), 'Injection of CO_2 for enhanced energy recovery: Coal-bed methane versus oil recovery', in P. Riemer, B. Eliasson and A. Wokaun (eds), *Greenhouse Gas Control Technologies*, Amsterdam: Elsevier, pp. 189–94.

PART III

Model Descriptions

9. Market Allocation Model (MARKAL) at ECN

Koen Smekens, Gerard Martinus and Bob van der Zwaan

MARKAL (MARKet ALlocation) is a family of dynamic bottom-up energy system models developed and supported by the Energy Technology Systems Analysis Programme (ETSAP), one of the Implementing Agreements of the International Energy Agency (ETSAP, 2006). While originally MARKAL models were of the linear programming (LP) type – which is still mostly the case – the framework today has been extended in principle also to include more refined modelling tools that allow for example for solving more complex programmes such as mixed integer problems (see, for example, Seebregts et al., 2001). MARKAL models are applied in a broad variety of settings, benefit from technical support by a large international research community, and are today implemented in more than 40 countries. This chapter gives an overview of the main features of MARKAL, in particular including concise descriptions of the objective function of the programme (Section 9.1), the simulation of technological change (Section 9.2), the representation of cluster learning (Section 9.3), the modelling of elastic energy demand (Section 9.4), and specific characteristics relevant for the European context (Section 9.5).

9.1 INTRODUCTION

In its basic formulation MARKAL is a linear optimization model with the total system costs as its objective function. By minimizing these total costs over the whole time period considered at once, it assumes perfect foresight. Thus, it reflects a perfectly transparent market with rational behaviour of all market players. Government interventions or specific social preferences, that essentially distort the free market, can be simulated through the use of constraints imposed by the modeller. These may range from generic instruments such as CO_2 taxes to technology-specific choices towards (gradually or abruptly) stimulating or abolishing certain energy options or resources.

The net present value of total costs, *NPV*, is the objective function, and consists of the sum over all regions of the discounted present value of the stream of annual costs incurred in each year of the overall time horizon (ETSAP, 2006):

$$NPV = \sum_{r=1}^{R} \sum_{t=1}^{NPER} (1+d)^{1-t} \cdot ANNCOST(r,t) \cdot \left(1+(1+d)^{-1}+\cdots+(1+d)^{1-NYRS}\right)$$

in which the indices *r* and *t* refer to the region and time period, respectively, *R* is the total number of regions, and *NPER* the number of periods in the overall planning horizon. The parameter *d* is the general discount rate, *ANNCOST(r,t)* the annual (or, rather, 'periodal') total energy system cost (per region and period), while the last factor in the expression represents the intra-period discount factor and *NYRS* the number of years in each period.

ANNCOST(r,t) is expressed as:

ANNCOST(r,t) =

Σ_k {*Annualized_Invcost(r,t,k)* · *INV(r,t,k)*

+*Fixom(r,t,k)* · *CAP(r,t,k)*

+ *Varom(r,t,k)* · Σ_s*ACT(r,t,k,s)*

+ Σ_c [*Delivcost(r,t,k,c)* · *Input(r,t,k,c)* · Σ_s*ACT(r,t,k,s)*]}

+ $\Sigma_{c,s}$ {*Miningcost(r,t,c,l)* · *MINING(r,t,c,l)*

+ *Tradecost(r,t,c)* · *TRADE(r,t,c,s,i/e)*

+ *Importprice(r,t,c,l)* · *IMPORT(r,t,c,l)*

− *Exportprice(r,t,c,l)* · *EMPORT(r,t,c,l)* }

+ Σ_p {*Tax(r,t,p)* · *ENV(r,t,p)*}

+ Σ_d *DemandLoss(r,t,d)*,

in which the indices *k*, *s*, *c*, *l* and *p* refer to the technology, year, commodity, price level and pollutant, respectively, while *e* and *i* refer to whether the commodity under consideration is sold (exported) or purchased (imported). Decision variables, representing the choices that can be made within the model, are in capitals: *INV(r,t,k)* is the new capacity added per technology, *CAP(r,t,k)* the installed capacity for each technology, *ACT(r,t,k,s)* the technology activity level, *MINING(r,t,c,l)* the quantity extracted of each commodity, *TRADE(r,t,c,s,i)* and *TRADE(r,t,c,s,e)* the quantities per commodity purchased (*i*) or sold (*e*), *IMPORT(r,t,c,l)* and *EXPORT(r,t,c,l)* the quantities per good exogenously imported or exported, and *ENV(r,t,p)* the emissions of each pollutant. *Annualized_Invcost(r,t,k)* is the lump sum unit investment cost, *Fixom(r,t,k)* and *Varom(r,t,k)* respectively fixed and variable operation and maintenance costs, *Delivcost(r,t,k,c)* the delivery cost per unit of commodity to the technology considered, *Input(r,t,k,c)* the amount of commodity required to operate one unit of technology, *Miningcost(r,t,c,l)* the cost of mining, *Tradecost(r,t,c)* the transport or transaction cost, *Importprice(r,t,c,l)* the (exogenous) import price per commodity, *Exportprice(r,t,c,l)* the (exogenous) export price, *Tax(r,t,p)* the tax on emissions, and *DemandLoss(r,t,d)* the welfare loss incurred by consumers when the service demand *d* is less than its value in the reference case.

The assumption of perfect foresight of the future concerns both 'external' pressures such as taxes or emission constraints and 'internal' changes such as technology availability or cost reductions. Model choices are thus made on the basis of the anticipation of both external and internal constraints or opportunities. As such, the programme minimizes the overall energy system costs, while both implicit and/or explicit modelling constraints are duly met. This feature is particularly instrumental for internalizing technology learning-by-doing and corresponding technology cost reductions: through perfect foresight the model accounts for the empirically observed phenomena that increased investments in technology deployment may be rewarded (at least partly compensated or even fully paid back) in the form of future cost decreases.

MARKAL is demand-driven, and in its standard formulation energy demand is exogenously determined. In other words, the modeller specifies the demand for energy services as external input. This exogenous energy demand determines the composition of the energy system, in which demand and supply of energy services are balanced. Energy requirements are fulfilled through end-use technologies that consume various types of fuel. Fuels are produced in conversion processes or directly supplied, so that (final) energy demand cascades through the system down to primary energy supply. The relative competitiveness of each of the chains from primary supply to end-use, together with physical constraints such as the availability of resources, determine which of the technologies enter the solution of MARKAL.

Technologies are characterized as: (i) resource, (ii) conversion, (iii) process, and (iv) end-use related. Depending on the classification of a technology, it is characterized by a number of specific parameters that may be technical in nature (related to for example efficiency, emission factors and fuel use) or more economically determined (such as its lifetime, required investment and operation costs, or the applicable discount rate). The use of technology-specific discount rates facilitates the inclusion of investment behaviour and preferences of different actors. Technology parameters are generally exogenous. As with the energy demand level, they have to be exogenously provided for all model periods. To facilitate their usage they are gathered in one database that serves as input to every model run. The set of data, their definition and classification, that is, the time series of all exogenous variables involved, in combination with the objective function and modelling constraints together constitute a specific MARKAL version.

9.2   TECHNOLOGICAL CHANGE

Originally, MARKAL used exogenously determined time-dependent trajectories for the investment costs of energy technologies. These cost trajectories were based on expert views and on the existing scientific and engineering literature. It was realized, however, that the underlying driver of the gradual decreases in energy technology costs may really be technology deployment, rather than time, and that the cost reductions were achieved through the experience obtained with fabricating and operating the technologies. Also, the exogenous simulation of technology costs implied that the model tended to postpone the deployment of a given technology until it became competitive compared to its alternatives, at which point its competitiveness often resulted in a sudden and usually unrealistically massive deployment of that technology. This necessitated the imposition of specific growth limitations allowing for a more gradual phasing in of technologies. The specification of such growth limitations required detailed modelling expertise and manual interference in the input data that did not always guarantee a consistent parameterization and often generated various modelling intricacies. Thus, to render MARKAL more realistic the modelling of time-dependent exogenous technology evolution and the implementation of growth limitations were gradually abandoned.

To reflect the observation that technology cost reductions are often the result of increasing physical deployment, learning curves were implemented in MARKAL. Indeed, many sources had meanwhile indicated that a learning-by-doing or learning-by-investing relationship could be observed between the evolution of investment costs, for example per unit of capacity, and the cumulated capacity or sales build-up (see, for example, IEA, 2000). The learning curves describing these phenomena, relating the costs of technologies to their capacity or sales, can be expressed by:

$$SC(t) = SC(0) \left(\frac{CC(t)}{CC(0)} \right)^{-b},$$

in which SC are the specific investment costs, for example in €/kW$_e$, and CC the cumulative capacity, in this case in kW$_e$. The constant b is the 'learning elasticity', generally rewritten into the more familiar progress ratio p:

$$p = 2^{-b}.$$

The progress ratio is a measure of how fast a technology learns, as it indicates the decrease in specific costs for each doubling of installed capacity. This means that by providing the initial values for capacity and investment costs, as well as the progress ratio, the potential for cost reductions is fully fixed. In an additional step made solely for the purpose of including learning curves in MARKAL, the learning curves are piece-wise linearized. For such a linearization an additional parameter has to be given, the maximal achievable capacity, determined in coherence with the chosen segmentation. With this endogenization of the investment costs, MARKAL calculates the optimal investment levels and timing thereof, using as knowledge the perfectly foreseeable investment cost decreases according to learning curves.

Over the years, the number of technologies for which learning curves were simulated in MARKAL gradually increased, and it became clear that learning spillovers between technologies had to be reflected. To account for the observation that different technologies may share a common component that is subject to learning, the concept of 'cluster learning' was introduced.

9.3 CLUSTER LEARNING

In order to diversify and correct the description of technological change, 'technology clusters' were modelled (Seebregts et al., 2000). With the previously simulated phenomenon of learning-by-doing, the basic assumption was that a technology learns as an integral and independent entity. In an extension of that formalism, the technologies that learn are viewed as being built up by underlying entities or components. These low-level components individually learn, rather than the high-level overall technologies. The set of technologies that share a certain component are referred to as a cluster. Consequently, a cluster of technologies also shares the same learning process of their common component. Since technologies may consist of several components that learn, and components may be part of several sets of clustering technologies at once, the formulation of cluster learning introduces the concept of spillovers between technologies.

For many of the technologies previously considered as independently learning entities the concept of technology clusters provides a more refined, consistent and correct description of the phenomenon of learning. For example, a natural gas combined cycle power plant consists of a gas turbine, a recovery boiler, and a steam turbine as principal elements, all three characterized by learning phenomena. As these elements or key components are also found in many other technologies, using the cluster learning approach accounts for the learning in these components of all the corresponding technologies at once.

Cluster learning quite naturally allows for the simulation of technology spillovers: if a technology containing a specific component that learns is deployed, all other technologies sharing this component will automatically benefit from that learning process as well. Thus, incurred experience naturally flows from one technology to all related technologies. In MARKAL the phenomenon of cluster learning is introduced through a single matrix, the so-called cluster matrix. In the cluster matrix, the key components serve as columns and the technologies as rows, while the entries in the matrix cells represent the capacity share of the key component in the technology on a unit per unit basis.

Joint learning does not need to be restricted to technologies within one sector, but can easily be extended to technology spillover effects between different sectors of the overall energy system. An intuitive example is provided by fuel cell technology. A basic fuel cell component is not only found in stationary applications such as for electricity and heat production but also in mobile applications like vehicle engines. While in an earlier stage the main focus was on learning and cross-technology spillovers within the power sector, later learning and spillover effects outside the power sector were included as well. The number of technologies and technology components that are subjected to learning is now so large that the limits of computability have been reached.

9.4   DEMAND ELASTICITY

As MARKAL is a demand-driven model, and can in principle only be run with an external specification of final demand for energy services for all time periods, projections of final energy demand have to be obtained from other sources or models. Traditionally, these demand levels are price-insensitive, that is, they remain unchanged if the prices of the supplied commodities change. The dash-dotted line in Figure 9.1 represents this fixed demand level. MARKAL generates a supply curve that satisfies the objective function and is stepwise because it is built up by discrete technologies. The total cost derived from the solution can be interpreted as the sum of the integrals under all supply curves.

Recently, MARKAL has been extended to simulate a price-elastic demand for energy. The exogenous demands for energy services have been replaced

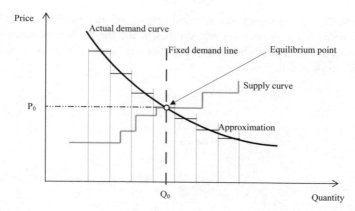

Figure 9.1 Price-independent Demand Level of a Standard MARKAL Model (dash-dotted line), and Supply and Demand Curves as Used in the Elastic-Demand Formulation of MARKAL

with energy demand functions that relate energy demand to market prices. The market price of energy services is assumed to be equal to the marginal cost as represented by the shadow price from the standard MARKAL solution. A rather simple demand function characterized by a prespecified price elasticity is assumed that does not allow for substitution between different demand categories. In order to solve the resulting non-linear problem through a mixed-integer programme, the demand curve is stepwise linearized, and to keep the variations of demand within the range deemed acceptable by the modeller, the maximum allowed deviations upwards and downwards from the equilibrium point are specified.

In the absence of an additional modelling constraint, MARKAL generates the same equilibrium point as it does in its non-elastic demand version. If, however, an external constraint is imposed on the energy system that effects the price level of one or more of the final energy services, for example when a CO_2 emission target is set, the model may adjust the demand levels and supply curves to minimize the overall system cost. Compared to the non-elastic version of MARKAL, an additional option for meeting such a modelling constraint is thus allowed for: in this case MARKAL can opt to change the demand level along the stepwise curve, rather than deploying (expensive) emission-reduction technologies.

Thus, in the elastic-demand form of MARKAL, a change in demand level can induce a change towards a different supply curve. Consequently, the equilibrium point will shift along the demand curve. The objective function now becomes the minimization of the area under the supply curves, or the maximization of the surface between the demand curves and the supply curves. The surface between the demand curve and the equilibrium price level is a measure for the consumers' surplus, while the surface between the equilibrium price level and the supply curve is a measure for the producers' surplus, as illustrated in Figure 9.2.

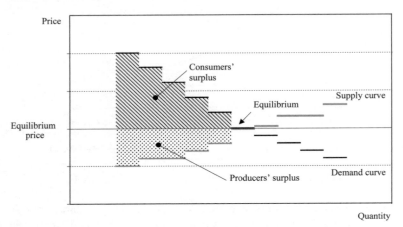

Figure 9.2   Producer and Consumer Surplus

The main reason for introducing a form of price-elasticity in MARKAL is that under stringent CO_2 reduction scenarios it is highly unlikely that the energy system will maintain its original demand level. For example, if a very high CO_2 tax is imposed, the corresponding expected carbon emission reductions are simply too significant to be realized by abatement technologies alone. While the currently employed partial equilibrium method to introduce a piece-wise linearized elastic energy demand does naturally not include the full complexity of the macroeconomy, it at least constitutes an option to include the most important effects of price-elasticity without forfeiting the technology richness of a bottom-up model like MARKAL. The results from this MARKAL version indeed point out the price-responsive behaviour of the different actors in a complex energy system when confronted with for example a binding climate constraint.

9.5   MARKAL FOR WESTERN EUROPE

The MARKAL model currently used by the Energy Research Centre of the Netherlands (ECN) (see Figure 9.3) is dedicated to the Western European energy system, with the 15 pre-2004 EU members together with Norway, Iceland and Switzerland treated as one single region. National boundaries or

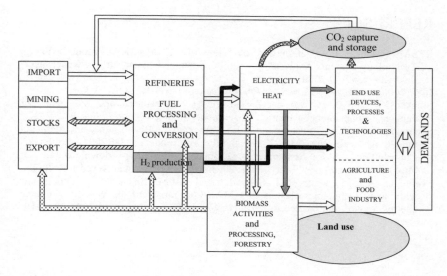

*Figure 9.3   Schematic Overview of the MARKAL Reference Energy System
at ECN*

intercountry exchanges of commodities (both energy and materials) are not
considered in this model version, but fuel and material imports into and
exports from the region are simulated. This MARKAL version covers the
1990–2100 time frame, modelled in periods of ten years each.

Some subregional aspects of the energy system are considered. For example,
in the residential sector the variability in space heat demand is sufficiently
relevant to warrant a distinction between the northern, middle and southern
part of the region. Consequently, both demand and end-use technologies
possess in this case additional regional characteristics. Also the influx from
solar radiation displays such variations that a more detailed technological
specification is required. In this case, only the corresponding technologies
have regional characteristics: associated hereto remains the electricity demand
in the entire region. For all other demands and technology chains, technologies
are of a generic type (for example a pulverized coal power plant, a diesel car,
a residential gas boiler, or an electric arc furnace for steel making).

MARKAL allows for the expansion and analysis of specific energy
technologies. For example, the existing model has recently been extended to
include a detailed description of the possible evolution towards a hydrogen
economy. For the TranSust project, the focus has been on the internal and
external cost features of CCS technologies and, as described elsewhere in this
volume, on the carbon and energy intensity of the overall energy economy
(see Smekens and van der Zwaan, 2006).

REFERENCES

ETSAP (2006), 'Introduction and overview of the MARKAL model', Energy
    Technology Systems Analysis Programme, downloadable at: http://www.etsap.org
    [last accessed July 2008].
IEA (2000), *Experience Curves for Energy Technology Policy*, OECD: Paris.
Smekens, K. and B.C.C. van der Zwaan (2006), 'Atmospheric and geological CO_2
    damage costs in energy scenarios', *Environmental Science and Policy*, **9**, 217–27.
Seebregts, A.J., G.A. Goldstein and K.E.L. Smekens (2001), 'Energy/environmental
    modelling with the MARKAL family of models', OR2001 Conference
    Contribution, 3–5 September, Duisburg, Germany, downloadable at:
    http://www.ecn.nl/docs/library/report/2001/rx01039.pdf [last accessed July 2008].
Seebregts, A.J., T. Kram, G.J. Schaeffer and A.J.M. Bos (2000), 'Endogenous
    learning of technology clusters in a MARKAL model of the Western European
    energy system', *International Journal of Global Energy Issues*, **14**(1–4), 289–319.

10. A Hybrid Model: DEMETER

Reyer Gerlagh and Bob van der Zwaan

This chapter describes the main features of the long-term dynamic top-down economy–energy–environment (EEE) model DEMETER,[1] which has been used for the analysis of a number of climate change issues (see Gerlagh and van der Zwaan, 2003, 2004; Gerlagh et al., 2004; van der Zwaan et al., 2002; van der Zwaan and Gerlagh, 2006). The DEMETER version described here simulates fossil fuels and non-fossil energy, as well as a decarbonization option through carbon dioxide capture and storage (CCS), in addition to a simple climate module and generic production and consumption behaviour. DEMETER connects to both models of endogenous growth (such as Bovenberg and Smulders, 1996; Chakravorty et al., 1997) and to (top-down) models particularly focusing on energy and climate change (for example Buonanno et al., 2003; Goulder and Mathai, 2000). While DEMETER fits into the tradition of models like DICE (Nordhaus, 1994, 2002), it is clearly much richer in technological detail than Nordhaus's pioneering top-down model. It shares the endogenization of technical change through learning curves with bottom-up models as developed by Messner (1997) and reported in Nakićenović et al. (2000). In this sense, DEMETER is hybrid and especially useful for deriving insight for policy-making (Jaccard et al., 2003). Below, after a short introduction, brief descriptions are given of how DEMETER models the representative consumer, the final good producer, energy producers, technological change, climate change, and carbon dioxide capture and storage (CCS).

10.1 INTRODUCTION

DEMETER models distinct time periods of five years, each denoted by $t = 1,\ldots,\infty$. The model distinguishes one representative consumer, three representative producers (also referred to as sectors), and a public agent that can set emission taxes to reduce carbon dioxide emissions. Producers are denoted by superscripts $j = C, F, N$, respectively for the producer of the final good or consumption good, the producer of energy based on fossil-fuel technology, and the producer of energy based on carbon-free technology.

There are four goods for which an equilibrium price is determined that brings supply and demand in equilibrium: the final good with price λ_t normalized to unity, $\lambda_t = 1$, fossil fuel energy, with price μ_t^F, carbon-free energy with price μ_t^N, and labour with price w_t. We use β_t^τ as the price deflator for the final good from period t to period τ. So, $\beta_t^\tau = 1/[(1+r_t)(1+r_{t+1})...(1+r_{\tau-1})]$, where r_t is the real interest rate. By definition, $\beta_t^t \equiv 1$ and $\beta_t^\tau = 1/\beta_\tau^t$. When convenient, we also use $\beta_t = \beta_t^{t+1} \equiv 1/(1+r_t)$. Figure 10.1 presents a schematic overview of the model flows. The time lag between investments and capital used as production factor is represented through an 'L' on top of the flow arrows.

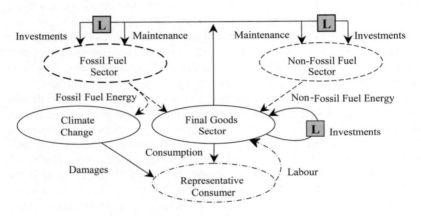

Figure 10.1   DEMETER Schematic Overview of Flows

The final good is produced by sector $j = C$, where output is denoted by Y^C. The same good is used for consumption, investments I in all three sectors and for operating and maintenance M (as usually distinguished in energy models) in both energy sectors $j = F,N$:

$$C_t + I_t^C + I_t^F + I_t^N + M_t^F + M_t^N = Y_t^C . \qquad (10.1)$$

We distinguish operating and maintenance costs, on the one hand, and investment costs, on the other hand (both in the energy sector), chiefly since the empirical data on learning rates often pertain to investment costs (see McDonald and Schrattenholzer, 2001) and we want to avoid overestimating learning rates. Fossil fuel energy is demanded by the final goods sector $j = C$ and supplied by the fossil fuel sector $j = F$. Carbon-free energy is demanded by the final goods sector $j = C$ and supplied by the carbon-free energy sector $j = N$. Labour L_t is demanded by the final goods sector $j = C$ and supplied inelastically by the consumers. Finally, the public agent may levy a tax τ_t on emissions Em_t produced by the final good sector when using fossil fuel energy sources.

10.2   THE REPRESENTATIVE CONSUMER

We assume there is one representative consumer who maximizes welfare subject to a budget constraint:

$$W = \sum_{t=1}^{\infty} (1+\rho)^{-t} L_t \ln(C_t / L_t), \tag{10.2}$$

where W is total welfare, ρ is the pure time preference, and C_t / L_t is consumption per capita. Welfare optimization gives the Ramsey rule as a first-order condition for consumption,

$$\beta_t = (C_t / L_t)/[(1+\rho)(C_{t+1}/L_{t+1})]. \tag{10.3}$$

10.3   THE FINAL GOOD PRODUCER

The representative producer maximizes the net present value of the cash flows:

$$\text{Max } \sum_{t=1}^{\infty} \beta_0^t (Y_t^C - I_t^C - w_t L_t - \mu_t^F Y_t^F - \mu_t^N Y_t^N - \tau_t Em_t), \tag{10.4}$$

subject to the production constraints (10.5)–(10.12), given below. Revenues consist of output Y_t^C, expenditures consist of investments, I_t^C (one period ahead), labour L_t at wage w_t, fossil-fuel energy Y_t^F at price μ_t^F, and carbon-free energy, Y_t^N at price μ_t^N, and the public agency levies a tax τ_t on emissions.

To describe production, DEMETER accounts for technology that is embodied in capital installed in previous periods. It therefore distinguishes between production that uses the vintages of previous periods, and production that uses the newest vintage for which the capital stock has been installed in the directly preceding period. The input and output variables, as well as prices, associated with the most recent vintages are denoted by tildes (~). For every vintage, the production of the final good is based on a nested CES-function (constant elasticity of substitution function), using a capital–labour composite, $\tilde{Z}_t$, and a composite measure for energy services, $\tilde{E}_t$, as intermediates:

$$\tilde{Y}_t^C = [(A_t^1 \tilde{Z}_t)^{(\gamma-1)/\gamma} + (A_t^2 \tilde{E}_t)^{(\gamma-1)/\gamma}]^{\gamma/(\gamma-1)}, \quad (\tilde{\lambda}_t^2) \qquad (10.5)$$

where A_t^1 and A_t^2 are technology coefficients, and γ is the substitution elasticity between $\tilde{Z}_t$ and $\tilde{E}_t$. Notice that the Lagrange variable for the profit maximization programme is given between brackets. The capital–labour composite $\tilde{Z}_t$ is defined as:

$$\tilde{Z}_t = (I_{t-1}^C)^\alpha (\tilde{L}_t)^{1-\alpha}, \quad (\tilde{\theta}_t) \qquad (10.6)$$

which says that the capital–labour composite has fixed value share α for capital. Note that new capital is by definition equal to the investments of one period ahead, $\tilde{K}_t^j = I_{t-1}^j$.

We model energy services $\tilde{E}_t$ as consisting of a CES aggregate of energy produced by the sectors F and N:

$$\tilde{E}_t = [(\tilde{Y}_t^F)^{(\sigma-1)/\sigma} + (\tilde{Y}_t^N)^{(\sigma-1)/\sigma}]^{\sigma/(\sigma-1)}, \quad (\tilde{\chi}_t) \qquad (10.7)$$

where σ is the elasticity of substitution between F and N. The CES aggregation allows for a strictly positive demand for the new technology N, if the price of the carbon-free energy exceeds the price of the fossil-fuel energy F even by an order of magnitude. By assuming the elasticity of substitution σ to have a (bounded) value larger than one, $1 < \sigma < \infty$, it is ensured that the (expensive) new technology has at least a small but positive value share. In this way, the CES aggregation effectively represents a niche market and enables the economic system to take advantage of a diversified energy production, for example because different technologies exist, each having their own markets for which they possess a relative advantage. In DEMETER, niche markets are represented on the macro level, while gradual substitution of one technology for the other technology takes place when prices change. Though one could argue that the competition between energy sources will intensify (and thus the elasticity of substitution will increase) once the market share of carbon-free technologies rises as a result of a carbon tax, we assume σ to be constant both for reasons of simplicity and for reasons of lack of empirical data. As we will argue in Section 10.3, there is not much empirical evidence on the value of σ.

Carbon dioxide emissions, Em_t, are linked to the production of the newest vintage through an emission intensity parameter ε_t^F (where $\varepsilon_t^N = 0$ for the carbon-free energy technology) that describes the level of emissions per unit of fossil fuel energy use:

$$\tilde{Em}_t = \varepsilon_t^F \tilde{Y}_t^F, \quad (\tilde{\tau}_t) \qquad (10.8)$$

One part of production employs the new vintage, the other part employs the old capital stock that carries over from the previous period. All flows, output, use of energy, labour and the output of emissions are differentiated between the old and the new vintages. The input–output flow in period t is equal to the corresponding flow for the new vintage, plus the corresponding flow for the old capital stock of the previous period, times a depreciation factor $(1 - \delta)$:

$$Y_t^C = (1-\delta)Y_{t-1}^C + \tilde{Y}_t^C, \qquad (\tilde{\lambda}_t^1) \tag{10.9}$$

$$Y_t^j = (1-\delta)Y_{t-1}^j + \tilde{Y}_t^j, \qquad (\tilde{\mu}_t^j ; j = F,N) \tag{10.10}$$

$$L_t^j = (1-\delta)L_{t-1}^j + \tilde{L}_t, \qquad (\tilde{w}_t) \tag{10.11}$$

$$Em_t = (1-\delta)Em_{t-1} + \tilde{E}m_t. \qquad (\tilde{\tau}_t) \tag{10.12}$$

where the last equation (10.12) presents the relation between total emissions Em_t and emissions of the new vintage $\tilde{E}m_t$. Note that the equations should not be read as describing accumulation over time, and related thereto, the variables Y_t^C, Y_t^F, Y_t^N, L_t^C, Em_t do not represent stock variables. Instead, the equations more or less describe the slow adjustment of production characteristics over time, as the capital stock slowly adjusts with new vintages in every period.

10.4   ENERGY PRODUCERS

Both energy producers, the fossil fuel sector $j = F$ and the non-fossil fuel sector $j = N$ are treated symmetrically. Production of energy, $\tilde{Y}_t^j$ $(j = F,N)$, requires investments I_{t-1}^j (in the previous period) and maintenance costs, M_t^j. Energy producers maximize the net present value of cash flows:

$$\text{Max } \sum_{t=1}^{\infty} \beta_0^t (\mu_t^j Y_t^j - I_t^j - M_t^j). \tag{10.13}$$

Each new vintage with output $\tilde{Y}_t^j$ requires proportional investments one period ahead, I_{t-1}^j, and maintenance costs $\tilde{M}_t^j$ according to:

$$\tilde{Y}_t^j = a_t^j I_{t-1}^j, \qquad (\zeta_{j,t}; j = F,N) \tag{10.14}$$

$$\tilde{Y}_t^j = b_t^j \tilde{M}_t^j, \qquad (\eta_{j,t}; j = F,N) \tag{10.15}$$

where we maintain subscripts t for the technology parameters a_t^j and b_t^j to describe decreasing costs of energy production (increasing levels for a_t^j and

b_t^j) resulting from learning-by-doing. We assume that knowledge gained is public, that is non-rival and non-exclusive. Thus firms will not internalize the positive spillovers from their investments in their prices. Hence, production parameters a_t^j and b_t^j are treated as exogenous by the firms, and the individual firms are confronted with constant returns to scale.[2] In a similar way as expressed in the production of consumer goods (10.9), energy output is distinguished by vintage (10.10), and the same vintage approach applies to maintenance costs, M_t^j:

$$M_t^j = (1-\delta)M_{t-1}^j + \tilde{M}_t^j . \quad (\xi_{j,t}; \ j = F,N) \tag{10.16}$$

Profit maximization of (10.13) subject to (10.10), (10.14), (10.15) and (10.16) gives zero profits.

In this formulation we have not explicitly modelled resource exhaustion. One may argue that resource depletion implies in principle increasing extraction costs that, in practice, however, is usually counterbalanced by continuous technological development that tends to reduce extraction costs over time. Looking at the expected future price trajectories for fossil fuels (for example, Nakicenovic et al., 1998, p. 111, medium scenario B), we see that the shadow prices for all fossil fuels increase over time. We may thus underestimate the costs of supplying fossil fuels, but not too much, since expected increases in fossil fuel prices are small.

10.5   TECHNOLOGICAL CHANGE

The DEMETER model incorporates various insights from the bottom-up literature that stresses the importance of internalizing learning-by-doing effects in climate change analyses. Energy production costs decrease as the experience increases through the installation of new energy vintages. In this version of DEMETER, the endogenous modelling of learning-by-doing is limited to the energy sectors; we have not included learning effects for overall productivity and energy efficiency. Thus, A_t^1 and A_t^2 as employed in (10.5) are exogenously determined by a benchmark (business-as-usual) growth path.

For the energy sector, the model describes the learning process through a scaling variable h_t^j the inverse of which measures the relative productivity a_t^j and b_t^j relative to long-term productivity levels, a_∞^j and b_∞^j:

$$h_t^j a_t^j = a_\infty^j, \quad (j = F,N) \tag{10.17}$$

$$h_t^j b_t^j = b_\infty^j. \quad (j = F,N) \tag{10.18}$$

Stated in other terms, the variable h_t^j measures the costs of one unit of output $\tilde{Y}_t^j$ as compared to potential long-term costs. For example, $h_t^j = 2$ means that one unit of energy output of sector j costs twice as much investments and maintenance costs as compared to the situation in the far future when the learning effect has reached its maximum value.

To capture the process of gaining experience and a decreasing value of h_t^j, we introduce the variable X_t that represents experience; it counts accumulated installed new capacity (vintage) at the beginning of period t:

$$X_{t+1}^j = X_t^j + \tilde{Y}_t^j. \quad (j = F,N) \tag{10.19}$$

Furthermore, we use a scaling function $g^j(X) \to [1,\infty)$ that returns the value for h_t^j as dependent on cumulative experience X_t^j. Employing discrete time steps, the value of h_t^j is given by the average value of $g^j(X)$ over a period:

$$h_t^j = \int_{X_t^j}^{X_{t+1}^j} g^j(x)\,\mathrm{d}x / (X_{t+1}^j - X_t^j), \quad (j = F,N) \tag{10.20}$$

We assume $g'(\cdot) \leq 0$, that is, production costs decrease as experience increases, and we assume $g'(\infty) = 1$, that is, production costs converge to a strictly positive floor price (minimum amount of input associated with maximum learning effect) given by the levels of a_∞^j and b_∞^j. Finally, we assume a constant learning rate $lr > 0$ for technologies at the beginning of the learning curve (that is, for small values of X). This means that, initially, production costs decrease by a factor $(1 - lr)$, for every doubling of installed capacity. Such decreases have been observed empirically for a large range of different technologies (IEA, 2000).

A function $g^j(\cdot)$ that supports all these assumptions is given by:

$$g^j(X) = c^j(1 - d^j)X^{-d^j} + 1. \tag{10.21}$$

where we omitted subscripts t and superscript j for the variable X, and $0 < d^j < 1$ measures the speed of learning, and c^j measures the size of the learning costs relative to the long-term production costs.[3] Finally, we notice that, in a model without learning-by-doing, we would have $g^j(\cdot) = 1$.

10.6   CLIMATE CHANGE

Emissions are included in the equilibrium through equations (10.12) and (10.8). Environmental dynamics are included by linking emissions to atmospheric

CO_2 concentrations, Atm_t, and, in turn, to temperature change, $Temp_t$:

$$Atm_{t+1} = (1 - \delta^M)Atm_t + \pi(Em_t + \overline{Em_t}), \qquad (10.22)$$

$$Temp_{t+1} = (1 - \delta^T)Temp_t + \delta^T \overline{T}^{\ 2} \ln(Atm_t / Atm_0), \qquad (10.23)$$

where δ^M is the atmospheric CO_2 depreciation rate, π is the retention rate, $\overline{Em_t}$ are emissions not linked to energy production, δ^T is the temperature adjustment rate due to the atmospheric warmth capacity, and $\overline{T}$ is the long-term equilibrium temperature change associated with a doubling of atmospheric CO_2 concentrations. The climate change submodel is essentially based on Nordhaus (1994; see also below).

10.7   DEMETER 2.0 WITH CCS

DEMETER's public agent can set carbon taxes, fossil fuel taxes and non-carbon energy subsidies. These three policy instruments may all serve to reduce the emissions of carbon dioxide. When the agent imposes a carbon tax, levied on carbon dioxide emissions, one of the possible reactions is a reduction in overall energy consumption (as modelled in DEMETER 1.0). Producers can also shift from fossil energy to carbon-free energy (DEMETER 1.0) or, alternatively (as included as additional carbon abatement option in DEMETER 2.0), decarbonize fossil-based energy production through the application of carbon dioxide capture and storage (CCS). Carbon dioxide emissions, Em_t, are proportional to the carbon content of fossil fuels, denoted by ε_t^F, while $CCSR_t$ represents the share of the emissions captured through CCS. The relation between emissions and fossil fuel energy production (and use) thus becomes:

$$Em_t = \varepsilon_t^F (1 - CCSR_t)Y_t^F. \qquad (10.24)$$

Today, there is no scientific guarantee that carbon dioxide stored underground will not start leaking back into the atmosphere. In that case, naturally, this leakage should be accounted for as a future additional source of CO_2 emissions. The central scenarios developed under the TranSust project abstract from such carbon leakage phenomena. As part of our sensitivity analyses, however, we do include carbon leakage in DEMETER.

The variable $CCSR_t$ can be understood as the carbon dioxide capture and storage ratio: it is the share of the total amount of CO_2 emissions from the combustion of fossil fuels that is prevented through the application of CCS. Alternatively, we can interpret $CCSR_t$ in a broader sense, that is, as a generic endogenous decarbonization measure, in which ε_t^F is the carbon intensity of a benchmark fuel mix that is optimal without carbon tax, and $CCSR_t$ represents an aggregation of all activities that reduce carbon dioxide emissions as a result of directed policies, not only through CCS implementation but also through for example fuel-switching options. The parameter ε_t^F decreases over time exogenously and describes *inter alia* the 'autonomous' substitution of for example gas for oil and coal. In principle, we do not simulate a carbon tax-induced substitution between fossil fuels, in any case not through the parameter ε_t^F. In practice, however, a broad interpretation of $CCSR_t$ implies that we do account for an endogenous simulation of fossil fuel substitution effects. Thus, while the thrust of this chapter's findings relates to the nature of endogenous energy decarbonization, with the parameter ε_t^F DEMETER also possesses a feature describing a particular kind of exogenous energy decarbonization (as reported in Gerlagh and van der Zwaan 2004).[4]

The carbon dioxide capture and storage process is described through an 'effort variable' Q_t^{CCS}, which is assumed to be a second-order polynomial function depending on the share of carbon dioxide that is captured and stored (10.25 below). In DEMETER all activities are described per vintage. Tildes on top of variables refer to the most recent vintage installed, as for the fossil fuel use Y_t^F in this equation. The parameter κ describes the increase in marginal costs when a higher share of fossil fuels is decarbonized. For $\kappa = 0$, in one period, costs of CCS are linear and marginal costs are constant. For $\kappa = 1$, marginal costs double when the share of fossil fuels to which CCS is applied increases from almost nothing to all fossil fuels being combusted. This specification constitutes an important extension in comparison to the work by Ha-Duong and Keith (2003) and Keller et al. (2003). In our case, the low-cost CCS options are used first, when carbon taxes are low, while more expensive CCS alternatives are added to the set of applied CCS technologies under higher carbon taxes: these higher taxes justify the more elevated expenses and effort per unit of reduced emissions. CCS technology is only implemented in response to carbon taxes. Under constant investment and maintenance prices, the share of fossil fuel energy from which carbon dioxide is captured and stored is assumed to be linear in the carbon tax.

The variable h_t^{CCS} is an inverse measure for the level of learning in CCS application. The higher its value, the lower the cumulative learning, the more effort is required to implement CCS. When CCS deployment accumulates and thus the amount of emissions avoided increases (10.26), the resulting (installation and operation) experience, X_t^{CCS}, leads to an enhancement of related knowledge, and a corresponding decrease in the cost parameter h_t^{CCS} (10.27). In equation (10.27), c^{CCS} and d^{CCS} are constant technology parameters describing the experience (or learning) curve for CCS.[5] When experience X_t^{CCS} accumulates, CCS options become cheaper, and, for constant carbon taxes, more CCS technology is applied. Investments, one period before, are proportional to the effort QtCCS (10.28), and so are maintenance costs (10.29). The parameters a^{CCS} and b^{CCS} define the investments and maintenance flows required for one unit of the effort Q_t^{CCS}. In every period, total CCS maintenance costs are summed over all vintages, through (10.30). The parameter δ denotes the share of vintage capital that is depreciated per period. Summarizing, we have:

$$Q_t^{CCS} = h_t^{CCS}(CCSR_t + \tfrac{1}{2}\kappa\ CCSR_t^2)\varepsilon_t^F \tilde{Y}_t^F, \qquad (10.25)$$

$$X_{t+1}^{CCS} = X_t^{CCS} + CCSR_t\varepsilon_t^F \tilde{Y}_t^F. \qquad (10.26)$$

$$h_t^{ccs} = 1 + c^{ccs}(1 - d^{ccs})(X_t^{ccs})^{-d^{ccs}}. \qquad (10.27)$$

$$I_{t-1}^{CCS} = Q_t^{CCS} / a^{CCS}, \qquad (10.28)$$

$$\tilde{M}_t^{CCS} = Q_t^{CCS} / b^{CCS}. \qquad (10.29)$$

$$M_t^{CCS} = (1-\delta)M_{t-1}^{CCS} + \tilde{M}_t^{CCS}. \qquad (10.30)$$

The particular climate change dynamics used for the TranSust project are as in DICE99 (Nordhaus and Boyer, 2000). They describe a multistratum system, including an atmosphere, an upper-ocean stratum, and a lower-ocean stratum.[6]

NOTES

1. A full model description with all equations and the complete GAMS code is available through the Internet, via the web page of the first author: http://personalpages.manchester.ac.uk/staff/Reyer.Gerlagh/.
2. An extended version of DEMETER 1.0 also includes subsidies for new technologies, as presented in van der Zwaan et al. (2002). These can be used to internalize learning-by-doing in order to reach a dynamically efficient allocation. In this chapter, however, we abstract from such subsidies.
3. The learning rate lr and the parameter d used in (10.21) are approximately related by the equation $d = -\ln(1-lr)/\ln2$. For small learning rates lr, we make the approximation $d = lr/\ln2$.
4. This exogenous decarbonization of fossil fuels amounts to 0.2 per cent per year.
5. For low values of X_t^{CCS}, the learning rate is given by $(1-2^{-d^{ccs}})$.
6. As DICE99 uses periods of ten years, we recalibrated the DICE99 climate module parameters to fit our five-year period structure.

REFERENCES

Bovenberg, A.L. and S.A. Smulders (1996), 'Transitional impacts of environmental policy in an endogenous growth model', *International Economic Review*, **37**, 861–93.

Buonanno, P., C. Carraro and M. Galeotti (2003), 'Endogenous induced technical change and the costs of Kyoto', *Resource and Energy Economics*, **25**,11–34.

Chakravorty U., J. Roumasset and K. Tse (1997), 'Endogenous substitution among energy resources and global warming', *Journal of Political Economy*, **105**, 1201–34.

Gerlagh, R. and B.C.C. van der Zwaan (2003), 'Gross world product and consumption in a global warming model with endogenous technological change', *Resource and Energy Economics*, **25**, 35–57.

Gerlagh, R. and B.C.C. van der Zwaan (2004), 'A sensitivity analysis of timing and costs of greenhouse gas emission reductions under learning effects and niche markets', *Climatic Change*, **65**, 39–71.

Gerlagh, R., B.C.C. van der Zwaan, M.W. Hofkes and G. Klaassen (2004), 'Impacts of CO_2-taxes in an economy with niche markets and learning-by-doing', *Environmental and Resource Economics*, **28**, 367–94.

Goulder, L.H. and K. Mathai (2000), 'Optimal CO_2 abatement in the presence of induced technological change', *Journal of Environmental Economics and Management*, **39**, 1–38.

Ha-Duong, M. and D.W. Keith (2003), 'Carbon storage: The economic efficiency of storing CO_2 in leaky reservoirs', *Clean Technology and Environmental Policy*, **5**, 181–9.

IEA (2000), *Experience Curves for Energy Technology Policy*, Paris: OECD.

Jaccard, M., J. Nyboer, C. Bataille and Bryn Sadownik (2003), 'Modeling the cost of climate policy: Distinguishing between alternative cost definitions and long-run cost dynamics', *The Energy Journal*, **24**, 49–73.

Keller, K., Z. Yang, M. Hall and D.F. Bradford (2003), 'Carbon dioxide sequestration: When and how much?', CEPS Working Paper 94, Princeton University.

McDonald, A. and L. Schrattenholzer (2001), 'Learning rates for energy technologies', *Energy Policy*, **29**, 255–61.

Messner, S. (1997), 'Endogenized technological learning in an energy systems model', *Journal of Evolutionary Economics*, **7**, 291–313.

Nakicenovic, N., A. Grübler and A. McDonald (eds) (1998), *Global Energy Perspectives*, IIASA-WEC. Cambridge: Cambridge University Press.

Nakicenovic, N., J. Alcamo, G. Davis, B. de Vries, J. Fenhann, S. Gaffin, K. Gregory, A. Grübler, T.Y. Jung, T. Kram, E.L. La Rovere, L. Michaelis, S. Mori, T. Morita, W. Pepper, H. Pitcher, L. Price, K. Raihi, A. Roehrl, H-H. Rogner, A. Sankovski, M. Schlesinger, P. Shukla, S. Smith, R. Swart, S. van Rooijen, N. Victor and Z. Dadi (2000), *Emissions Scenarios: Special report of Working Group III of the Intergovernmental Panel on Climate Change*, Cambridge: Cambridge University Press.

Nordhaus W.D. (1994), *Managing the Global Commons*, Cambridge, MA: MIT Press.

Nordhaus, W.D. (2002), 'Modeling induced innovation in climate change policy', in A. Grübler, N. Nakićenović and W.D. Nordhaus (eds), *Modeling Induced Innovation in Climate Change Policy*, Washington DC: Resources for the Future Press, pp. 182–209.

Nordhaus, W.D. and J. Boyer (2000), *Warming the World, Economic Models of Global Warming*, Cambridge, MA: MIT Press.

van der Zwaan, B.C.C. and R. Gerlagh (2006), 'Climate sensitivity uncertainty and the necessity to transform global energy supply', *Energy*, **31**, 2571–87.

van der Zwaan, B.C.C., R. Gerlagh, G. Klaassen and L. Schrattenholzer (2002), 'Endogenous technological change in climate change modelling', *Energy Economics*, **24**, 1–19.

11. Impact Assessment of Climate Policies (IMACLIM-S)

Frédéric Ghersi

11.1 INTRODUCTION

This text provides a technical description of the aggregated one-region (global) two-good version of IMACLIM-S used in the TranSust project. The two goods are energy E and an aggregate of all other productions, or composite good, Q.

Notwithstanding such a high level of aggregation, IMACLIM-S is presented in a generalised i-sector format, to limit the number of equations to be commented upon and give a sense of how the composite sector is disaggregated in other versions of the model. The formulary is preceded by a short overview describing the purpose of the model and its general architecture.

11.2 IMACLIM-S: AN OVERVIEW

IMACLIM-S is a static general equilibrium framework designed to assess the macroeconomic impacts of a price- or quantity-based carbon policy at some medium- to long-term horizon. It focuses on the sensitivity of such impacts to the technical abatement costs and the particulars of the policy tools (tax reforms, trading systems, technical or emission standards) triggering abatement. It is built to allow for the description of economies with: (i) a suboptimal equilibrium on the labour market; and (ii) behaviours of the underlying technical systems that cannot be approximated by 'well-behaved' production or utility functions for large departures from the reference scenario. The shifts of technical systems impact upon an aggregated induced technical change encompassing learning by doing and research and development activities; IMACLIM-S thus operates in an endogenous technical change framework.

Relying on the method of comparative-static analysis, it provides insights that are valid under the assumption that the transition from the reference growth path to a carbon-constrained equilibrated growth path is completed, and does not imply any transitory disequilibrium that would affect the derived equilibrium.

The main feature of IMACLIM-S is that assumptions regarding both the baseline projection of the energy system and its price-response at the projected time horizon are harmonised with information from a bottom-up energy model, completed by a limited set of exogenous assumptions:

- The baseline projection to the time horizon is devised to be price- and quantity-consistent with a bottom-up projection of the energy system, based on shared assumptions regarding main economic and demographic drivers.
- At the time horizon, the response of the input–output (IO) coefficients and of consumers to new relative prices is captured through envelopes of the functions generated by various carbon prices, as reconstructed from bottom-up information. This method amounts to capturing the bias in technical change induced by the carbon constraint through a set of varying point elasticities. As opposed to conventional production specifications, the use of envelope functions allows for representing technical asymptotes and technological breakthroughs.[1]

In order to capture the rate and not only the direction of technical progress, IMACLIM-S carries out a comparative-static analysis of an endogenous growth mechanism: investment triggers a Hicks-neutral technical progress affecting factor productivity. Crowding-out effects of biasing the direction of technical change are computed by withdrawing the investment dedicated to carbon abatement from total investment (under the assumption of a constant saving ratio), modulo spillover assumptions.

The most extensive calibrated version of IMACLIM-S to date pictures 14 world regions and three goods (composite, transformed energy, fossil fuels); for more in-depth scrutiny of issues such as the role of fiscal reforms, competitiveness of exposed carbon-intensive industry or distributive effects, a nine-sector two-region (country or region analysed and rest of the world) version is preferred.

11.3   TECHNICAL DESCRIPTION

The following technical description presents the one-region two-good version of IMACLIM-S used during the TranSust project. It entails a nomenclature of notations and a formulary of 28 equations, completed by a brief comment on each of the latter.

11.4   MODEL NOMENCLATURE

As a comparative-static model, IMACLIM consists in a system of equations:

$$f_1(x_1,..., x_n, z_1,..., z_m) = 0$$
$$f_2(x_1,..., x_n, z_1,..., z_m) = 0$$
$$...$$
$$f_n(x_1,..., x_n, z_1,..., z_m) = 0$$

with: x_i, $i \in [1, n]$, a set of variables (as many as equations); zi, $i \in [1, m]$, $m < n$, a set of parameters; fi, $i \in [1, n]$, a set of functions, some of them non-linear in x_i.

Calibration consists in defining a set of $x_1,..., x_n$ and solving the system for $z_1,..., z_m$. In the case of TranSust simulations, the x vector used for the calibration of IMACLIM-S – its business-as-usual (BAU) equilibrium – is based on a global projection of 1997 accounting matrices matrices built on the Global Trade Analysis Program (GTAP) 5.0 database.[2] In more recent exercises, it is derived from a harmonised reference projection of the IMACLIM-R (a dynamic recursive version of IMACLIM) and the POLES model of global energy systems.[3] In both instances, the economic equilibria expressed in monetary flows are disaggregated in prices and quantities by fixing the vector of prices, thereby defining quasi-units for all goods (including labour), without loss of generality.

A limited set of parameters is exogenous to the calibration, based either on econometric specifications, or on mere assumptions (control variables).

The following presentation of the notations used in the model is divided into the three categories outlined above: variables, calibrated parameters, exogenous parameters and control variables. Within each category the notations are sorted in alphabetical order.[4]

Variables (x Vector)

α_{EE} Energy intensity of energy (unit intermediate consumption of energy E in the production of energy E, input–output coefficient).

α_{EQ} Energy intensity of the composite good (unit intermediate consumption of energy E in the production of the composite good Q, input–output coefficient).

C_i Household consumption of good i (in real terms).

γ_{Ci} Carbon (or CO_2, depending on calibration) emitted per unit of final consumption of good i.

γ_{ij} Carbon (or CO_2, see above) emitted per unit of consumption of good i in the production of good j.

IPC Consumer price index.

k_{AQ} Carbon tax-induced investment per unit of production of good i (in real terms). Nil per definition in the BAU projection.

k_E Unit fixed capital consumption in the production of energy E (in real terms).

K_i Consumption of good i in fixed capital formation (in real terms). In the two-sector version of the model, K_E is irrelevant and K_i boils down to K_Q.

l_Q Labour intensity of the composite good (unit labour consumption in the production of good Q, in real terms).

p_{Ci} Consumer price of good i, household consumption.

p_{Gi} Consumer price of good i, public consumption.

Φ_Q Endogenous technical progress coefficient applying to the composite production. Normalised in the BAU projection (see below). Energy production is not corrected by a similar coefficient: it is assumed that the more detailed bottom-up (BU) expertise providing the basis of energy technology shifts (endogenous variations of the α_{EE} and k_E coefficients) takes into account all sources of factor productivity variations.

p_K Capital price index (weighted average of the price of capital goods). With K_Q the only relevant component of fixed capital formation p_K boils down to p_{KQ}.

p_{Ki} Price of good i used in fixed capital formation.

p_{Li} Unit labour cost in the production of good i.

p_{Yi} Producer price of good i.

R Household income (gross disposable income).

R_T Transfer income.

σ_i Payroll tax rate in the production of good i.

T Total tax and social security contributions.

Θ_Q Decreasing returns coefficient applying to composite production. Normalised in the BAU projection. Energy production is not corrected by a similar coefficient (see Φ_Q above).

u Unemployment rate.

w_E Net wage in the production of energy.

Y_i Output of good i (in real terms).

Calibrated Parameters

α_{QQ} Composite intensity of the composite good (unit consumption of the composite good Q in its own production, input–output coefficient).

α_{QE} Composite intensity of the energy good (unit consumption of the composite good Q in the production of energy E, input–output coefficient). The degree of approximation stemming from fixing α_{QQ} and α_{QE} is limited by the highly aggregated nature of good Q.

G_i Public (government) consumption of good i (in real terms). Is held constant for lack of behavioural assumptions regarding governments, and as this makes the shifts in final consumption a better qualitative indicator of welfare variations.

k_Q Unit fixed capital consumption in the production of the composite good Q (in real terms). The baseline data, unavailable from the GTAP database, is calibrated so that the difference between total investment and households' savings should equal total fixed capital consumption (in monetary terms).

L Labour supply (unit defined by the numeraire w_Q, see below).

l_E Labour intensity of energy (unit consumption of labour in the production of energy E). Is held constant, considering both its relatively small weight in the energy cost structure, and impact on the aggregate labour market.

π_i Mark-up rate in the production of good i.

r_C Households' saving rate.

r_T Ratio of fiscal contributions to total output. A constant r_T applies only in the payroll tax-recycling version of the model, where it defines the revenue neutrality of the fiscal reform accompanying the carbon policy.

t_{Ci} Tax rate on the sales of good i to households.

t_{Gi} Tax rate on the sales of good i to public agents.

t_i Output tax rate (on the production of good i).

τ_{IR} Income tax rate.

τ_{IS} Corporate tax rate.

t_{ji} Tax rate on the sales of good j entering the production of good i.

t_{Ki} Tax rate on the sales of good i to form fixed capital.

Econometrically Estimated Parameters and Control Variables

$\varepsilon_{\Phi K}$ Elasticity of the technical progress coefficient Φ_Q to the evolution of total fixed capital consumption in the composite sector. The latter argument is intended as a proxy of the investment differential cumulated between the BAU and the policy-induced growth path. An econometric analysis made for France has not been extended to other regions yet. For the time being, a conservative learning curve assumption is used for all sectors: a doubling of real investment leads to a 10 per cent decrease in factor consumption. This assumption corresponds to a 0.15 value for $\varepsilon_{\Phi K}$.

ε_{wu} Elasticity of the real wage to the unemployment rate. Set to 0.1 following a seemingly robust empirical estimate.[5]

τ_{ev} Crowding-out assumption: share of the investment dedicated to carbon abatement that is subtracted from general productivity investment (see below). Sensitivity analysis reveals a paramount importance of the choice of τ_{ev}.

t_C Tax per unit of carbon as defined by γ_{ij} and γ_{Ci}. The main control variable in the model.

w_Q Net wage in the production of the composite good Q. Following common practice, w_Q is exogenously set in the calibration process to disaggregate prices and quantities on the labour market (thereby defining a unit for labour L, without loss of generality). With labour used as the numeraire it is then kept constant.[6]

11.5   FORMULARY

In the following equations, notations with a '0' subscript stand for values in the BAU projection.

Prices

$$p_{Yi} = \frac{\Theta_i}{\Phi_i} \left(\sum_{j=E,Q} (p_{Yj} + t_C\, \gamma_{ji})\, (1+t_{ji})\, \alpha_{ji} + p_{Li}\, l_i + p_K\, k_i \right) + t_i\, p_{Yi} + p_{Yi}\, \pi_i \quad (11.1)$$

$$p_{Ci} = (p_{Yi} + t_C\, \gamma_{Ci})\, (1+t_{Ci}) \quad\quad\quad\quad (11.2)$$

$$p_{Gi} = p_{Yi}\, (1+t_{Gi}) \quad\quad\quad\quad\quad\quad (11.3)$$

$$p_{Ki} = p_{Yi}\, (1+t_{Ki}) \quad\quad\quad\quad\quad\quad (11.4)$$

$$IPC = \frac{\displaystyle\sum_{i=E,Q} p_{Ci}\, C_{i0}}{\displaystyle\sum_{i=E,Q} p_{Ci0}\, C_{i0}} \quad\quad\quad\quad (11.5)$$

$$p_K = \frac{\displaystyle\sum_{i=E,Q} p_{Ki}\, K_{i0}}{\displaystyle\sum_{i=E,Q} p_{Ki0}\, K_{i0}}\, p_{K0} \quad\quad\quad\quad (11.6)$$

$$p_{Li} = w_i\, (1+\sigma_i) \quad\quad\quad\quad\quad\quad (11.7)$$

Households

$$R = (1-\tau_{IR}) \sum_{i=E,Q} w_i\, \frac{\Theta_i}{\Phi_i}\, l_i\, Y_i + (1-\tau_{IS}) \sum_{i=E,Q} p_{Yi}\, \pi_i\, Y_i + R_T \quad (11.8)$$

$$r_C\, R = \sum_{i=E,Q} p_{Ci}\, C_i \quad\quad\quad\quad (11.9)$$

$$\frac{p_{CE}\,C_E}{r_C\,R} = f_1\left(\frac{p_{CE}}{p_{CQ}}\right) \tag{11.10}$$

Government

$$T = \sum_{j=E,Q}\sum_{i=E,Q} t_{ij}\,(p_{Yi} + t_C\,\gamma_{ij})\,\frac{\Theta_i}{\Phi_j}\,\alpha_{ij} + \sum_{i=E,Q}\sigma_i\,w_i\,\frac{\Theta_i}{\Phi_i}\,l_i\,Y_i + \sum_{i=E,Q} t_i\,p_{Yi}\,Y_i$$

$$+ \tau_{IR}\sum_{i=E,Q} w_i\,\frac{\Theta_i}{\Phi_i}\,l_i\,Y_i + \tau_{IS}\sum_{i=E,Q} p_{Yi}\,\pi_i\,Y_i + \sum_{i=E,Q} t_{Ci}\,p_{Yi}\,C_i + \sum_{i=E,Q} t_{Gi}\,p_{Yi}\,G_i$$

$$+ \sum_{i=E,Q} t_{Ki}\,p_{Yi}\,K_i + t_C\left(\sum_{j=E,Q}\sum_{i=E,Q}\gamma_{ij}\,\frac{\Theta_i}{\Phi_j}\,\alpha_{ij}\,Y_j + \sum_{i=E,Q}\gamma_{Ci}\,C_i\right) \tag{11.11}$$

$$T = \sum_{i=E,Q} p_{Gi}\,G_i + R_T \tag{11.12}$$

$$T = r_T\sum_{i=E,Q} p_{Yi}\,Y_i \tag{11.13}$$

$$\sigma_i = \sigma_{i0}\,\frac{\sigma_Q}{\sigma_{Q0}} \tag{11.14}$$

Investment Market

$$\sum_{i=E,Q} p_{Ki}\,K_i = p_K\sum_{i=E,Q}\frac{\Theta_i}{\Phi_i}\,k_i\,Y_i + (1-r_C)\,R \tag{11.15}$$

Labour Market

$$L = \sum_{i=E,Q}\frac{\Theta_i}{\Phi_i}\,l_i\,Y_i + u\,L \tag{11.16}$$

$$\frac{w_Q}{IPC}\,u^{\varepsilon_{wu}} = w_{Q0}\,u_0^{\varepsilon_{wu}} \tag{11.17}$$

Goods Market

$$Y_i = \sum_{j=E,Q}\frac{\Theta_i}{\Phi_j}\,\alpha_{ji}\,Y_j + C_i + G_i + K_i \tag{11.18}$$

Technology Biases

$$k_Q = k_{Q0} + (1 - \tau_{ev})\, k_{AQ} \tag{11.19}$$

$$k_{AQ} = f_2\left(\frac{t_C}{IPC}\right) \tag{11.20}$$

$$k_E = k_{E0}\, f_3\left(\frac{t_C}{IPC}\right) \tag{11.21}$$

$$\alpha_{EQ} = \alpha_{EQ0}\, f_3\left(\frac{(p_{YE} + t_C\, \gamma_{EQ})\,(1 + t_{EQ})}{p_{LQ}}\right) \tag{11.22}$$

$$\frac{\alpha_{EQ}}{l_Q} = \frac{\alpha_{EQ0}}{l_{Q0}}\, f_4\left(\frac{(p_{YE} + t_C\, \gamma_{EQ})\,(1 + t_{EQ})}{p_{LQ}}\right) \tag{11.23}$$

$$\alpha_{EE} = \alpha_{EE0}\, f_5\left(\frac{(p_{YE} + t_C\, \gamma_{EE})\,(1 + t_{EE})}{IPC}\right) \tag{11.24}$$

Carbon Emission Coefficients

$$\gamma_{Ci} = f_6\left(\frac{t_C}{IPC}\right) \tag{11.25}$$

$$\gamma_{ij} = f_7\left(\frac{t_C}{IPC}\right) \tag{11.26}$$

Productivity Factors

$$\Phi_Q = \left(\frac{k_{Q0}\, Y_Q - \tau_{\acute{e}v}\, k_{AQ}\, Y_Q}{k_{Q0}\, Y_{Q0}}\right)^{\mathcal{E}_{\Phi KQ}} \tag{11.27}$$

$$\Theta_Q = \left(\frac{Y_Q}{Y_{Q0}}\right)^{\frac{\pi_Q}{1 - \pi_Q}} \tag{11.28}$$

11.6   COMMENTS ON THE EQUATIONS

(1)   Producer prices are defined according to the cost structure of production, that is, the sum of intermediate consumption, labour costs, capital amortisement, an output tax and a relative mark-up. Input–output coefficients α_{ji}, labour consumption l_i and capital amortisement k_i are (i) multiplied by a decreasing returns coefficient Θ_i and (ii)

divided by a technical progress coefficient Φ_i.[7] The underlying theoretical stance is that the quantity – together with the substitutability and eventually the balance – of physical factors consumptions in the production are linked to the particular capital structure induced by the carbon policy under scrutiny.

(2–4) Consumer prices equal the producer prices plus taxes, including, for the consumption of households,[8] a tax on the related carbon emissions.

(5) Consumer price index (Laspeyres defined).

(6) Investment price index. Irrelevant in the two-sector version of the model, where the composite good Q is the only eligible good for capital formation.

(7) Labour costs equal net wages plus *ad valorem* payroll taxes. Contributions from the employer and the employee are not distinguished.

(8) Households' income R equals revenues from labour (wages net of payroll taxes and income tax) and profits (net of corporate tax) plus public transfers R_T.

(9) Households' budget constraint: households' consumption amounts to a constant share r_C of total income.

(10) The households' budget share of energy expenditures is a function f_1 of the energy price relative to the price of the competing composite good. f_1 is an envelope of the point demand functions induced by increasing price signals, calibrated on bottom-up results.[9]

(11) Public revenues accrue from taxes on intermediate consumptions, payroll taxes, output taxes, the income and corporate taxes, final consumption taxes, public consumption taxes, investment taxes, and the carbon tax (levied on the carbon emissions related to the intermediate and final consumptions).

(12) Government's budget constraint: public income equals public consumption plus transfers to the households.

(13) Revenue neutrality assumption: r_T the ratio of total public revenues over total nominal output is held constant (at its calibrated value); another possible assumption, with non-negligible impacts on the simulation results, is a constancy of the public revenue to gross domestic product (GDP) ratio.

(14) Payroll tax rates evolve identically in all sectors.

(15) Balance on the investment market: total investment equals the sum of total fixed capital consumption and of a constant share of households' revenues (constant saving ratio).

(16) Balance on the labour market: total labour equals the sum of employed and unemployed labour. Not detailing this equilibrium for every production amounts to the implicit assumption of 'mobile' – not sector-specific – labour.[10]

(17)   Wage curve: real wages in the production of good Q are inversely correlated to unemployment. Resorting to a wage curve allows for picturing unemployment, which is of particular interest when analysing specific carbon-levy recycling schemes.

(18)   Balance on good i's market: total output equals the sum of intermediate consumption, household's consumption, public consumption and investment.

(19)   Real fixed capital consumption in the production of good Q is equal to its BAU value plus a share of the amortisement of the abatement-specific unitary investment, modulo the extent of crowding-out effects: outside such effects ($\tau_{ev} = 0$) abatement-dedicated investments enter the cost structure on top of BAU investments (cost increases are entirely passed through to consumers); if crowding-out occurs to some extent ($0 < \tau_{ev} \leq 1$) they are partly substituted to BAU investments.

(20)   Unitary investment linked to abatement-dedicated capital in the production of good Q is a function f_2 of the IPC-corrected carbon tax. f_2 is calibrated on bottom-up results.

(21)   Capital intensity of energy (real fixed capital consumption in the production of good E) is a function f_3 of the IPC-corrected carbon tax. f_1 is an envelope of the point factor demand functions induced by increasing price signals, calibrated on bottom-up results.

(22–3) The energy and labour intensities of the composite good are functions of the corresponding relative prices. f_3 and f_4 are again envelope specifications built on bottom-up results. As stated in the commentary to equation (11.1), the underlying theoretical viewpoint is that any carbon policy primarily induces changes in the structure of capital, resulting in a 'capital vintage' eventually characterised by a trade-off between the remaining factors – trade-off grounded on an envelope function of the results from an associated bottom-up model.

(24)   Energy intensity of energy (real energy consumption in the production of good E) is a function f_5 of the relative price of energy. f_5 is an envelope of point factor demand functions calibrated on bottom-up results.

(25) γ_{Ci} is a function of t_C as drawn from the results of an associated bottom-up model, accounting for implicit fuel substitution in the composition of final fossil fuel and transformed energy demands.

(26)   Same as γ_{Ci}, it is a function of t_C as drawn from the results of an associated bottom-up model.

(27)   Induced technical change coefficient in the production of good Q – see comment (1). The amount of real investment positively correlated to a rise in productivity ($\varepsilon_{\phi KQ} > 0$) is computed net of the share of the abatement-specific investment substituted to, rather than added up to, general-productivity investment.

(28)   Decreasing returns in the production of good Q are a function of Y_Q dictated by analytical calculus on equation (11.1) to allow for marginal cost pricing. They cause an exponential rise in factor consumptions as production supersedes its baseline level – which is thus used as a reference level for all alternative growth scenarios at the time horizon explored.

NOTES

1.   For an extensive presentation of the hybridising methodology behind these envelopes see Ghersi and Hourcade (2006).
2.   This projection is again a comparative-static exercise, based on a simplified version of IMACLIM, IMACLIM-PROJTES, and grounded on an evolution of the energy systems as projected by the POLES model (with which it shares the two central assumptions of GDP and population growth).
3.   See Criqui (2001).
4.   The Greek letters are sorted following their English denomination rather than their Latin equivalent.
5.   See Blanchflower and Oswald (1995).
6.   The model is conventionally homothetic in prices, and a numeraire must be defined in which all prices can be measured. With labour the numeraire, prices fluctuation are intuitively interpretable as the variations of the quantity of work necessary to buy one good.
7.   As previously indicated the two coefficients impact the composite cost structure only (that is, $\Theta_E = \Phi_E = 1$).
8.   Neither investment nor public expenditures consume any energy goods in national accounting systems – public expenditures are concentrated on a single 'public good' produced by a public sector with its own cost structure.
9.   Again, see Ghersi and Hourcade (2006).
10.   The assumption is arguably reasonable, bearing in mind the comparative-static nature of IMACLIM simulation: the alternate growth path leading to the derived equilibrium at a mid- to long-term horizon allows for qualitative labour adjustments.

REFERENCES

Blanchflower, D.G. and A.J. Oswald (1995), 'An introduction to the wage curve', *Journal of Economic Perspectives*, **9**(3), 153–67.
Criqui, P. (2001), 'POLES: Prospective outlook on long-term energy systems', Institut d'Économie et de Politique de l'Énergie, Grenoble, France, available at: http://www.upmf-grenoble.fr/iepe/textes/POLES8p_01.pdf [accessed August 2006].
Ghersi, F. and J.-C. Hourcade (2006), 'Macroeconomic consistency issues in E3 modeling: The continued fable of the elephant and the rabbit', in J.-C. Hourcade, M. Jaccard, C. Bataille and F. Ghersi (eds), *The Energy Journal*, Special Issue 2: *Hybrid Modeling of Energy–Environment Policies: Reconciling Bottom-up and Top-down*, 39–62.

12. The Energy–Environment–Economy Model for Europe (E3ME)

Terry Barker, Sebastian De-Ramon and Hector Pollitt

12.1 INTRODUCTION

This section provides a short non-technical description of the Energy–Environment–Economy Model for Europe (E3ME), developed by Cambridge Econometrics (CE). More details are available at www.e3me.com. For acknowledgements and references please refer to the online manual at: http://www.camecon-e3memanual.com/cgi-bin/EPW_CGI.

12.2 AN OVERVIEW OF THE E3ME MODEL

Short- and Long-term Effects of E3 Policies

E3ME is intended to meet an expressed need of researchers and policy-makers for a framework for analysing the long-term implications of Energy–Environment–Economy (E3) policies, especially those concerning research and development (R&D) and environmental taxation and regulation. The model is also capable of addressing annual short-term and medium-term economic effects as well as, more broadly, the long-term effects of such policies over the next 20 years, such as those from the supply side of the labour market. E3ME includes the EU-25 (as of 2006), Norway and Switzerland; it is being expanded to include for new EU member states.

The E3ME Approach

E3ME is an annual medium-term sectoral simulation model, estimated by formal econometric methods. It is not an equilibrium model, but it has the detail and adopts some of the methods of computable general equilibrium (CGE) models. It provides an analysis of the movement of the long-term outcomes for key E3 indicators in response to policy changes. It can be used for dynamic policy simulation and for forecasting and projecting over the medium and long terms. As such, it is a valuable tool for E3 policy analysis in Europe. E3ME has the following advantages over many competing models:

Model disaggregation. The detailed nature of the model allows the representation of fairly complex scenarios, especially those that are differentiated according to sector and to country. Similarly, the impact of any policy measure can be represented in a detailed way. E3ME's classifications are ESA95-compatible and include 42 industry sectors (including 16 service sectors), 28 categories of consumer spending, 19 different fuel user groups and 12 energy carriers. A full list of model classifications is available on the model website (www.e3me.com).

Econometric pedigree. The econometric grounding of the model makes it better able to represent and forecast performance in the short to medium run. It therefore provides information that allows for dynamic responses to changes in policy and that is closer to the time horizon of many policy-makers than pure CGE models, which provide long-term equilibrium solutions.

E3 linkages. E3ME is a hybrid model. An interaction (two-way feedback) between the economy, energy demand/supply and environmental emissions is an undoubted advantage over models that may either ignore the interaction completely or only assume a one-way causation. For example, the EU Emission Trading Scheme (ETS) includes a cap on CO_2 emissions: the model can be used to solve for the CO_2 allowance price, allowing for effects on electricity prices and demand, as well as on macroeconomic variables.

Model data sources. Like its predecessors, HERMES (Barker et al., 1993) and MDM-E3 (Barker et al., 1995), E3ME is an estimated model. Version 4.2 (E3ME42) is based on international data sources, including Eurostat and the Organisation for Economic Co-operation and Development (OECD).

12.3   A DESCRIPTION OF E3ME

The Theoretical Background to E3ME

Economic activity undertaken by persons, households, firms, governments, trade unions and other groups has effects on all groups after a time lag, and the effects may persist into future generations, although many of the effects soon become so small as to be negligible. However, although the individual effects may be small, there are many of them, both beneficial and damaging, and they accumulate in economic and physical stocks. The effects are transmitted through the environment (with externalities such as greenhouse gas emissions contributing to global warming), through the economy and through the price and money system (for example via the markets for labour and commodities), and through the global transport and information networks. The markets transmit policy effects in three main ways: through the level of activity creating demand for inputs of materials, fuels and labour; through wages and prices affecting incomes; and through incomes leading in turn to further demands for goods and services. These interdependencies suggest that an E3 model should be comprehensive, and include the relevant linkages between different parts of the economic and energy systems.

The economic and energy systems have the following characteristics: economies and diseconomies of scale in both production and consumption; markets with different degrees of competition; the prevalence of institutional behaviour whose aim may be utility maximisation, but may also be the satisfaction of more limited, satisfying objectives; and rapid and uneven changes in technology and consumer preferences, certainly within the time scale of greenhouse gas mitigation policy. Labour markets in particular may be characterised by long-term unemployment. The E3ME model is capable of representing these features by embodying a variety of behaviours, and by simulating a dynamic system. This approach can be contrasted with that adopted by most general equilibrium models: they typically assume constant returns to scale; perfect competition in all markets; maximisation of social welfare measured by total discounted private consumption; no involuntary unemployment; and exogenous technical progress following a constant time trend (see Barker, 1998a, 1998b, 2004 for more detailed discussion).

E3ME as an E3 Model

The E3ME model comprises:

- the accounting balances for:
  - commodities from input–output tables;
  - energy carriers from energy balances;
  - institutional incomes and expenditures from the national accounts;
- environmental emission flows.

The model contains 22 sets of time-series econometric equations, each one estimated by country and sector. They are aggregate energy demands, fuel substitution equations for coal, heavy oil, gas and electricity; intra-EU and extra-EU commodity exports and imports; total consumers' expenditure; disaggregated consumers' expenditure; industrial capital formation; industrial employment; industrial hours worked; labour participation; industrial prices;

export and import prices; industrial wage rates; residual incomes; investment in dwellings; and normal output equations.

Energy supplies and population stocks and flows are treated as exogenous.

The E3 Interactions

Figure 12.1 shows how the three components (modules) of the model – energy, environment and economy – fit together. Each component is shown in its own box with its own units of account and sources of data. Each data set has been constructed by statistical offices to conform with accounting conventions. Exogenous factors coming from outside the modelling framework are shown on the outside edge of the chart as inputs into each component. For the EU economy, these factors are economic activity and prices in non-EU world areas and economic policy (including tax rates, growth in government expenditures, interest rates and exchange rates). For the energy system, the outside factors are the world oil prices and energy policy (including regulation of energy industries). For the environment component, exogenous factors include policies such as reduction in SO_2 emissions by means of end-of-pipe filters from large combustion plants. The linkages between the components of the model are shown explicitly by the arrows that indicate which values are transmitted between components.

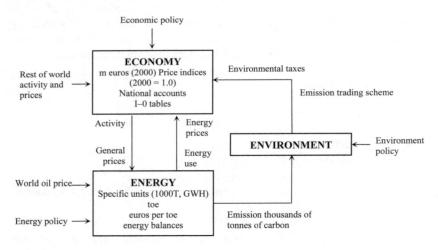

Figure 12.1   E3ME as an E3 Model

The economy module provides measures of economic activity and general price levels to the energy module; the energy module provides measures of emissions of the main air pollutants to the environment module, which in turn gives measures of damage to health and buildings (estimated using the most recent ExternE[1] coefficients). The energy module provides detailed price levels for energy carriers distinguished in the economy module and the overall price of energy as well as energy use in the economy.

The E3ME Regional Econometric Input–Output Model

Figure 12.2 shows how the economic module is solved as an integrated EU regional model. Most of the economic variables shown in the chart are at a 42-industry level. The whole system is solved simultaneously for all industries and all 27 regions, although single-region solutions are also possible. The chart shows interactions at three spatial levels: the outermost area is the rest of the world; the next level is the European Union outside the country in question; and finally, the inside level contains the relationships within the country.

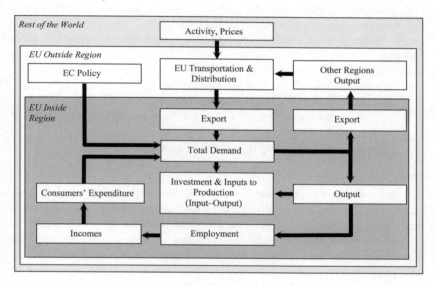

Figure 12.2   E3ME41 as a regional Econometric Input–Output Model

The chart shows three loops or circuits of economic interdependence, which are described in some detail below. These are the export loop, the output–investment loop and the income loop. The arrows indicate the direction of causal effects in the model, which take place over varying time lags, estimated (except for the input-output and similar coefficient tables) in sets of dynamic co-integrating equations, each with long-term estimated solutions.

The Export Loop

The export loop runs from the EU transport and distribution network to the region's exports, then to total demand. The region's imports feed into other EU regions' exports and output and finally to these other regions' demand from the EU pool and back to the exports of the region in question.

Treatment of international trade

An important part of the modelling concerns international trade. The basic assumption is that, for most commodities, there is a European 'pool' into which each region supplies part of its production and from which each region satisfies part of its demand. This might be compared to national electricity supplies and demands: each power plant supplies to the national grid and each user draws power from the grid and it is not possible or necessary to link a particular supply to a particular demand.

The demand for a region's exports of a commodity is related to three factors:

- domestic demand for the commodity in all the other EU regions, weighted by their economic distance from the region in question;
- activity in the main external EU export markets, as measured by GDP or industrial production;
- relative prices, including the effects of exchange rate changes.

Economic distance

Economic distance is measured by a special distance variable. For a given region, this variable is normalised to be 1 for the home region and values less than one for external regions. The economic distance to other regions is inversely proportional to trade between the regions. In E3ME regional imports are determined from econometric equations that include demand and relative prices by commodity and region. In addition, measures of innovation (including spending on R&D) have been introduced into the trade equations to pick up an important long-term dynamic effect on economic development.

The Output–Investment Loop

The output–investment loop includes industrial demand for goods and services and runs from total demand to output and then to investment and back to total demand. For each region, total demand for the gross output of goods and services is formed from industrial demand, consumer expenditure, government consumption, investment (fixed domestic capital formation and stock-building) and exports. These totals are divided between imports and output depending on relative prices, levels of activity and utilisation of capacity. Industrial demand represents the inputs of goods and services from other industries (required for current production), and is calculated using input–output coefficients. The coefficients are calculated as inputs of commodities from whatever source, including imports, per unit of gross industrial output.

Determination of investment demand
Forecast changes in output are important determinants of investment in the model. Investment is determined from equations that include past and expected output. Expectations are normally treated as adaptive, but the model can be solved assuming rational expectations for GDP and energy price projections (that is, the model solutions for these variables are consistent with the expected values in the investment and other equations). A set of 'normal' output equations is estimated for the model. Investment in new equipment and new buildings is one of the ways in which companies adjust to the new challenges introduced by energy and environmental policies. Consequently, the quality of the data and the way data are modelled are of great importance to the performance of the whole model. Regional investment by the investing industry is determined in the model as intertemporal choices depending on capacity output and investment prices. When investment by user industry is determined, it is converted, using coefficients derived from input–output tables, into demands on the industries producing the investment goods and services, mainly engineering and construction. These demands then constitute one of the components of total demand.

Accumulation of knowledge and technology
Gross fixed investment, enhanced by R&D expenditure in constant prices, is accumulated to provide a measure of the technological capital stock. By avoiding the conventional treatment of depreciation (Scott, 1989), there are fewer problems with the usual definition of the capital stock and lack of data on economic scrapping. The accumulation measure is designed to get round the worst of these problems. Investment is central to the determination of long-term growth and the model embodies a theory of Post-Keynesian endogenous growth (described for the companion model E3MG in Barker et al., 2006), which underlies the long-term behaviour of the trade and employment equations.

The Income Loop

In the income loop, industrial output generates employment and incomes, which leads to further consumer expenditure, adding to total demand. Changes in output are used to determine changes in employment, along with changes in real wage costs, interest rates and energy costs. With wage rates explained by price levels and conditions in the labour market (see Barker and Gardiner, 1996) the wage and salary payments by industry can be calculated from the industrial employment levels. These are some of the largest payments to the personal sector, but not the only ones. There are also payments of interest and dividends, transfers from government in the form of state pensions, unemployment benefits and other social security benefits. Payments made by the personal sector include mortgage interest payments and personal income taxes. Personal disposable income is calculated from these accounts, and deflated by the consumer price index to give real personal disposable income.

Determination of consumers' demand

Totals of consumer spending by region are derived from consumption functions also estimated from time-series data (this is a similar treatment to that adopted in the HERMES model). These equations relate consumption to regional personal disposable income, a measure of wealth for the personal sector, inflation and interest rates. Sets of equations have been estimated from time-series data relating the spending per capita to the national spending using the CBS[2] version of the consumption allocation system. The incorporation of this system into the solution is complex: the allocation system has been adapted to provide the long-run income and relative price parameters in a two-stage procedure, with a standardised co-integrating equation including demographic effects providing the dynamic solution. The substitution between categories as a result of changes in relative prices is achieved at the regional level.

12.4   ENERGY–ENVIRONMENT LINKS

Top-Down and Bottom-Up Methodologies

E3ME is intended to be an integrated top-down, bottom-up model of E3 interaction. In particular, the model includes a detailed engineering-based treatment of the electricity supply industry (ESI). Demand for energy by the other fuel-user groups is top-down, but it is important to be aware of the comparative strengths and weaknesses of the two approaches. Top-down economic analyses and bottom-up engineering analyses of changes in the pattern of energy consumption possess distinct intellectual origins and distinct strengths and weaknesses (see Barker et al., 1995).

A Top-Down Submodel of Energy Use

The energy submodel in E3ME is constructed, estimated and solved for 19 fuel users, 12 energy carriers (termed fuels for convenience below) and 27 regions. Figure 12.3 shows the inputs from the economy and the environment into the components of the submodel.

Determination of Fuel Demand

Aggregate energy demand, shown at the top of Figure 12.3, is determined by a set of co-integrating equations,[3] whose main explanatory variables are:

- economic activity in each of the 19 fuel users;
- average energy prices by the fuel users relative to the overall price levels;
- technological variables, represented by R&D expenditure in key industries producing energy-using equipment and vehicles.

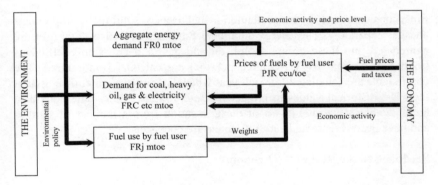

Figure 12.3   Input to the Energy Submodel

Fuel substitution
Fuel use equations are estimated for four fuels – coal, heavy oils, gas and electricity – and the four sets of equations are estimated for the fuel users in each region. These equations are intended to allow substitution between these energy carriers by users on the basis of relative prices, although overall fuel use and the technological variables are allowed to affect the choice. Since the substitution equations cover only four of the 12 fuels, the remaining fuels are determined as fixed ratios to similar fuels or to aggregate energy use. The

final set of fuels used must then be scaled to ensure that it adds up to the aggregate energy demand (for each fuel user and each region).

Emissions Submodel

The emissions submodel calculates air pollution generated from end-use of different fuels and from primary use of fuels in the energy industries themselves, particularly electricity generation (Bruvoll et al., 2000). Provision is made for emissions to the atmosphere of carbon dioxide (CO_2), sulphur dioxide (SO_2), nitrogen oxides (NOx), carbon monoxide (CO), methane (CH_4), black smoke (PM10), volatile organic compounds (VOCs), nuclear emissions to air, lead emissions to air, chlorofluorocarbons (CFCs) and the other four greenhouse gases: nitrous oxide (N_2O), hydrofluorocarbons (HFCs), perfluorocarbons (PFCs), sulphur hexafluoride (SF_6). These four gases together with CO_2 and CH_4 constitute the six greenhouse gases (GHGs) monitored under the Kyoto Protocol. Using estimated (ExternE) damage coefficients, E3ME may also estimate ancillary benefits relating to reduction in associated emissions, for example PM10, SO_2, NOx.

CO_2 Emissions

Emissions data for CO_2 are available for fuel users of solid fuels, oil products and gas separately. The energy submodel estimates of fuel by fuel user are aggregated into these groups (solid, oil and gas) and emission coefficients (tonnes of carbon in CO_2 emitted per toe) are calculated and stored. The coefficients are calculated for each year when data are available, then used at their last historical values to project future emissions. Other emissions data are available at various levels of disaggregation from a number of sources and have been constructed carefully to ensure consistency.

Feedback to the Rest of the Economy

Feedback from the energy demand equations to the rest of the economy, including the electricity and the power generation sectors, is modelled via changes in the input–output coefficients. The exception to this is the household sector, where changes in energy demand are reflected by changes in consumer expenditure.

Material Demands

The current version of E3ME is being extended to include explicitly the physical demand for eight material goods (plus the energy carriers). Demand will be disaggregated by up to 14 user groups and the model will include economic feedbacks, using a similar system to that of the energy submodel. For more information about this major development, please refer to the model website, www.e3me.com.

Parameter Estimation

The econometric model has a complete specification of the long-term solution in the form of an estimated equation that has long-term restrictions imposed on its parameters. Economic theory, for example the recent theories of endogenous growth, informs the specification of the long-term equations and hence properties of the model; dynamic equations that embody these long-term properties are estimated by econometric methods to allow the model to provide forecasts. The method utilises developments in time-series econometrics, in which dynamic relationships are specified in terms of error correction models (ECMs) that allow dynamic convergence to a long-term outcome. The specific functional form of the equations is based on the econometric techniques of co-integration and error-correction, particularly as promoted by Engle and Granger (1987) and Hendry et al. (1984).

12.5 CONCLUSION

E3ME is a dynamic estimated time-series cross-section model of Europe covering the EU-25 (as of 2006) member states and Norway and Switzerland. E3ME is a fully integrated E3 model with detailed sectoral coverage including 42 industrial sectors, 19 fuel users and 12 energy carriers. The model is intended to meet an expressed need of researchers and policy-makers for a framework for analysing the long-term implications of E3 policies, especially those concerning R&D and environmental taxation and regulation. The model is also capable of addressing the short-term and medium-term economic effects as well as, more broadly, the long-term effects of such policies. The current version of E3ME is capable of forecasting annual macroeconomic and sectoral economic effects, energy use and emissions in the period up to 2030.

NOTES

1. http://www.externe.info/tools.html.
2. Centraal Bureau voor de Statistiek (CBS; Bracke and Mayermans, 1997) allocation of consumption, where consumption of any one good is a function of its price, the average real consumption and the price of each of the other $(n - 1)$ commodities.

3. Co-integration is an econometric technique that defines a long-run relationship between two variables resulting in a form of 'equilibrium'. For instance, if income and consumption are cointegrated, then any shock (expected or unexpected) affecting temporarily these two variables is gradually absorbed since in the long-run they return to their 'equilibrium' levels. Note that a co-integration relationship is a much stronger relationship than a simple correlation: two variables can show similar patterns simply because they are driven by some common factors but without necessarily being involved in a long-run relationship.

REFERENCES

Barker, T.S. (1998a), 'Use of energy–environment–economy models to inform greenhouse gas mitigation policy', *Impact Assessment and Project Appraisal*, **16**(2), 123–31.

Barker, T.S. (1998b), 'Large-scale energy–environment–economy modelling of the European Union', in I. Begg and B. Henry (eds), *Applied Economics and Public Policy*, Cambridge: Cambridge University Press, pp. 15–40.

Barker, T.S. (2004), 'Economic theory and the transition to sustainability: A comparison of general equilibrium and space-time-economics approaches', Tyndall Working Paper 62, Tyndall Centre, University of East Anglia.

Barker, T.S. and B. Gardiner (1996), 'Employment, wage formation and pricing in the European Union: empirical modelling of environmental tax reform', in C. Carraro and D. Siniscalco (eds), *Environmental Fiscal Reform and Unemployment*, Dordrecht: Kluwer, pp. 229–72.

Barker, T.S., P. Ekins and N. Johnstone (1995), *Global Warming and Energy Demand*, London: Routledge.

Barker, T.S., H. Pan, J. Köhler, R. Warren and S. Winne (2006), 'Decarbonizing the global economy with induced technological change: Scenarios to 2100 using E3MG', *The Energy Journal*, **27**, 241–58.

Barker, T.S., R. van der Putten and I. Stern (1993), 'HERMES: A macrosectoral model for the UK economy', in CEC (eds), *HERMES: Harmonised Econometric Research for Modelling Economic Systems*, Amsterdam: North-Holland, pp. 533–68.

Bracke, I. and E. Meyermans (1997), 'Construction of an allocation model for private consumption in Europe', E3ME working paper 4.5a, Reference: JOS3-CT95-011.

Bruvoll, A., G. Ellingsen and K.E. Rosendahl (2000), 'Inclusion of six greenhouse gases and other pollutants into the E3ME model', Working Paper 9b, Statistics Norway, Oslo.

Engle, R.F. and C.W.J. Granger (1987), 'Cointegration and error correction: Representation, estimation and testing', *Econometrica*, **55**, 251–76.

Hendry, D.F., A. Pagan and J.D. Sargan (1984), 'Dynamic specification', in Z. Griliches and M.D. Intriligator (eds), *Handbook of Econometrics*, Vol. 2, Amsterdam: North-Holland, pp. 1023–100.

Scott, M.F.G. (1989), *A New View of Economic Growth*, Oxford: Clarendon Press.

13. An Endogenous Technical Change Model: FEEM-RICE

Valentina Bosetti, Carlo Carraro and Marzio Galeotti

13.1 INTRODUCTION

The FEEM-RICE model presented below is an extended version of the so-called RICE-99 model by Nordhaus and Boyer (2000). RICE-99 is a Ramsey–Koopmans single-sector optimal growth model suitably extended to incorporate the interactions between economic activities and climate. There is one such model for each of the eight macro-regions into which the world is divided: USA, Other High Income countries (OHI), OECD Europe (Europe), Russia and Eastern European countries (REE), Middle Income countries (MI), Lower Middle Income countries (LMI), China (CHN) and Low Income countries (LI).[1]

The Model General Structure

Within each region a central planner chooses the optimal paths of two control variables, fixed investment and carbon energy input, so as to maximize welfare, defined as the present value of per capita consumption. The value added created via production (net of climate change) according to a constant returns technology is used for investment and consumption, after subtraction of energy spending. The technology is Cobb–Douglas and combines the inputs from capital, labour and carbon energy together with the level of technology. Population (taken to be equal to full employment) and technology levels grow over time in an exogenous fashion, whereas capital accumulation is governed by the optimal rate of investment.

Compared to the previous RICE-96 model of Nordhaus and Yang (1996), this specification contains a more detailed regional disaggregation of the world. However, the main novelty of the new model is the introduction of an energy input. Because carbon dioxide is the only greenhouse gas considered, the input is directly measured in carbon units. The carbon energy input can be thought of as the energy services derived from fossil fuel consumption (for example derived from coal, petroleum and natural gas). An implication of the introduction of this crucial input is that its market must be specified. While the demand for carbon energy stems naturally from the first principles of the entrepreneur's (or social planner's) problem, a supply curve for this input is introduced in a somewhat ad hoc fashion, and it implies rising marginal costs. Because of the optimal growth framework, carbon energy is efficiently allocated across time, which implies that low-cost carbon resources have scarcity prices (Hotelling rents) and that carbon energy prices rise over time.[2] The carbon energy input is modelled as being the source of greenhouse gas (GHG) emissions in the production process, and the cumulated emissions (that is, concentrations) cause an increase in the worldwide temperature. To close the circle, global temperature (relative to pre-industrial levels) is responsible for the wedge between gross output and output net of climate change effects.

The control variables are determined within a game-theoretic framework. Each country plays a non-cooperative Nash game in a dynamic setting which yields an open loop Nash equilibrium. In each region the planner maximizes its utility subject to the individual resource and capital constraints and the climate module for a given emission production of all the other players.[3] Kyoto-type international environmental agreements can be easily accommodated by adding a constraint stating that regional emissions cannot exceed a given upper limit. It is also possible to use the model in the presence of international emission trading. In this case the standard identity between sources and uses of resources specifies that output is used for consumption and investment, to which proceeds or sales from net imports of permits are be added.

Under the possibility of emission trading, the sequence whereby an equilibrium à la Nash is reached must be revised as follows. Each region maximizes its utility subject to the individual resource and capital constraints, the emission target constraint, and the climate module for a given optimal set of strategies of all the other players and a given price of permits (in the first round this is set at an arbitrary level). When all regions have made their optimal choices, the overall net demand for permits is computed at the given price. If the sum of net demands in each period is approximately zero, a Nash equilibrium is obtained; otherwise the price is revised in proportion to the market imbalance and each region's decision process starts again. The price of a unit of tradable emission permits is expressed in terms of the numeraire output price and there is an additional policy variable, that is, the net demand for permits.

13.2   THE TREATMENT OF TECHNICAL CHANGE IN FEEM-RICE

The original RICE-99 model specifies the following production function (n indexes regions, t time periods):

$$Q(n,t) = A(n,t)[K_F(n,t)^{1-\gamma-\alpha_n} CE(n,t)^{\alpha_n} L(n,t)^{\gamma}] - p_n^E CE(n,t) \quad (13.1)$$

where Q is output (gross of climate change effects), A the exogenously given level of technology and K_F, CE and L are the inputs from physical capital, carbon energy and labour, respectively, and p^E is fossil fuel price. Carbon emissions are proportional to carbon energy, that is:

$$E(n,t) = \zeta(n,t) \, CE(n,t) \quad (13.2)$$

where E is industrial CO_2 emissions, while ζ is an idiosyncratic carbon intensity ratio which also exogenously declines over time.[4] In this way, Nordhaus and Boyer (2000) make the assumption of a gradual, costless improvement of the green technology gained by the agents as time goes by. For the reasons discussed in the previous section, we consider this treatment of technical change (TC) inadequate for a model designed to study issues related to climate change.

In previous work (see Carraro and Galeotti, 2002, 2003) we explored the consequences of two ways of endogenizing the process of TC. First, in the 'learning-by-researching' (LbR) model, an endogenously generated stock of knowledge affected both factor productivity and the emission–output ratio (there was no energy input and emissions were linked directly to unabated output). Knowledge was the result of intertemporal optimal accumulation of research and development (R&D), where R&D is a choice variable describing a new investment opportunity in addition to consumption and physical investment. Secondly, in the 'learning-by-doing' (LbD) model, knowledge, conceived as a stock of experience, was approximated by installed capacity, in turn represented by physical capital accumulating through periodic investment. Again, this stock of experience affected both factor productivity and the emission–output ratio. This LbD approach entailed one less choice variable with respect to the R&D approach, but no further claim on resources created, in addition to consumption and physical investment, was made.

The main shortcomings of these formulations mainly derive from the absence, in the core model, of an explicit energy module. The absence of an energy production factor made it impossible to capture the effects of TC on the energy intensity of production. Moreover, the 'learning-by-researching' and the 'learning-by-doing' features of TC were modelled separately, while it would appear appropriate to include both sources of TC in the same model. Finally, approximating the stock of experience with physical capital was not very accurate, but the presence of the abatement rate as a model control variable made it difficult, if not impossible, to account for cumulated abatement efforts as the force driving the learning process.[5]

In the newly developed model, the above shortcomings have been explicitly addressed and solved. In FEEM-RICE, we consider simultaneously both LbD and LbR as inputs of induced TC and we focus on the effects of TC on both the energy intensity of production and the carbon intensity of energy use. These features of the model allow us to address both energy-saving and energy-switching issues.

To clarify the importance of this two-input–two-output specification of TC, it is perhaps useful to refer to a time-honoured concept in environmental economics, the so-called Kaya's identity. In its generalized form, it can be represented as follows. Let $i = 1,..., I$ be the various GHG emissions, E, $j = 1,..., J$ be the various energy sources, S, $k = 1,..., K$ be the sectors in the economy, Y, and $n = 1,..., N$ be the countries in the world. Then, the world emissions of GHGs, E_t, can be decomposed as follows:

$$E_t = \sum_n \sum_k \sum_j \sum_i \left(\frac{E_{ijkn}}{S_{jkn}} \right) \left(\frac{S_{jkn}}{Y_{kn}} \right) \left(\frac{Y_{kn}}{Y_n} \right) \left(\frac{Y_n}{L_n} \right) L \qquad (13.3)$$

where L is total world population. Hence, world emissions are a product of two 'forces': techno-economic forces, given by carbon intensity (E/S) and energy intensity (S/Y), and socio-economic forces, given by output composition (Y_k/Y) and output levels (Y/L), as well as demographic dynamics L. Similarly to the RICE-99 model, FEEM-RICE has a single economic sector, a single energy source, namely carbon energy, CE, and endogenous emissions are limited to industrial CO_2. Thus, the relationship stated in (13.3) can be rewritten for our specific case as:

$$E_t = \sum_n \left(\frac{E_n}{CE_n} \right) \left(\frac{CE_n}{Y_n} \right) \left(\frac{Y_n}{L_n} \right) L \qquad (13.3')$$

In addition to socio-economic forces – income and population – which are commonly modelled in endogenous growth models, our model allows us to endogenize both techno-economic forces, namely energy and carbon intensity.[6]

The main novelty of our new formulation hinges on the relationship between TC and both learning-by-researching and learning-by-doing at the same time. We assume that innovation is brought about by R&D spending which contributes to the accumulation of the stock of existing knowledge.[7] In addition to this learning-by-researching effect, the model also accounts for the effect of learning-by-doing, now modelled in terms of cumulated abatement efforts. Thus, our index of technical change *TP* (technical progress) is defined as follows:

$$TP(n,t) = f[ABAT(n,t), K_R(n,t)] \qquad (13.4)$$

The variable *TP* is assumed to affect both energy intensity (that is, the quantity of carbon energy required to produce one unit of output) and carbon intensity (that is, the level of carbonization of primarily used fuels). More specifically *TP* is formulated as a convex combination of the stocks of knowledge and abatement:

$$TP(n,t) = ABAT_s(n,t)^c K_R(n,t)^d \qquad (13.5)$$

where $K_R(n,t)$ is the stock of knowledge and $ABAT_S$ represents the stock of cumulated abatement, in turn defined as:

$$ABAT_S(n,t+1) = \delta_A ABAT(n,t) + (1-\delta_B) ABAT_s(n,t) \qquad (13.6)$$

ABAT the abatement flow, δ_A the learning factor, that is, the amount of abatement which translates into a learning experience, and δ_B being the depreciation rate of cumulated experience. The stock of knowledge $K_R(n,t)$ accumulates in the usual fashion:

$$K_R(n,t+1) = R \& D(n,t) + (1-\delta_R) K_R(n,t) \qquad (13.7)$$

where δ_R is the depreciation rate of knowledge.

How does technical progress affect the rest of the economy? As seen in equation (13.1), the factors of production are labour, physical capital and carbon energy. Let us first consider the effect of technical progress on factor productivity (the energy-intensity effect). In our model, the production function (13.1) is replaced by the following equation:

$$Q(n,t) = A(n,t)[K_F(n,t)^{1-\alpha_n(TP)-\gamma} CE(n,t)^{\alpha_n(TP)} L(n,t)^\gamma] - p_e(n,t) CE(n,t) \quad (13.1')$$

where:

$$\alpha_n = \alpha_n[TP(n,t)] = \frac{\beta_{1n}}{2 - \exp[-\beta_{0n} TP(n,t)]} \qquad (13.8)$$

and β_{0n} and β_{1n} are region-specific parameters. Thus, an increase in the endogenously determined technical progress variable reduces – *ceteris paribus* – the output elasticity of the energy input. It is worth noting that the output technology in (13.1′) also accounts for a fraction of TC which evolves exogenously, thus following an explicit suggestion by Clarke and Weyant (2002) and the discussion of the previous section.

Let us now turn to the effect of technical progress on the carbon intensity of energy consumption. As shown in (13.2), effective energy results from both fossil fuels input use and (exogenous) TC in the energy sector. In our model, we assume that *TP* serves the purpose of reducing, *ceteris paribus*, the level of carbon emissions. More precisely, equation (13.2) is replaced by:

$$E(n,t) = h[CE(n,t), TP(n,t)] = \varsigma(n,t) \left\{ \frac{1}{2 - \exp[-\psi_n TP(n,t)]} \right\} CE(n,t) \qquad (13.2')$$

Here an increase in *TP* reduces progressively the amount of emissions generated by a unit of fossil fuel consumed. Finally, we recognize that R&D spending absorbs some resources, that is:

$$Y(n,t) = C(n,t) + I(n,t) + R\&D(n,t) + p(t)NIP(n,t) \qquad (13.9)$$

where Y is output net of climate change effects, C is consumption, I gross fixed capital formation, $R\&D$ research and development expenditures, p^P is the equilibrium price on the emissions rights, and NIP is the net demand for permits.

It may be noted that there is only one type of R&D effort that helps in both saving energy and switching the energy needs away from fossil fuels. Although in principle it could be argued that the innovation activity resulting in technologies using less energy is different from the innovation activity resulting in the development in clean energy technologies, in practice accounting for this fact in highly aggregate models like FEEM-RICE is probably not worth the complications. Finally, 'red' TC – that is, purely productivity-enhancing TC (captured by the A index in the production function) – has been kept exogenous, albeit time-varying, though we believe that 'red' R&D can also be endogenized (this is something we plan to do in future work).

To clarify further our formulation of induced TC, let us highlight the dynamic interrelationships between the different variables and their role in the model. First of all, let us notice that R&D is a control variable, whereas stock of knowledge and cumulated abatement are state variables. Therefore, R&D can be used strategically by regulators in each region of the model, whereas LbD is an output of the regulator's strategic behaviour (which also includes the optimal path of other control variables, for example investment and demand for permits). This is quite clear at the beginning of the game (see Figure 13.1). At stage one, only LbR through R&D investments occurs. This modifies TP (which evolves both endogenously and exogenously) and yields some amount of abatement, that is, some abatement experience which becomes LbD. Both LbR and LbD then affects TP in the subsequent stages.

Summing up, the fundamental driver of technical progress is basic research and R&D investments. This induces knowledge accumulation and experience in emission abatement in various regions of the world. In turn, these variables move technology towards a more environment-friendly dynamic path.

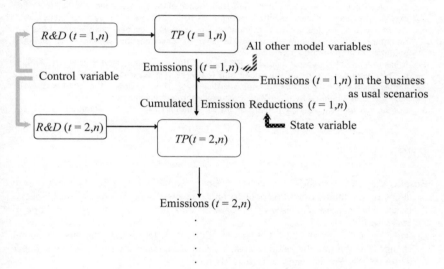

Figure 13.1   Effects of LbR and LbD on Technical Progress

Our quite general solution to account for induced TC comes obviously at a cost. Basically, little information to calibrate the model parameters is available.[8] The strategy followed was to 'guesstimate' the critical TC parameters and then compare the output of the models with data on observed variables. At the same time, an extensive sensitivity analysis on the parameters of our formulation of induced TC has been performed, as extensively discussed in Bosetti et al. (2006b). The model has also been applied to the valuation of long term stabilization scenarios. Results are presented in Bosetti et al. (2006a).

NOTES

1. The countries belonging to each one of the macro-regions above indicated are listed in Nordhaus and Boyer's book. We refer to it as RICE-99 because it has been made available by the authors through the web in 1999.
2. Thus the new version of RICE incorporates a treatment of energy supply, which is seen as an exhaustible resource. Another addition is a revised and extended climate module which now includes a three-reservoir model calibrated to existing carbon-cycle models. The equation of the original model retained in FEEM-RICE are reported in the appendix.
3. As there is no international trade in the model, regions are interdependent just through climate variables. The absence of trade of goods among regions is an important limitation of all regional versions of RICE. We plan to address this issue in the near future.
4. Throughout the chapter we will indifferently refer to 'environmental' technology or 'green' technology when mentioning the time-varying coefficient ς.
5. Recall that cumulated abatement was the variable used by Goulder and Mathai (2000) in the LbD version of their cost minimization model. The absence of the energy input, and therefore of an explicit price, made it also impossible to carry out any policy exercise in energy or carbon taxation.
6. As in most of models present in literature, population is exogenously determined. An important future development would be that of endogenizing demographic changes, including migration flows across regions.
7. It has to be pointed out that analysing R&D expenditure is complicated because: (i) R&D is not always amenable to measurement; and (ii) there is a great deal of uncertainty in the ability of R&D to generate technological change. These words of caution should be therefore borne in mind by the reader when going through the chapter.
8. For this reason we give some parameters the same numerical value for all regions.

REFERENCES

Bosetti, V., C. Carraro and M. Galeotti (2006a), 'The dynamics of carbon and energy intensity in a model of endogenous technical change', *The Energy Journal*, Special Issue: *Endogenous Technological Change and the Economics of Atmospheric Stabilisation*, 93–107.

Bosetti, V., C. Carraro and M. Galeotti (2006b), 'Stabilisation targets, technical change and the macroeconomic costs of climate change control', Working Paper 02.06, Milan: Fondazione Eni Enrico Mattei.

Carraro, C. and M. Galeotti (2002), 'Traditional environmental instruments, Kyoto mechanisms and the role of technical change', in C. Carraro and C. Hegenhofer (eds), *Firms, Governments and Climate Policy: Incentive-based Policies for Long-term Climate Change*, Cheltenham, UK and Northampton, MA, USA: Edward Elgar, pp. 222–66.

Carraro, C. and M. Galeotti (2003), 'Does endogenous technical change make a difference in climate policy analysis? A robustness exercise with the FEEM-RICE Model', Fondazione Eni Enrico Mattei, October.

Clarke, L.E. and J.P. Weyant (2002), 'Modeling induced technological change', in A. Grübler, N. Nakicenovic and W.D. Nordhaus (eds), *Technological Change and the Environment*, Washington, DC: Resources for the Future, pp. 320–63.

Goulder, L.H. and K. Mathai (2000), 'Optimal CO_2 abatement in the presence of induced technological change', *Journal of Environmental Economics*, **39**, 1–38.

Nordhaus, W.D. and J. Boyer (2000), *Warming the World*, Cambridge, MA: MIT Press.

Nordhaus, W.D. and Z. Yang (1996), 'A regional dynamic general-equilibrium model of alternative climate-change strategies', *American Economic Review*, **4**, 741–65.

APPENDIX 13.1   OTHER MODEL EQUATIONS

In this appendix we reproduce the remaining equations that make up the whole model. These equations are reported here for the sake of completeness and are the same as the ones found in the original RICE-99 model.

In each region, n, there is a social planner who maximizes the following utility function (n indexes the world's regions, t are ten-year time spans):

$$W_n = \sum_t U\left[C_n(t), L_n(t)\right] R(t) = \sum_t L_n(t)\left\{\log\left[c_n(t)\right]\right\} R(t) \quad \text{(A13.1)}$$

where the pure time preference discount factor is given by:

$$R(t) = \prod_{v=0}^{t}\left[1+\rho(v)\right]^{-10} \quad \text{(A13.2)}$$

and the pure rate of time preference $\rho(v)$ is assumed to decline over time.

The maximization problem is subject to:

$$Q_n(t) = \Omega_n(t)\left\{A_n(t)K_{nF}(t)^{1-\gamma-\alpha} L_n(t)^\gamma CE_n(t)^\alpha - p_n^E(t)CE_n(t)\right\} \quad \text{(A13.3)}$$

$$c_n(t) = \frac{C_n(t)}{L_n(t)} \quad \text{(A13.4)}$$

$$K_{nF}(t+1) = (1-\delta_K)K_{nF}(t) + I_n(t+1) \quad \text{(A13.5)}$$

$$Q_n(t) = C_n(t) + I_n(t) \quad \text{(A13.6)}$$

$$E_n(t) = \varsigma_n(t)CE_n(t) \quad \text{(A13.7)}$$

$$p_n^E(t) = q(t) + markup_n^E \quad \text{(A13.8)}$$

$$M_{AT}(t+1) = \sum_n\left[E_n(t) + LU_j(t)\right] + \varphi_{11}M_{AT}(t) + \varphi_{21}M_{UP}(t) \quad \text{(A13.9)}$$

$$M_{UP}(t+1) = \varphi_{22}M_{UP}(t) + \varphi_{12}M_{AT}(t) + \varphi_{32}M_{LO}(t) \quad \text{(A13.10)}$$

$$M_{LO}(t+1) = \varphi_{33}M_{LO}(t) + \varphi_{23}M_{UP}(t) \quad \text{(A13.11)}$$

$$F(t) = \eta\left\{\log\left[M_{AT}(t)/M_{AT}^{PI}\right] - \log(2)\right\} + O(t) \quad \text{(A13.12)}$$

$$T(t+1) = T(t) + \sigma_1\left\{F(t+1) - \lambda T(t) - \sigma_2\left[T(t) - T_{LO}(t)\right]\right\} \quad \text{(A13.13)}$$

$$\Omega_n(t) = \frac{1}{1 + \theta_{1,n}T(t) + \theta_{2,n}T(t)^2} \tag{A13.14}$$

List of Variables

W	welfare
U	instantaneous utility
C	consumption
L	population
R	discount factor
Q	production
Ω	damage
A	productivity or technology index
K_F	capital stock
CE	carbon energy
p^E	cost of carbon energy
I	fixed investment
E	carbon emissions
M_{AT}	atmospheric CO_2 concentrations
LU	land-use carbon emissions
M_{UP}	upper oceans/biosphere CO_2 concentrations
M_{LO}	lower oceans CO_2 concentrations
F	radiative forcing
T	temperature level
q	costs of extraction of industrial emissions

List of Parameters

α, γ	parameters of production function
δ_K	rate of depreciation of capital stock
ζ	exogenous technical change effect of energy on CO_2 emissions (carbon intensity)
$\phi_{11}\,\phi_{12}\,\phi_{21}\,\phi_{22}\,\phi_{23}\,\phi_{32}\,\phi_{33}$	parameters of the carbon transition matrix
η	increase in radiative forcing due to doubling of CO_2 concentrations from pre-industrial levels
σ_1, σ_2	temperature dynamics parameters
λ	climate sensitivity parameter
$markup^E$	regional energy services markup
θ_1, θ_2	parameters of the damage function
M_{AT}^{PI}	pre-industrial atmospheric CO_2 concentrations
O	increase in radiative forcing over pre-industrial levels due to exogenous anthropogenic causes

ρ discount rate
T_{LO} lower ocean temperature

14. Policy Analysis Based on Computable Equilibrium (PACE)

Christoph Böhringer, Andreas Löschel and Thomas F. Rutherford

---

14.1 OVERVIEW

PACE (Policy Analysis based on Computable Equilibrium) is a flexible system of computable general equilibrium (CGE) models which integrates the areas of economy, energy and environment. The generic core of PACE is a standard multisector, multiregion CGE framework of global trade and energy use designated to assess major policy initiatives in a world that is increasingly integrated through trade. Departing from the generic core, the various PACE modules allow for the problem-specific analysis of policy interference at different regional and sectoral levels as well as time treatments (static, dynamic-recursive, intertemporal). The different PACE modules account for issue-driven priorities in the representation of details and functional relationships. There is a module that emphasizes discrete technological choice in the energy system thereby featuring a bottom-up representation of alternative electricity supply options. Another module incorporates a detailed description of labor market imperfections and public taxation to trace back the interaction of tax policies and involuntary unemployment (for example due to union-bargaining). Further modules include a disaggregate representation of different household types or overlapping generations in order to allow for more detailed incidence analysis or a vintage approach to car stocks in order to investigate the implications of alternative emission regulation policies for automobile industries. More recently, an integrated assessment module has been added that links a reduced-form representation of climate relationships with a comprehensive intertemporal multisector, multiregion model for the world economy.

The PACE modeling system has been primarily used for the economic analysis of energy and environmental policy initiatives. Examples include the assessment of carbon abatement policies (Kyoto and Post-2012), multi-gas analysis of long-term climate policy scenarios, sectoral impacts of the EU emissions trading scheme, environmental tax reforms, nuclear phase-out, green quotas and fossil fuel subsidies. However, several submodules allow for the problem-specific investigation of trade, tax and labor market policies without a focus on energy or environmental markets. Recent applications in these fields include the assessment of value-added tax and income tax reforms, labor market regulation and trade integration.

Below, we provide a description of the dynamic multisector, multiregion PACE module designed to assess the impacts of major policy initiatives for open economies that linked through international trade flows. Section 14.2 summarizes key model features in a non-technical manner. Section 14.3 features an algebraic model summary.

14.2 NON-TECHNICAL MODEL DESCRIPTION

The multisector, multiregion module of PACE is a standard computable general equilibrium representation of production, consumption and international trade. General equilibrium provides a comprehensive microeconomic-sound framework for studying price-dependent market interactions. Furthermore, the simultaneous explanation of the origination and the spending of income of economic agents (here: regions) permits addressing both economy-wide efficiency as well as equity implications of policy intervention. Therefore, computable (or applied) general equilibrium models have become a central method for the assessment of the economy-wide impacts of emission policies on resource allocation and the associated implications for incomes of economic agents.

Beyond the consistent representation of market interactions as well as income and expenditure flows, policy analysis often calls for an explicit dynamic framework as policy problems are of an inherently dynamic nature and problem and happen on larger time scales. To build dynamic features in the modeling of the economic behavior of households and firms requires an assumption on the degree of foresight of the economic agents. In a deterministic setting, the only consistent approach is to assume that agents in the model know as much about the future as the modeler: agents have rational (intertemporal) expectations and consistently anticipate all current and future prices. In this vein, the dynamic PACE versions are typically implemented as standard Ramsey-type intertemporal models which allows for the assessment of the adjustment path of economies to exogenous (energy and climate) policy constraints.

Static Single-Period Module

Figure 14.1 lays out the diagrammatic structure of the model's intra-period structure. Primary factors of a region r include labor $\bar{L}_r$, capital K_r, and resources of fossil fuels $\bar{Q}_{ff}$ ($ff \in$ {coal, gas, oil}). The specific resource used in the production of coal, gas and oil results in upward-sloping supply schedules consistent with exogenous fossil fuel supply elasticities.

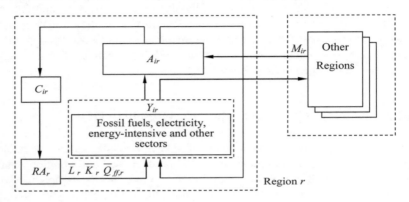

Figure 14.1   Structure of the Intra-Period Submodule

Production Y_{ir} of commodities i in region r, other than primary fossil fuels, is captured by aggregate production functions which characterize technology through substitution possibilities between various inputs. Nested constant elasticity of substitution (CES) cost functions with several levels are employed to specify the *KLEM* substitution possibilities in domestic production sectors between capital (K), labor (L), energy (E) and non-energy intermediate inputs, that is, material (M).

Final aggregate consumption demand C_r of the representative agent RA_r in each region is given as a CES composite which combines consumption of an energy aggregate with a non-energy consumption bundle. The substitution patterns within the non-energy consumption bundle as well as the energy aggregate are described by nested CES functions.

Non-energy goods used in the domestic market in intermediate and final demand correspond to a so-called Armington good, that is, a CES composite A_{ir} of the domestically produced variety and a CES import aggregate M_{ir} of the same variety from the other regions. Domestic production either enters the formation of the Armington good or is exported to satisfy the import demand of other regions. Fossil fuels are treated as homogenous goods across regions.

Endowments of labor and the specific resources are fixed exogenously.

Within any time period, factor markets and commodity markets function according to the competitive paradigm, that is, flexible prices adjust to clear these markets. Carbon emissions are associated with fossil fuel demand in production and final consumption.

Dynamic Setting

As to the dynamic model setting, the representative household in each region chooses to allocate lifetime income, that is, the intertemporal budget, across consumption in different time periods in order to maximize lifetime utility. In each period, the agent faces the choice between current consumption and future consumption purchased via savings. Investment takes place as long as the marginal return on investment equals the marginal cost of capital formation. The rates of return are determined by a uniform and endogenous world interest rate such that the marginal productivity of a unit of investment and marginal utility of a unit of consumption is equalized within and across countries. Capital stocks evolve through constant geometric depreciation and new investment. Figure 14.2 sketches the basic dynamics of the economic module.

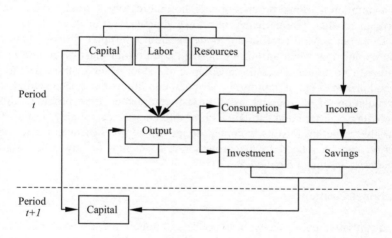

Figure 14.2   Dynamic Model Settings

The notion of consistent expectations is coupled with the simplifying assumption of an infinitely lived representative agent who makes explicit choices at the margin between current and future consumption. The representative agent maximizes welfare subject to an intertemporal budget constraint. In equilibrium the present value of consumption equals the present value of income over the infinite horizon. Within a given period, however, a region may run a current account surplus or deficit, depending on the difference between national income and expenditure (note: closure of financial flows within the model implies that the deficit is equal to the difference between the value of commodity imports and commodity exports). Figure 14.2 illustrates the basic dynamics of the model.

The representative agent for each region maximizes his discounted utility over the model's time horizon. The primary factors, capital, labor and energy, are combined to produce output in period t. In addition, energy is delivered directly to final consumption. Output is divided between consumption and investment, and investment augments the (depreciated) capital stock in the next period. Capital, labor and the energy resource earn incomes, which are either spent on consumption or retained for savings, that is, investment. Investment is driven by consistent expectations where the return on investment (with quadratic adjustment costs) is balanced against the cost of capital. In equilibrium, investments are placed in the region (sectors) where they will receive the highest return. International capital flows are thus endogenous, and the demand and supply of savings jointly determine the international interest rate. The baseline equilibrium growth path is calibrated to a common marginal product of capital in all regions. Capital stocks evolve through constant geometric depreciation and new investment.

Dynamic general equilibrium models exhibit a turnpike property, and one can exploit this when an infinite horizon equilibrium must be approximated with a finite model. To assure invariance of model results with respect to the time horizon, a set of appropriate terminal conditions must be specified. The formulation of the model as a mixed complementarity problem allows including post-terminal capital stock as an endogenous variable. Using state variable targeting for this variable, the growth of investment in the terminal period can be related to the growth rate of capital or any other 'stable' quantity variable in the model.

Parameterization

In quantitative policy analysis, the effects of policy interference are measured with respect to a reference situation – usually termed business-as-usual (BaU) – where no policy changes apply. To perform numerical simulations, the concrete forms of the production functions (characterizing the technological options in production) and the utility functions (characterizing the consumption preferences of agents) must be specified.

The procedure most commonly used in CGE analysis to select parameter values is known as calibration. Calibration of the free parameters of functional forms requires a consistent one-year's data in prices and quantities (or a single observation represented as an average over a number of years), together with exogenous elasticities that are usually taken from literature surveys. The calibration is a deterministic procedure and does not allow for statistical tests of the model specification. Within the policy simulations, policy control parameters – such as carbon taxes or emission constraints – are assigned and a new (counterfactual) equilibrium is computed. Comparison of the counterfactual and the benchmark equilibrium then provides information on the policy-induced changes of economic variables such as employment, production, consumption, relative prices, and so on.

For the base-year calibration, the GTAP database is employed which provides detailed input–output tables as well as bilateral trade and physical energy flows for a large number of commodities and regions.

In dynamic policy analysis, there is the need for additional information on the future BaU development. Apparently, the BaU projections are a crucial determinant for the overall magnitude of adjustment effects to policy interference. For example, exogenous policy constraints such as mid-term greenhouse gas emission constraints will bind future economies the more, the higher the projected BaU growth in greenhouse gas emissions. Substantial differences in model-based analysis can often be traced back to different assumptions about the baseline development. Regarding long-term climate policy analysis, the issue of baseline projections becomes very critical in view of the tremendous uncertainties regarding BaU developments over several decades. Not only is there the question of why one baseline should be preferable over another, but official projections based on expert analyses often stand out for their large internal inconsistencies as the endogeneity of system relationships are not sufficiently incorporated.

Considering the regional resolution of an intertemporal CGE model, the most restrictive constraint comes from the availability of long-term baseline projections. Official projections on the future development of GDP, fossil fuel production, international fuel prices and carbon emissions across various world regions are, for example, provided by the US Department of Energy until 2030. In order to incorporate the exogenous projections, a two-step recalibration of the model (after an initial calibration to a steady-state uniform growth path) is performed. First, the exogenous baseline intensities for fossil fuel demands are used to rescale baseline cost shares in production: In order to preserve the initial total costs per unit of production, capital cost shares are inversely adjusted, meaning that energy efficiency improvements are not costless but are linked to the increased use of capital services. Within the baseline recalculation, fossil fuel resource endowments get endogenously adjusted in order to calibrate the model to given exogenous target prices for fossil fuels. In a second step, fossil fuel supply functions are locally recalibrated to match exogenous estimates of fossil fuel supply elasticities.

14.3 ALGEBRAIC MODEL SUMMARY

This section presents the algebraic equilibrium conditions for the basic intertemporal multiregion, multisector submodule of the PACE CGE model system designed to investigate the economic adjustment path to policy regulation. The following key assumptions apply for the 'generic' model:

- Output and factor prices are fully flexible and markets are perfectly competitive.
- Labor force productivity increases at an exogenous growth rate (Harrod-neutral technological progress).
- In equilibrium, there is a period-by-period balance between exports from each region and global demand for those goods. The model differentiates between commodities produced for the domestic market and imports adopting the Armington assumption. Fossil fuels can be treated either as perfect substitutes or imperfect substitutes on international markets.
- In each region, a representative consumer (likewise the social planner) maximizes the present value of lifetime utility subject to: (i) an intertemporal balance-of-payments constraint; (ii) the constraint that the output per period is either consumed (including intermediate demand and exports) or invested; and (iii) the equation of motion for the capital stock, that is, capital stocks evolve through depreciation and new investment. This renders the optimal level of consumption and investment over time.
- The agents have an infinite horizon, and their expectations are forward-looking and rational. To approximate an infinite horizon model with a finite horizon model we assume that the representative consumer purchases capital in the model's post-horizon period at a price which is consistent with steady-state equilibrium growth (terminal condition).

The model is formulated in the complementarity format as a system of nonlinear inequalities using GAMS/MPSGE and solved using PATH. The inequalities correspond to the three classes of conditions associated with a general equilibrium: (i) exhaustion of product (zero-profit) conditions for constant-returns-to-scale producers; (ii) market clearance for all goods and factors; and (iii) income balance for the representative consumers in each region. The fundamental unknowns of the system are three vectors: activity levels (production indices), non-negative prices and consumer incomes. In equilibrium, each of these variables is linked to one inequality condition: an activity level to an exhaustion of product constraint, a commodity price to a market clearance condition, and a consumer income variable to an income definition equation. An equilibrium allocation determines production, prices and incomes.

In the following algebraic exposition, the notation Π_j^X is used to denote the zero-profit function of activity X. Formally, all production activities exhibit constant returns to scale, hence differentiating Π_j^X with respect to input and output prices provides compensated demand and supply coefficients, which appear subsequently in the market-clearance conditions. All prices are expressed as present values.

Exhaustion of Product Conditions

Production
In domestic production, nested, separable, constant elasticity of substitution (CES) cost functions are employed to specify the substitution possibilities between inputs of capital (K), labor (L), an energy composite (E) and a material composite (M). The energy composite is made up of the outputs of the energy industries. The materials composite consists of the outputs of the other non-energy industries. At the top level, the materials composite is employed in fixed proportions with an aggregate of energy, capital and labor. A constant elasticity describes the substitution possibilities between the energy aggregate and the aggregate of labor and capital at the second level. Finally, at the third level capital and labor trade off with a unitary elasticity of substitution.

Aggregate output in region r describes the supply of the non-energy macro-good to the domestic market and export market. A separable nested constant elasticity of substitution (CES) cost function is employed to specify the substitution possibilities between capital (K), labor (L) and an energy composite (E). At the top level, a constant elasticity describes the substitution possibilities between the energy aggregate and the aggregate of labor and capital. At the second level capital and labor trade off with a unitary elasticity of substitution. On the output side, production is split between goods produced for the domestic market and goods produced for the export market according to a constant elasticity of transformation. The (intra-period) zero-profit condition for the production of the macro-good is:

$$\Pi_{irt}^Y = P_{irt} - (1-\theta_{ir}^{KLE}) P_{irt}^M - \theta_{ir}^{KLE} \left[\theta_{ir}^E p_{irt}^E{}^{1-\sigma_{ir}^{KLE}} + (1-\theta_{ir}^E)\left(w_{rt}^{\alpha_{ir}} v_{rt}^{1-\alpha_{ir}} \right)^{1-\sigma_{ir}^{KLE}} \right]^{\frac{1}{1-\sigma_{ir}^{KLE}}} = 0$$

where:

P_{irt} output price of commodity i produced in region r and period t,

p_{irt}^E price of aggregate energy input to the production of commodity i in region r and period t,

w_{rt} wage rate in region r and period t,

v_{irt} rental price of capital services in region r and period t,

θ_{ir}^{E} benchmark cost share of aggregate energy input to the production of commodity i in region r,

α_{ir} benchmark share of labor in value-added of macro-good production in region r,

σ_{ir}^{KLE} elasticity of substitution between the energy aggregate and value-added in production of commodity i in region r, and

Y_{irt} associated dual variable which indicates the activity level of production of commodity i in region r and period t.

Fossil fuel production. The production of fuels requires intermediate inputs together with primary factors and a fuel-specific factor which can be thought of as a sector-specific resource.[1] The zero-profit condition has the form:

$$\Pi_{ff,rt}^{F} = p_t^{ff} - \left[\theta_r^{ff} q_{rt}^{ff\,1-\sigma_r^{ff}} + (1-\theta_r^{ff})\left(\Sigma_i \theta_{ir}^{ff} p_{irt}^{A} + \theta_{wr}^{ff} w_{rt} + \theta_{vr}^{ff} v_{rt} \right)^{1-\sigma_r^{ff}} \right]^{\frac{1}{1-\sigma_r^{ff}}} = 0$$

ff $\in$ {COA, OIL, GAS}

where:

p_t^{ff} a_{jr}^{KLE} world market price of fossil fuel ff in period t,

q_{rt}^{ff} price of fuel-specific resource for production of fossil fuel ff in region r and period t,

p_{irt}^{A} Armington price of commodity i in region r and period t,

θ_r^{ff} benchmark share of fuel-specific resource for fossil fuel production in region r,

θ_{ir}^{ff} benchmark cost share of Armington good i in fossil fuel production in region r,

θ_{wr}^{ff} benchmark cost share of labor in fossil fuel production in region r,

θ_{vr}^{ff} benchmark cost share of capital in fossil fuel production in region r,

σ_r^{ff} elasticity of substitution between the fuel-specific resource and non-energy inputs in fossil fuel production of region r, and

$F_{ff,rt}$ associated dual variable which indicates the activity level of fossil fuel production ff in region r and period t.

The value of the elasticity of substitution $\theta_{i'rr}^{MM}$ between non-energy inputs and the fuel-specific resource determines the price elasticity of fossil fuel supply $\theta_{i'rr}^{MM}$ at the reference point, according to the relation:

$$\varepsilon_r^{ff} = \sigma_r^{ff} \frac{\theta_r^{ff}}{1-\theta_r^{ff}}.$$

Armington production. Intermediate inputs into commodity production, investment demand, and final consumption are a composite of a domestic and imported variety which trade off at a constant elasticity of substitution. The corresponding zero profit condition for the production of the Armington good is given by:

$$\Pi_{irt}^A = p_{irt}^A - \left[\theta_{ir}^A p_{irt}^{1-\sigma_{ir}^A} + (1-\theta_{ir}^A) \left(\sum_s \theta_{isr}^M p_{ist}^{1-\sigma_{ir}^M} \right)^{\frac{1}{1-\sigma_{ir}^M}} \right]^{\frac{1}{1-\sigma_{ir}^A}} = 0$$

where:

θ_{ir}^A benchmark cost share of domestically produced commodity i into Armington production of commodity i in region r,

θ_{isr}^M benchmark cost share of imported commodity i from region s (aliased with index r) in the production of the import composite of commodity i to region r,

σ_{ir}^A Armington elasticity of substitution between domestically produced commodity i and the import composite of the same variety for region r,

σ_{ir}^M Armington elasticity of substitution between imports within the import composite of commodity i for region r, and

A_{irt} associated dual variable which indicates the activity level of Armington production of commodity i in region r and period t.

Production of the sectoral energy aggregate. Aggregate energy inputs to production of commodity i (other than fossil fuels) are a nested separable CES aggregation of oil, gas and coal. Gas and oil trade off as relatively close substitutes in the lower nest of the energy composite; at the next level the oil and gas composite combines with coal at a lower rate. The zero-profit condition for the production of the industrial energy aggregate to sector i is:

$$\Pi_{irt}^E = p_{irt}^E - \{\theta_{ir}^{COA} (p_t^{COA} + pcarb_{rt} CO2_{COA})^{1-\sigma_{ir}^{COA}} + (1-\theta_{ir}^{COA})$$
$$[\theta_{ir}^{OIL} (p_t^{OIL} + pcarb_{rt} CO2_{OIL})^{1-\sigma_{ir}^{LQ}}$$
$$+ (1-\theta_{ir}^{OIL})(p_t^{GAS} + pcarb_{rt} CO2_{GAS})^{1-\sigma_{ir}^{LQ}}]^{\frac{1-\sigma_{ir}^{COA}}{1-\sigma_{ir}^{LQ}}} \}^{\frac{1}{1-\sigma_{ir}^{COA}}} = 0$$

where:

$pcarb_{rt}$ carbon price in region r and period t,

$CO2_{ff}$ physical carbon coefficient for fossil fuels,

θ_{ir}^{COA} benchmark cost share of coal input into the energy aggregate of sector i in region r,

θ_{ir}^{OIL} benchmark cost share of the oil input into the gas and oil composite of the energy aggregate of sector i in region r,

σ_{ir}^{COA} elasticity of substitution between coal and the gas and oil composite in the energy aggregate of sector i in region r,

σ_{ir}^{LQ} elasticity of substitution between gas and oil in the energy aggregate of sector i in region r, and

E_{irt} associated dual variable which indicates the activity level of production for the energy aggregate to sector i in region r.

Production of the household energy aggregate. Energy demanded by the household is a CES aggregate of fossil fuels. The zero-profit condition for the production of the household energy aggregate has the form:

$$\Pi_{rt}^{EC} = p_{rt}^{EC} - \left(\sum_{ff} \theta_{r,ff}^{EC} (p_t^{ff} + pcarb_{rt} CO2_{ff})^{1-\sigma_r^{EC}} \right)^{\frac{1}{1-\sigma_r^{EC}}} = 0$$

where:

$p_{rt}^{EC} \; a_{jr}^{KLE}$ price of household energy aggregate for region r and period t,

$\theta_{r,ff}^{EC}$ benchmark cost share of fossil fuel input ff in the household energy aggregate of region r,

σ_r^{EC} elasticity of substitution between fossil fuel inputs within the household energy aggregate, and

EC_{rt} associated dual variable which indicates the activity level of household energy aggregate production in region r and period t.

Production of the household consumption aggregate. In final consumption demand the household energy aggregate trades off with the macro-good at a constant elasticity of substitution:

$$\Pi_{rt}^C = p_{rt}^C - \left(\theta_r^C \left(\prod_i (p_{irt}^A)^{\gamma_{ir}} \right)^{1-\sigma_r^C} + (1-\theta_r^C) p_{rt}^{EC\,1-\sigma_r^C} \right)^{\frac{1}{1-\sigma_r^C}} = 0$$

where:

p_{rt}^C a_{jr}^{KLE} price of household consumption aggregate for region r and period t,

θ_r^C benchmark cost share of the non-energy composite in aggregate household demand in region r,

γ_{ir} benchmark cost share of Armington commodity i in the non-energy composite of aggregate household demand in region r,

σ_r^C elasticity of substitution between the non-energy composite and the energy aggregate in household consumption demand in region r, and

C_{rt} associated dual variable which indicates the activity level of household consumption in region r and period t.

Capital stock formation and investment. An efficient allocation of capital, that is, investment over time assures the following intertemporal zero-profit conditions which relates the cost of a unit of investment, the return to capital and the purchase price of a unit of capital stock in period t:[2]

$$\Pi_{rt}^K = p_{rt}^K - v_r^\tau - (1-\delta)p_{r,t+1}^K = 0$$

and

$$\Pi_{rt}^I = p_{r,t+1}^K - p_{CGD,rt} = 0$$

where:

P_{t+1}^K value (purchase price) of one unit of capital stock in region r and period t,

δ_r depreciation rate in region r,

$p_{CGD,rt}$ cost of a unit of investment in period t where $p_{CGD,rt}$ is equal to $p_{i,rt}$ for $i = CGD$ (savings good or likewise investment production), and

K_{rt} associated dual variable, which indicates the activity level of capital stock formation in region r and period t,

I_{rt} associated dual variable, which indicates the activity level of aggregate investment in region r and period t.[3]

Market Clearance Conditions

Labor. The supply–demand balance for labor is:

$$\overline{L}_{rt} = \sum_i Y_{irt} \frac{\partial \Pi_{irt}^Y}{\partial w_{rt}} + \sum_{ff} Y_{ff,rt} \frac{\partial \Pi_{ff,rt}^F}{\partial w_{rt}}$$

where $\overline{L}_{rt}$ is exogenous endowment of time in region r and period t.[4]

Capital. The supply–demand balance for capital is:

$$\overline{K}_{rt} = \sum_i Y_{irt} \frac{\partial \Pi_{irt}^Y}{\partial v_{rt}} + \sum_{ff} Y_{ff,rt} \frac{\partial \Pi_{ff,rt}^F}{\partial v_{rt}}$$

Fuel-specific resources. The supply–demand balance for fuel-specific resources is:

$$\overline{Q}_{rt}^{ff} = F_{rt,ff} \frac{\partial \Pi_{rt,ff}^F}{\partial q_{rt}^{ff}} \qquad ff \in \{COA, OIL, GAS\}$$

where $\overline{Q}_{rt}^{ff}$ is exogenous endowment with fuel-specific resource *ff* for region *r* and period *t*.

Fossil fuels. The supply–demand balance for fossil fuels is:

$$\sum_r F_{rt}^{ff} = \left(\sum_r \left(\sum_i E_{irt} \frac{\partial \Pi_{irt}^E}{\partial (p_t^{ff} + pcarb_t CO2_{ff})} \right) + EC_{rt} \frac{\partial \Pi_{rt}^{EC}}{\partial (p_t^{ff} + pcarb_t CO2_{ff})} \right)$$

$$ff \in \{COA, OIL, GAS\}$$

Domestic commodity markets. The market clearance condition for the macro-good produced for the domestic market is:

$$Y_{irt} \frac{\partial \Pi_{irt}^Y}{\partial p_{irt}} = A_{irt} \frac{\partial \Pi_{irt}^A}{\partial p_{irt}}$$

Sectoral energy aggregate. The market clearance condition for the energy aggregate of sector *i* is:

$$E_{irt} = Y_{irt} \frac{\partial \Pi_{irt}^E}{\partial p_{irt}^E}$$

Household energy aggregate. The market clearance condition for the household energy aggregate is:

$$EC_{rt} = EC_{rt} \frac{\partial \Pi_{rt}^{EC}}{\partial p_{rt}^{EC}}$$

Armington aggregate. The market clearance condition for Armington aggregate is:

$$A_{irt} = \sum_i Y_{irt} \frac{\partial \Pi_{irt}^Y}{\partial p_{irt}^A} + \sum_{ff} Y_{ff,rt} \frac{\partial \Pi_{ff,rt}^F}{\partial p_{irt}^A} + C_{rt} \frac{\partial \Pi_{rt}^C}{\partial p_{irt}^A}$$

Household consumption aggregate. The market clearance condition for the household consumption aggregate is:

$$C_{rt} = D_{rt}$$

$$C_r = \frac{(1 - mps_r)(w_r \overline{L}_r + R \overline{K}_r + \sum_j r_{jr} K_{jr}^S + PCO\ CRTS_r - P_r^G \overline{G}_r - \overline{B}_r)}{P_r^C}$$

where D_{rt} is uncompensated final demand which is derived from maximization of lifetime utility (see below).

Income Balance of Households

Consumers choose to allocate lifetime income across consumption in different time periods in order to maximize lifetime utility. The representative agent in each period solves:

$$\text{Max} \sum_t \left(\frac{1}{1+\rho_r}\right)^t u_r(C_{rt})$$

$$\text{s.t.} \sum_t p_{rt}^C C_{rt} = M_r$$

where:

u_r instantaneous utility function of representative agent in region r,
ρ_r time preference rate of representative agent in region r, and
M_r lifetime income of representative agent in region r.

Lifetime income M is defined as:

$$M_r = p_{r0}^K \overline{K}_{r0} + \sum_t w_{rt} \overline{L}_{rt} + \sum_{ff} q_{rt}^{ff} \overline{Q}_{rt}^{ff}$$

$$+ \sum_t \sum_{ff} pcarb_{rt} CO2_{ff} \left(\sum_i E_{irt} \frac{\partial \Pi_{rt}^{EY}}{\partial(p_t^{ff} + CO2_{ff}\ pcarb_{rt})} + EC_{rt} \frac{\partial \Pi_{rt}^{EC}}{\partial(p_t^{ff} + CO2_{ff}\ pcarb_{rt})} \right)$$

where $\overline{K}_{r0}$ is initial capital stock in region r.

With isoelastic lifetime utility the instantaneous utility function is given as:

$$u_r(C_{rt}) = \frac{C_{rt}^{1-\frac{1}{\mu_r}}}{1-\frac{1}{\mu_r}}$$

where μ_r is constant intertemporal elasticity of substitution.

The uncompensated final demand function D_{rt} is then derived as:

$$D_{rt}(p_{rt}^C, M) = \frac{(1+\rho_r)^{-t\mu_r}}{\sum_t (1+\rho_r)^{-t\mu_r} p_{rt}^{C1-\mu_r}} \frac{M}{p_{rt}^{C\mu_r}}$$

Terminal Constraints

The finite horizon poses some problems with respect to capital accumulation. Without any terminal constraint, the capital stock at the end of the model's horizon would have no value and this would have significant repercussions for investment rates in the periods leading up to the end of the model horizon. In order to correct for this effect we define a terminal constraint which forces terminal investment to increase in proportion to final consumption demand:[5]

$$\frac{I_{Tr}}{I_{T-1,r}} = \frac{C_{Tr}}{C_{T-1,r}}.$$

NOTES

1. A constant-returns-to-scale production function with convex level sets exhibits decreasing returns to scale in remaining factors when one or more inputs are in fixed supply. We exploit this result in representing a decreasing-returns-to-scale function through a constant returns-to-scale activity which uses the fuel-specific factor.
2. The optimality conditions for capital stock formation and investment are directly derived from the maximization of lifetime utility by the representative household taking into account its budget constraint, the equation of motion for the capital stock and the condition that output in each period is either invested or consumed. Note that in our algebraic exposition we assume an investment lag of one period.
3. As written, we have taken explicit account of the non-negativity constraint for investment.
4. Time endowment grows at a constant rate *g*, which determines the long-run (steady-state) growth rate of the economy.
5. This constraint imposes balanced growth in the terminal period but does not require that the model achieves steady-state growth.

BIBLIOGRAPHY

Böhringer, C. (1996), 'Fossil fuels subsidies and environmental constraints', *Environmental and Resource Economics*, **8**(3), 331–49.

Böhringer, C. (2000), 'Cooling down hot air: A global CGE analysis of Post-Kyoto carbon abatement strategies', *Energy Policy*, **28**, 779–89.

Böhringer, C. (2002a), 'Industry-level emissions trading between power producers in the EU', *Applied Economics*, **34**(4), 523–33.

Böhringer, C. (2002b), 'Climate politics from Kyoto to Bonn: From little to nothing?', *The Energy Journal*, **23**(2), 51–71.

Böhringer, C. (2004), 'Sustainability impact assessment: The use of computable general equilibrium models', *Economie Internationale*, **99**, 9–26.

Böhringer, C., S. Boeters and M. Feil (2005), 'Taxation and unemployment: An applied general equilibrium approach for Germany', *Economic Modelling*, **22**(1), 81–108.

Böhringer, C., K. Conrad and A. Löschel (2003), 'Carbon taxes and joint implementation: An applied CGE analysis for Germany and India', *Environmental and Resource Economics*, **24**(1), 49–76.

Böhringer, C. and A. Lange (2005a), 'Economic implications of alternative allocation schemes for emission allowances', *Scandinavian Journal of Economics*, **107**(3), 563–81.

Böhringer, C. and A. Lange (2005b), 'Mission impossible!? On the harmonization of national allocation plans under the EU emission trading directive', *Journal of Regulatory Economics*, **27**(1), 81–94.

Böhringer, C. and A. Löschel (2005), 'Climate policy beyond Kyoto: Quo vadis? A computable general equilibrium analysis based on expert judgements', *KYKLOS*, **58**(4), 467–93.

Böhringer, C. and A. Löschel (2006), 'Promoting renewable energy in Europe: A hybrid CGE approach', *The Energy Journal, Hybrid Modelling: New Answers to Old Challenges*, 123–38.

Böhringer, C., A. Löschel and J. Francois (2004), 'A computable general equilibrium model for climate and trade policy anaysis', in C. Böhringer and A. Löschel (eds), *Climate Change Policy and Global Trade*, ZEW Economic Studies, 26, Physica (Springer), pp. 111–44.

Böhringer, C., A. Löschel and T.F. Rutherford (2006), 'Efficiency gains from "what"-flexibility in climate policy: An integrated CGE assessment', *The Energy Journal*, Special Issue 3, 405–24.

Böhringer, C., A. Löschel and T.F. Rutherford (2007), 'Decomposing integrated assessment of climate change', *Journal of Economic Dynamics and Control*, **31**(2), 683–702.

Böhringer, C. and T.F. Rutherford (1997), 'Carbon taxes with exemptions in an open economy: A general equilibrium analysis of the German tax initiative', *Journal of Environmental Economics and Management*, **32**, 189–203.

Böhringer, C. and T.F. Rutherford (2002), 'Carbon abatement and international spillovers', *Environmental and Resource Economics*, **22**(3), 391–417.

Böhringer, C. and T.F. Rutherford (2009), 'Combining bottom-up and top-down', *Energy Economics*, **30**(2), 574–6.

Böhringer, C. and C. Vogt (2003), 'Economic and environmental impacts of the Kyoto Protocol', *Canadian Journal of Economics*, **36**(2), 475–94.

Böhringer, C. and C. Vogt (2004), 'The dismantling of a breakthrough: The Kyoto Protocol as symbolic policy', *European Journal of Political Economy*, **20**(3), 597–617.

Böhringer, C. and H. Welsch (2004), 'C&C – contraction and convergence of carbon emissions: The implications of permit trading', *Journal of Policy Modeling*, **26**, 21–39.
Böhringer, C. and H. Welsch (2006), 'Burden sharing in a greenhouse: Egalitarianism and sovereignty reconciled', *Applied Economics*, **38**, 981–96.

PART IV

Synthesis of TranSust

15. Economic Impacts of GHG Emission Reductions: An Overview of Multiple Model Calculations

Reyer Gerlagh, Stefan P. Schleicher, Walter Hyll and Gregor Thenius

15.1 INTRODUCTION

This chapter explores the effects of CO_2 taxes on CO_2 emissions, energy use and gross domestic product (GDP), based on a simulation exercise carried out as part of the TranSust network.[1] The TranSust network stimulated economic modeling targeted to support policies that aim at the transition to sustainable economic structures. Eleven research partners cooperate in TranSust on developing the next generation of economic models explicitly targeted to sustainability issues. These partners employ various types of models for the economic analysis of sustainability. Our aim is to understand better the relation between these models and results of the analysis. We therefore grouped the models used by the project partners into computable general equilibrium (CGE), econometric, growth and energy system models. This breakdown allows us to see common patterns among models of the same kind, when assessing, for example, the marginal abatement costs of emission reductions.

In the first part of the chapter we briefly report on an earlier model comparison study by Resources for the Future (RFF). That study assessed the linkage between various model features and assumptions of economic–energy models and (different) outcomes with respect to estimates of marginal abatement costs for reducing carbon emissions. The second part of the chapter describes the results of the TranSust model comparison. In the third part of the chapter we look at the (marginal) abatement costs from an aggregate perspective. More precisely, we define (marginal) abatement costs as the GDP loss (per ton CO_2 reduced), following Weitzman and others who argue that GDP is the most proper measure available for welfare when measuring at one instant in time only (Weitzman, 1976). We note that our (marginal) cost estimates deviate from private (marginal) costs of emission reductions, where the latter is better captured by the level of carbon tax or the price of emission permits, since these price signals measure the marginal costs with which the individual is confronted, when deciding to emit more or less carbon. In the fourth part of the chapter, we focus on the mechanisms of emission reductions. We analyze the paths for the carbon intensity of energy and energy intensity of output for different carbon tax scenarios. The issue here is whether emission reductions are achieved through energy savings, that is, an enhanced decrease in energy intensity, or through a switch from high-carbon to low-carbon fuels, that is, an enhanced decrease in carbon intensity, as a reaction to the imposition of a carbon tax.

15.2   FACTORS OF CARBON ABATEMENT COSTS

In this section we briefly report on an earlier study by Resources for the Future that identified the main factors that lead to different results among economic–energy models in marginal abatement costs for reducing carbon emissions (Fischer and Morgenstern, 2003). This study identified four factors often mentioned in the literature as the main causes for the differences in emission reduction costs: (i) the baseline emission projections; (ii) the structural characteristics of the models; (iii) the climate policy regimes; and (iv) the benefits of pollution reductions (ancillary benefits).

An earlier study by Repetto and Austin (1997) identified differences in the policy regimes and the treatment of ancillary benefits as the main causes for different model results, paying only limited attention to differences in baseline emission projections and model characteristics. In a subsequent study of the Stanford Energy Modeling Forum (1999), a controlled experiment was set up where the differences between model simulations in terms of policy regimes and ancillary benefits were minimized, so that the baseline emission projections and the structural characteristics of the models became the two main factors in explaining the different outcomes of the models with respect to emission reduction costs.

The Fischer and Morgenstern study follows up on the earlier analysis, using a model survey where model results differ with respect to both baseline emission projections and various structural model characteristics. A priori, one expects the baseline emissions to be important as a higher baseline emissions path increases the need for emission reductions to reach a certain emission target, and subsequently one expects higher (marginal) emission reduction costs to reach. Nonetheless, Fischer and Morgenstern did not find a significant relationship between the level of baseline projections and the level of (marginal) abatement costs. A probable explanation of this absent relation lies in the link between baseline emission levels and other structural model characteristics. The authors hypothesize that baseline emissions are not an exogenous assumption, but a predictable output of the model, determined by a vast number of factors and assumptions within the model. Thus, when baseline emissions are an outcome of the structural characteristics of the model, the effect of the baseline emissions may be captured through the structural parameters. We will now list the structural parameters assessed by Fischer and Morgenstern.

The first factors, labeled 'energy' and 'non-energy' look at the degree of disaggregation in the models. The representation of many non-energy sectors lowers marginal abatement costs. This is possibly due to the increased possibility of substitution for energy. In contrast to that, a more disaggregated representation of the energy sector produces higher marginal abatement costs. On the one hand, a variety of energy sources allows for more substitution options, and this tends to decrease abatement costs. But also, a more detailed modeling of energy sources better pictures the rigidities in many energy markets. The latter effect, that increases marginal abatement costs, outweighs the former. The modeling of technology in the model is also important. The inclusion of a low-carbon backstop technology as well as the modeling of endogenous technological change lowers marginal abatement costs.

Then we come to the international linkages in the models. A more detailed regional disaggregation tends to lower marginal abatement costs, because there may be more room for trade and specialization. The modeling of an international finance sector does not show significant effects on the marginal abatement costs and has a different sign for different regions. As far as trade is concerned, the comparison concludes that models with traded goods as perfect substitutes produce lower marginal abatement costs than those using assumptions with imperfect substitution between foreign and domestic goods.

As to the dynamic features, the study checks whether models assume dynamic optimization of consumers (neglecting possible dynamic optimization of producers). We note that dynamic optimization is most often connected to an assumed infinitely lived household. Though one might expect that the possibility of distributing abatement efforts optimally over time would lead to lower marginal abatement costs, the model comparison gives mixed results in this issue. Dynamic optimization is not clearly linked to lower abatement costs.

The model comparison included only one fully macroeconometric model, which produced relatively high marginal abatement costs. This finding was insufficient to draw a robust conclusion, but it was noted that it was supported by other model comparisons.

Fischer and Morgenstern are aware of many other factors in the models that can explain the differences in outcomes. Elasticities of substitution in consumption and production for example determine the possibilities for consumers and producers to react flexibly to the introduction of a carbon tax. Specifically for the energy market, it is of high importance whether it is assumed to be easy to switch from one fuel to another, or not.

15.3   SIMULATIONS IN THE TRANSUST PROJECT

Within the TranSust project, a series of scenarios was developed that could be analysed by the various models. In a first step, a baseline path (BaU) was defined, in which it is assumed that the Kyoto emission targets for 2010 are maintained after this period. This assumption is labelled 'Kyoto forever'. Second, it was assumed that applied CO_2 taxes that are already effective before 2005, or that will become implemented based upon agreed political decisions of before 2005, will be maintained. In a second step, five carbon tax scenarios were created. In those scenarios carbon taxes were increased (in addition to existing ones in BaU) linearly from 2000 to 2050, reaching by 2050 the levels of €10, €20, €30, €50 and €100 per ton CO_2. This brings us to Table 15.1, showing scenarios and tax paths.

Table 15.1   Tax Scenarios (€/tons of CO_2)

Year	2000	2005	2010	2015	2020	2030	2040	2050
BaU	0	0	0	0	0	0	0	0
SCEN10	0	1	2	3	4	6	8	10
SCEN20	0	2	4	6	8	12	16	20
SCEN30	0	3	6	9	12	18	24	30
SCEN50	0	5	10	15	20	30	40	50
SCEN100	0	10	20	30	40	60	80	100

The scenario specification is incomplete, however, without an assumption on the use of tax revenues, known as recycling, as the effect of CO_2 taxes on the economy are known to be rather sensitive to recycling schemes. We therefore asked each modeler group to specify, when possible, two sets of tax scenarios. In the first set, carbon tax revenues should not be used to lower other existing taxes. Instead, taxes may be returned to the citizen in a lump-sum fashion, or to lower the budget deficit (or increase a budget surplus). In the second set, carbon tax revenues should be recycled. As an example, they could be used to cut existing taxes, lower payroll taxes and social security payments, or subsidize renewable energy sources.

For each model, for each scenario, for each five-year period, data were collected on GDP levels, CO_2 emissions and energy use. These data were then used to analyse the effects of carbon taxes on output, emissions, energy use, energy intensity of output, and carbon intensity of energy. We paid specific attention to marginal effects of emission reductions on GDP to answer the question how much GDP decreases (or increases in some cases) for an additional decrease in carbon dioxide emissions, and in what way this depends on the period and the use of a recycling option.

Below, we will show, for each model when available, three types of graphs. The first graph presents the relative change in GDP in relation to the relative change in emissions. It depicts the relative loss of GDP as dependent on the relative cut in emissions, through the use of a carbon tax with and without the recycling option, and for different periods. The second graph shows the marginal costs of emission reductions, in terms of euros per ton CO_2 abated. The measure presented in this figure is more or less equal to the derivative of the first figure. It shows how much it costs in terms of GDP loss to abate an additional ton of carbon dioxide. The third graph compares the two channels of emission reduction: energy savings and decarbonization of energy supply. The graphs make it possible to conclude immediately, for each model, whether the major emission reduction goes through an improvement of energy efficiency, or alternatively, through a fuel switching towards less carbon-rich energy sources. For all graphs, we compare three periods when data are available: 2010, 2020 and 2050.

15.4 GDP COSTS OF EMISSION REDUCTIONS

In summary the following report can be made. We recall from theory that without other pre-existing distortions to the economy, the costs of a reduction in emissions more or less follow a quadratic curve. For small reduction levels, marginal costs are almost nill. For higher emission reduction levels, marginal costs increase. That is, the marginal abatement cost curve (MACC) goes through the origin. In a more complex model with other distortions, the above argument does not carry over, and thus, we do not expect the marginal cost curve to go through the origin.

In our model overview, we find two cases of zero marginal social costs of emission reductions at the origin, calculated by the DART and the FEEM-RICE models. Thus, the results of these two models suggest a context in which other pre-existing distortions are either absent, or not too important, or effects of different distortions might cancel out one another. Most other models find strictly positive marginal social costs for the whole range of reduction levels, when there is no tax recycling. Another outstanding finding is that calculated costs without tax recycling are high, especially for econometric models. When tax recycling is introduced, however, the picture turns around, and the econometric models find substantial negative costs under smart tax recycling schemes.

CGE Models

We will now first look at the CGE models DART and PACE. The DART model does not run to 2050, but ends after 2040. Also, data suggest that calculated numbers for 2040 are sensitive to the terminal conditions, so that we present graphs for 2010, 2020 and 2030. In 2010, almost 20 percent of emissions can be reduced at 0.16 percent loss of GDP. The cost curves are almost constant over time, by which we mean to say that the same relative reduction can be reached at the same relative costs in 2020 and 2030. In 2030, about 32 percent of emissions can be reduced at about 0.55 percent of GDP loss.

As mentioned above and as can be seen from the diagrams (Figures 15.1–15.2), the DART model is one of the two cases where the costs curves are

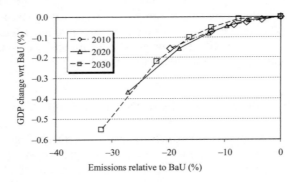

Figure 15.1   GDP and Emissions for DART Model

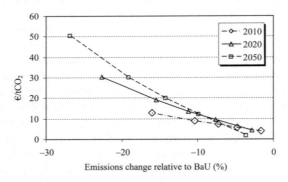

Figure 15.2   MACCs for DART Model

almost quadratic, so that the marginal abatement costs curve goes through the origin. According to the modelers, the reason for this does not lie in absent pre-existing distortions, but in the fact that CO_2 tax revenues are recycled lump-sum to the consumers, thus government budgets are not kept constant.[2] The costs are low for small emission reductions and go up until about €50 per ton of CO_2 in 2030 when taxes are increased from €30 to €60 /tonCO$_2$. Thus, in this model, the marginal loss of GDP (social costs) seems to be almost equal to (slightly above) the level of the carbon tax (private costs). This finding reiterates the conclusion that the DART model suggests economic costs close to the typical outcome of a first-best model.

The PACE model (Figures 15.3–15.4) shows a similar picture as the DART model, but at higher abatement and higher cost levels. Emissions are about twice as elastic with respect to the carbon tax, and costs are about four times higher, so that at equal reduction levels, costs are about two times higher. In PACE, marginal costs start at about €50 per ton of CO_2. In this

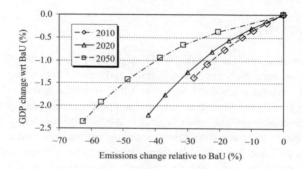

Figure 15.3   GDP and Emissions for PACE Model

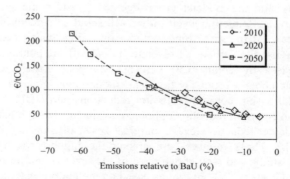

Figure 15.4   MACCs for PACE Model

model, even a low carbon tax leads to a substantial loss of GDP. In the PACE model, tax interaction effects seem to play a significant role in increasing the social costs of carbon taxes. Another, more subtle, difference between the two CGE models is that whereas in the DART model the relative cost structure seems to be almost constant over time (Figure 15.1), in the PACE model, the marginal costs structure (Figure 15.4) seems the same for 2010, 2020 and 2050.

Both CGE models give us GDP/emissions curves that show a negative relationship between emission reductions and the level of GDP. Thus emission reductions are costly and cause a loss in GDP. The costs for achieving emission reduction targets vary in their magnitude but are positive in both models. As mentioned above, the higher costs in PACE compared to the tax level suggests that tax interactions play a role, and we would expect a clever recycling scheme to make it possible to reduce costs substantially, but unfortunately, for both models, no data are available for scenarios with revenue recycling.

Econometric Models

The econometric models E3ME, W8D, MULTIMAC and MIDE show very high gains or very high costs of emission reductions depending on whether carbon tax revenues are used to lower other existing taxes, or not. When abstracting from recycling, this outcome supports the finding of the Fischer and Morgenstern study and other studies that econometric models give higher marginal abatement costs than other modeling approaches. But the outcomes of econometric models seem to be very sensitive to the assumptions about the use of the revenues from the carbon tax, and various options for double dividends seem available.

In the E3ME model (Figures 15.5–15.6), emissions are relatively inelastic to tax levels, and the modeler group decided to add some scenarios with higher tax levels. Reduction levels only reach about 15 percent in 2020, for a €100/tCO_2 tax. At the same time, without recycling, which means that the governments use the carbon tax revenues to pay off the public sector debts, GDP decreases by about 0.50 percent. Marginal abatement costs are calculated at about €150/tCO_2 tax. The model thus gives a very strong negative relationship between emission reductions and GDP. Also, we see that no cheap emission reduction option are available. Though marginal costs are less for lower reduction levels, marginal costs still start at €60 per ton of CO_2 in 2010. These numbers are among the highest we found in our comparative study, and well above most of the levels found in the literature for the social costs of CO_2 emissions based on the net present value of losses due to expected future climate change.

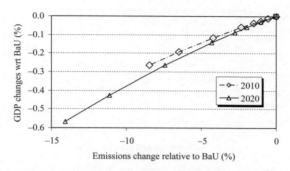

Figure 15.5   GDP and Emissions for E3ME Model without Recycling

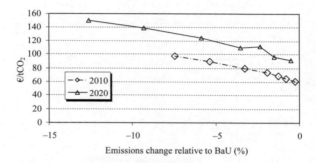

Figure 15.6   MACCs for E3ME Model without Recycling

The picture changes drastically if we allow for tax recycling. The E3ME team has developed two recycling schemes. In the first scheme, carbon tax revenues are returned to consumers in a lump-sum fashion. According to the modelers, this recycling scheme introduces an income benefit to the consumers, who increase their consumption, which in turn stimulates production. Employment increases, income increases further, and turning the wheel, a multiplier effect arises where a modest initial carbon tax recycling leads to a large GDP gain. The second recycling scheme calculated by the E3ME model group is based on a reduction of social security contribution (SSC). For both recycling schemes, we show the marginal abatement costs curve in Figure 15.7 and Figure 15.8, respectively. In both cases, the (negative) costs are of the same magnitude and for low emission reduction levels are about €200 per ton of CO_2. Both recycling schemes drive on different mechanisms, however. In the high tax scenarios (€100/tonCO_2 in 2050), in 2020, European unemployment falls by 2 million under SSC recycling, but only by 200 000 in the lump-sum recycling scenario. But, in the end, the positive impulse to the economy seems to be comparable for both

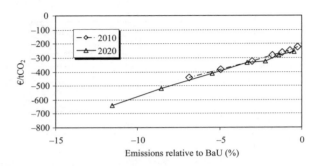

*Figure 15.7   MACCs for E3ME Model with Recycling through Lump-Sum
            Transfers to Households*

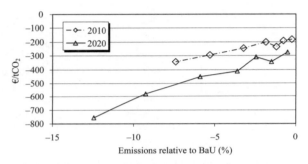

*Figure 15.8   MACCs for E3ME Model with Recycling through Social
            Security*

recycling schemes. The figures show a strong double dividend; emissions
decrease at negative costs. Remarkably, we even find an upward-sloping
marginal costs curve, which means that the relative size of the second
dividend increases with the level of emission reductions.

This finding of increasing marginal benefits from emission reductions
raises the question of how long such a double dividend can go on. Can one
extend the positive effect of tax recycling to go on without end? Certainly
not, but the figure suggests that substantial emission reductions can be
reached, far beyond the level calculated in the scenarios, with a strong double
dividend effect as long as taxes are recycled. The multiplier effects of
revenue recycling in E3ME depend critically on the dynamics of the labor
market. As long as unemployment remains high, the double dividend will
continue to show up in the results. When unemployment is reduced to below
its 'natural' rate, this trigger a non-linear response in wage rates and prices,
leading to loss of price competitiveness, increases in imports and decreases in

exports, and so brings an end to the double dividend. But the bottom of the double dividend is not reached in the calculated scenarios.

Alternatively, in the second recycling scheme studied with the E3ME model (Figure 15.8), carbon tax revenues are used to cut the employers' social security contribution (SSC), and in this case, the double dividend will continue until either unemployment is cut to its friction level, or until the SSC is completely eliminated. Again, none of these breaks applies to the considered scenarios.

We notice that costs (without recycling) or benefits (with recycling) of the emission reductions outweigh typical Pigouvian tax levels for carbon of €0–100/tCO$_2$ found in the literature (Tol, 2003). This finding implies that according to the above model calculations, the carbon tax deserves consideration as a tax instrument per se. There is no direct need of bringing in climate change policies as the main driving factor for a tax reformation scheme.

A similar picture emerges from the MULTIMAC model. Under tax recycling – in this case a payroll tax cut – GDP increases while emissions decrease. First we note that MULTIMAC is only run until the year 2010 and in this year the highest tax rate level is €20 per ton of CO$_2$. Figures 15.9 and 15.10 show a clear double dividend with negative marginal costs. According to the modelers, the main mechanism behind the double dividend is a combination of Keynesian mechanisms and shifting factor demand. The carbon tax shifts demand from energy to labor, the payroll tax cut enhances the demand in labor and thereby increases total income. This stimulates demand and a multiplier arises with higher employment and income levels. In this model, there is also a role for wage bargaining between the union and the employers, which increases the income share of labor when unemployment is lowered. When involuntary unemployment reaches a floor, the double dividend should fade out, because the effect of the payroll tax cut on employment stops, but such is not visible in the scenario exercises carried out here.

A rather different picture appears from the W8D model (Figures 15.11–15.12). In this model, public expenditures are a function of public revenues, and when these revenues increase due to a carbon tax, they are spent in fixed proportions. Part of additional revenues is spent on public investments, increasing the supply of a future production factor. Another part of tax revenues leads to increasing demand through increasing wages of the employees in the public sector or increasing public payments for social and unemployment benefits. Still another part of carbon tax revenues is used for repayment of public debt. The W8D model calculates GDP gains for small emission reduction levels, up to 5 percent, and sharply increasing costs thereafter. For higher emission reduction levels, further abatement becomes very costly.

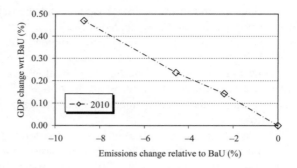

Figure 15.9   GDP and Emissions for MULTIMAC Model with Recycling

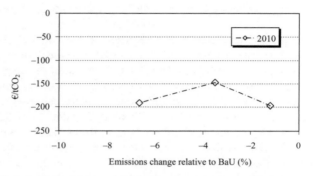

Figure 15.10   MACCs for MULTIMAC Model with Recycling

According to the modelers, the negative costs in the short term should not be interpreted as a case of a double dividend, but should be viewed as part of a dynamic interplay between supply and demand. When machine utility is not at its maximum, that is when production capacities are not exhausted by current production, then the increased public expenditures will stimulate final demand which leads to an increase in output and an increased GDP. In the longer term, this mechanism probably cannot be sustained because of increased production costs due to the carbon tax.

At first instance, the MIDE model seems to show a somewhat peculiar behavior (Figures 15.3–15.14), but in a certain way, it shows the behavior also described by the W8D modeler group (though not visible in their own graphs). Emission reductions have a strongly positive effect on GDP in 2010, and an almost as strong but negative effect in 2020. In the short term, the extra carbon tax revenues are used for public spending which increases demand, output, and GDP. Moreover, demand both by the private and public sector shifts from carbon-intensive to carbon-extensive sectors. As the

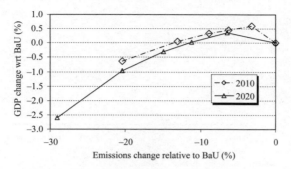

Figure 15.11   GDP and Emissions for W8D Model

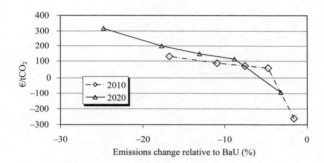

Figure 15.12   MACCs for W8D Model

carbon-extensive sectors have, on average, a higher share of value added and more linkages to other domestic sectors, this shift in demand increases GDP. But as time goes by, and other goods substitute for energy, this shift reduces the carbon tax base. Carbon tax revenues fall, the stimulus generated by it through the additional amount of public spending falls, and increasing production costs then lead to a fall in output. Having said this, we notice that the MIDE model has about the lowest elasticity of emissions with respect to the carbon tax (emissions decrease by only 2 percent in 2020 given a carbon tax of €40/tonCO$_2$). In fact, we would expect the carbon tax base erosion to be of least importance in this model.

The MIDE model finds extremely high numbers for marginal costs of emission reductions, either negative or positive. In this sense, the model fits well in the group of econometric models. Be it costs or benefits, the GDP effect of a carbon tax outweighs the typical estimated climate damage associated with carbon emissions. The modelers group explains the large numbers by the energy-intensive character of the Spanish economy. Historically, Spain has shown a high GDP–oil elasticity ranging from 0.5 to

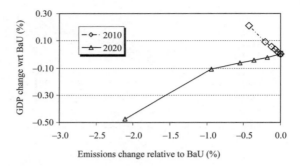

Figure 15.13   GDP and Emissions for MIDE Model

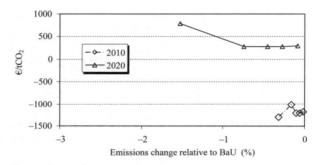

Figure 15.14   MACCs for MIDE Model

0.7, depending on the year and the author who calculated the estimate. Overall, the dependency on oil is greater than for any other member state of the EU-15. In general, Spain's tradition in environmental protection is very weak and recent and, accordingly, little effort has been made in decoupling energy consumption and emissions. Spanish industry dumps more pollutants and emissions into the environment per unit of value added than other EU countries.

Growth Models

We now turn to the IMACLIM, FEEM-RICE and DEMETER models, which are long-term stylized models of growing economies. The IMACLIM modeler group developed two recycling schemes, the first using carbon tax revenues for lump-sum payments to the consumers, the second spending carbon tax revenues on reductions in payroll taxes (Figures 15.15–15.16). Within the group of growth models, the IMACLIM model calculates relatively high and almost constant costs under both lump-sum and payroll recycling schemes. The modeler group determined two reasons for the relatively high costs. First, these are due to the inflexibilities of the model's energy system, which, according to the modelers, presents a somewhat pessimistic view of future low- and non-carbon energy technologies. These inflexibilities imply that it becomes very costly to switch to other energy technologies. Second, the model describes the crowding-out of abatement-specific investment on general productivity investment, which is perhaps stronger than in most other models. As can be seen from the diagrams, employing the payroll-recycling scheme reduces costs of abatement by about 30 percent, so that they remain on a high level.

The reason for the almost flat marginal abatement costs curves can probably be traced back to the energy system assumptions made in the POLES model, as IMACLIM's energy submodel is calibrated on POLES' results. The POLES model addresses long-term energy, technology and climate change issues and assumes more or less linear energy system profiles.

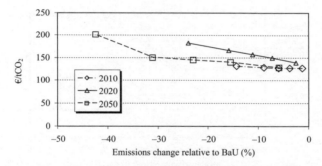

Figure 15.15   MACCs for IMACLIM Model with Lump-Sum Recycling

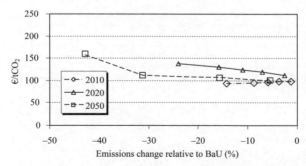

Figure 15.16   MACCs for IMACLIM Model with Recycling through Payroll Tax Reduction

The FEEM-RICE (Figures 15.17–15.18) is different from the other models in the sense that it does not specify a scenario in terms of the carbon tax imposed, but in terms of emission reduction levels to be achieved. *Ex post*, carbon taxes consistent with the reduction target can be calculated. With the DART model, the FEEM-RICE model shares the result that marginal costs are almost zero for low levels of emission reduction, and increasing for higher emission reduction levels. Indeed, the feature is explained by the FEEM-RICE model structure, which abstracts from most other distortions, and entirely focuses on the climate change distortion. Different from the DART model is the clear reduction over time in abatement costs. This cost reduction is due to assumed technological change in energy savings options and the assumed future availability of more low-carbon or carbon-free options.

The DEMETER model (Figures 15.19–15.20) is without doubt the model in which emission reductions have the least effect on GDP, negative or

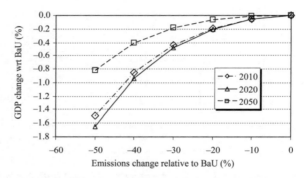

Figure 15.17   GDP and Emissions for FEEM-RICE Model

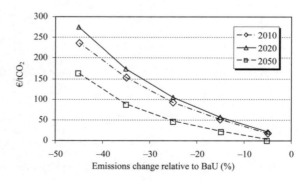

Figure 15.18   MACCs for FEEM-RICE Model

positive. Without recycling carbon tax revenues, the DEMETER model calculates costs below €10/tonCO₂, and most importantly, marginal costs decrease with higher abatement levels. An explanation for the low level of costs in DEMETER is an assumption that non-carbon energy sources can easily substitute for fossil fuels and that there are various energy markets where these non-carbon energy sources are almost competitive with fossil fuels. Thus, at the aggregate level, substitution takes place at low social costs. Second, consistent with the immediate increase in the deployment of non-carbon energy sources following small emission reductions, it is assumed that the increased use leads to an enhanced development of carbon-free energy sources at low costs. Thus, costs of emission reductions are mainly transition costs and decrease over time, and when for a given reduction level the non-carbon energy sources have become competitive with fossil fuels, a further reduction in emissions becomes relatively cheap.

The DEMETER modelers group also worked out a recycling scheme in

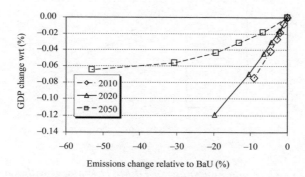

Figure 15.19   GDP and Emissions for DEMETER Model without Recycling

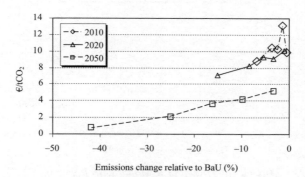

Figure 15.20   MACCs for DEMETER Model without Recycling

which the carbon tax revenues are used to subsidize non-carbon energy sources (Figures 15.21–15.22). Under this recycling scheme, they find a double dividend. The reason for this GDP benefit is twofold. First, non-carbon energy sources require higher investment levels compared to higher levels of maintenance costs for fossil fuels. Since investments count positively in GDP (which is consumption plus gross investments), the shift in energy sources will increase GDP, even when consumption levels (and welfare) are unaffected. Second, non-carbon energy sources are assumed to have substantial potential for learning-by-doing, and the learning spillover effect of non-carbon energy assumption is assumed not to be internalized in the benchmark scenario. A subsidy for the non-carbon energy source thus to some extent internalizes the learning externality, and this will improve welfare. Notice however, that benefits of emission reductions decrease with the level of emission reductions. There is thus a clear end to the double dividend.

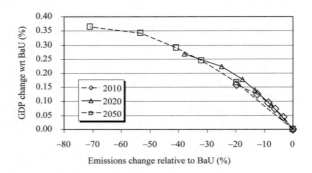

Figure 15.21   GDP and Emissions for DEMETER Model with Recycling

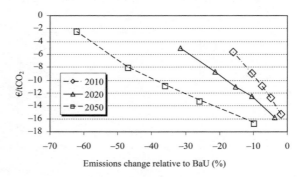

Figure 15.22   MACCs for DEMETER Model with Recycling

Energy System Model

Finally, we report on the MARKAL model (Figures 15.23–15.24), which is the single-energy system model in the set of TranSust models. It incorporates a wide range of energy technologies, of which many can serve as an alternative to carbon technologies. Thanks to these features of the model, substantial emission reductions are achieved at low costs. As much as 30 percent emission reductions in the year 2050 can be achieved at almost no loss in GDP. This is because of many energy sources substitution possibilities. Restrictions on the scale of non-carbon technologies lead to a relatively sharp increase in costs for higher emission reduction levels. A 66 percent emission reduction level is achieved at a 0.37 percent loss in GDP. This figure is still low compared with most other models.

Notably, marginal costs decrease between 0 and 10 percent reduction and rise thereafter. This feature is yet unexplained. The model group emphasizes

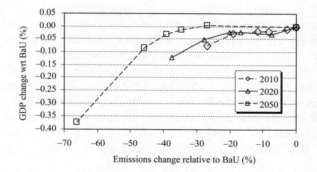

Figure 15.23   GDP and Emissions for MARKAL Model

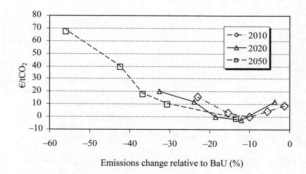

Figure 15.24   MACCs for MARKAL Model

that MARKAL is a multiperiod dynamic optimization model, for which the profile over time of some variables need not be smooth. In some periods, specific investments strongly increase, while in other periods, these investments fall. Depicting a graph for a specific year may then produce an image that is too dependent on modeled specific investment decisions.

15.5   MECHANISMS OF EMISSION REDUCTIONS

In this part we compare the two mechanisms for emission reduction: the reduction in energy intensity (energy savings) or the reduction in carbon intensity of energy supply (decarbonization). A main finding is that a substantial role for decarbonization requires the model to put sufficient emphasis on non-fossil fuels. DART and E3ME (Figures 15.25–15.26) almost entirely describe energy savings as the main mechanism for emission reduction. Fuel switching seems almost absent in DART, and only modest in E3ME. In DART, the CO_2-intensity remains practically constant, and the modeler group explains this feature by the different supply elasticities for the fossil fuels. The supply elasticities for coal, gas and crude oil are calibrated to produce a scenario consistent with most projections for 2030. The resulting supply elasticitiy for gas (2.5) is much higher than the elasticities for coal (0.57) and for crude oil (0.36). Due to the higher elasticity, gas supply reacts stronger to a price decrease. When we take together the higher carbon content of coal and oil, and the lower supply elasticity of the latter two, we find a lower decrease in gas prices compared to oil and coal prices, but a fall in supply that is about equal for the three major fossil fuels. Thus, the carbon

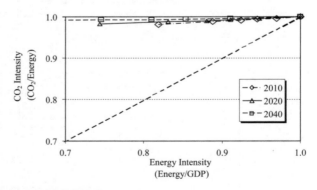

Note: Relative to BaU (BaU = 1).

Figure 15.25   Energy Savings versus Decarbonization for DART Model

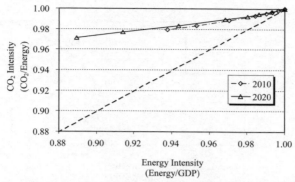

Figure 15.26 Energy Savings versus Decarbonization for E3ME Model

content of the fossil fuel mix remains almost constant. There are no non-carbon energy sources in DART. For E3ME, we are not certain whether the same mechanism applies, but it is true that non-carbon energy sources are not covered. Inter-fossil fuel substitution goes through a complex interaction between domestic supply and demand, import and export, and this requires further analysis.

In PACE (Figure 15.27) there is more room for decarbonization, but it ends when the carbon content reaches about 80 percent of the benchmark level. Fuel substitution is apparently limited, and energy savings are required for more substantial emission reductions. The IMACLIM model (Figure 15.28) portrays the inverse pattern. The deeper the cut in emission levels, the larger the role for fuel substitution. Especially in the long term, there is a substantial decrease in CO_2-intensity. This feature is consistent with IMACLIM's use of the POLES model as a source for its energy substitution possibilities.

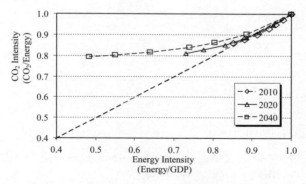

Figure 15.27 Energy Savings versus Decarbonization for PACE Model

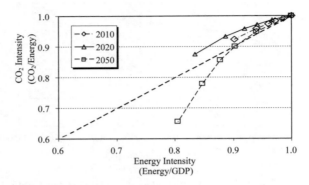

Note: Relative to BaU (BaU = 1).

Figure 15.28   Energy Savings versus Decarbonization for IMACLIM Model

The trade-off between energy savings and decarbonization in the DEMETER model depends on the recycling of taxes (see Figures 15.29 and 15.30). If there is no tax recycling, the path is comparable with the IMACLIM model. For low emission reduction levels, energy savings are most important, while for more substantial cuts in emissions, fuel substitution becomes dominant as the main mechanism. As we would expect, when carbon tax revenues are recycled through a subsidy on non-carbon technologies, fuel substitution becomes more prominent, also for low carbon tax levels.

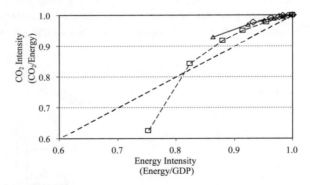

Note: Relative to BaU (BaU = 1).

Figure 15.29   Energy Savings versus Decarbonization for DEMETER Model without Recycling

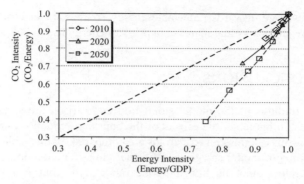

Note: Relative to BaU (BaU = 1).

Figure 15.30   Energy Savings versus Decarbonization for DEMETER
Model with Recycling

MARKAL, with its focus on the energy system and its detailed description
of energy technologies entirely focuses on fuel substitution, and more or less
abstracts from energy savings. As can be seen from Figure 15.31, in this
model, the major part of emission reductions is due to a decrease in the
carbon intensity. We even find a slight increase in energy intensity above 1.0
in 2020 and 2050 for moderate carbon tax levels. This somewhat surprising
result may be due to a measurement problem. Energy is measured in primary
energy equivalents, and the deployment of renewable energy sources for
electricity (end use in GJ) is multiplied by a fixed factor (which accounts for
the average conversion loss when fossil fuels are combusted to produce
electricity) to calculate a fictitious primary energy equivalent. When the
model switches from efficient coal combustion which has a lower conversion

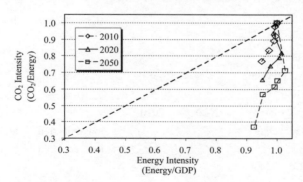

Note: Relative to BaU (BaU = 1).

Figure 15.31   Energy Savings versus Decarbonization for MARKAL Model

loss than average, towards renewable energy sources for electricity, such a shift may result in a virtual increase in primary energy use.

15.6 CONCLUSIONS

The main findings of the model simulation comparison are summarized in Table 15.2. In this table, the effects of the emission reductions on GDP and the mechanisms of emission reductions are compared. In this table, we see no clear grouping of model categories. Whether emission reductions increase or decrease GDP cannot be linked to the model type, but is linked to the assumptions about how the income from the carbon tax is used. Only under tax recycling – but not in all recycling schemes – is a double dividend sometimes found. On the other hand, no model produced an increase in GDP without a smart tax recycling scheme. For MIDE, the effect of a carbon tax is time-dependent. The econometric models stand out as a group in two ways. First, emissions are relatively inelastic. Reduction levels reached through the common carbon tax scenarios are systematically lower for the econometric models, when compared to the other models. Second, and logically following therefrom, marginal income effects in terms of changes in GDP divided by changes in emissions are systematically higher.

Table 15.2   Model Simulation Comparison

	GDP		Major Mechanism	
	Decrease	Increase	Energy Savings	Decarbonization
DART	✓	.	✓	.
PACE	✓	.	high reduction	low reduction
E3ME	✓	.	✓	.
E3ME recycling	.	✓	✓	.
MULTIMAC recycling	.	✓	n.a.	n.a.
W8D recycling	✓	.	n.a.	n.a.
MIDE	2020	2010	✓	.
IMACLIM recycling	✓	.	low reduction	high reduction
DEMETER	✓	.	low reduction	high reduction
DEMETER recycling	.	✓	.	✓
FEEM-RICE	✓	.	n.a.	n.a.
MARKAL	✓	.	.	✓

As to the mechanisms of emission reduction, most models give an important role to energy savings. Some models also describe fuel switching between carbon-rich and carbon-poor fossil fuels, from coal to gas. The results by the DART model make clear that for a proper calculation of this mechanism, we need a better understanding of the elasticity of supply to changing prices. Only a few models also describe the substitution of non-carbon fuels for fossil fuels, and in these models, decarbonization plays a major role for deep cuts in emissions.

For the three models MIDE, IMACLIM and DEMETER, the sign of some of the effects depends on the year we are looking at.

NOTES

1. See www.transust.org.
2. The explanation given by the modelers group is not entirely clear to the authors of this chapter, but as noticed in the introduction, the objective of this chapter is not to make an elaborate and independent assessment of all mechanisms over the variety of models, but to present a forum where various model groups present their own understanding of the mechanisms at work, under a unified format.

REFERENCES

Energy Modeling Forum (1999), 'The costs of the Kyoto protocol: A multi-model evaluation', *The Energy Journal*, Special Issue, edited by J.P. Weyant.

Fischer, C. and R.D. Morgenstern (2003), 'Carbon abatement costs: Why the wide range of estimates?', Discussion Paper no. 03–42, Washington, DC: Resources for the Future.

Repetto, R. and D. Austin (1997), 'The costs of climate protection: A guide for the perplexed', World Resources Institute, Washington, DC.

Tol, R.S.J. (2003), 'The marginal costs of carbon dioxide emissions: An assessment of the uncertainties', Working Paper FNU-19, University of Hamburg, Germany.

Weitzman, M.L. (1976), 'On the welfare significance of national product in a dynamic economy', *Quarterly Journal of Economics*, **90**(1), 156–62.

16. Transition to Sustainability: Some Preliminary Conclusions

Valentina Bosetti and Carlo Carraro

There has been much debate among economists, and between economists and nearly everyone else, regarding the meaning of the frequently employed concept of 'sustainability'. Many economists define sustainability as in the Brundtland Report (WCED, 1987), which identifies sustainable economic development as:

> development that meets the needs of the present without compromising the ability of future generations to meet their own needs.

Implicit in this definition are two basic concepts: intergenerational fairness and optimality. Sustainability is a question of intergenerational equity, asking about the fair or just distribution of productive capacity and welfare between the present and future generations. Optimality, or dynamic efficiency as in Stavins et al. (2002), on the other hand, is concerned with attaining the highest feasible level of social welfare over the long run. Therefore, contrary to some claims, sustainability is not only about intergenerational equity; rather, widely held views of sustainability encompass elements of both efficiency and distributional equity. This leaves room for the contribution of economic analysis, which can identify the mechanisms and policies that enhance the optimality of economic development.

The search for an economic development path that is both optimal and sustainable has occupied economists as far back as Ramsey (1928). To show the importance of the role of economists and the linkage between intergenerational equity issues and optimality in the definition of sustainability, let us consider, as an example, the choice of the discount rate to be used to evaluate present and future needs (an issue recently fashionable again, thanks to the Stern Review). As is well known, Ramsey objected to the discounting of future utilities as 'ethically indefensible'. However, several authors (see Farzin, 2007, for a recent analysis) formally showed that:

following the moral principle of treating the welfare of all generations equally (i.e., applying no discount rate) could result in an optimal outcome which is intergenerationally highly inequitable.

This is not new to economists. Koopmans (1956) was the first economist who questioned the reasonableness of the moral principle that requires the welfare of all generations to be equally treated in the social welfare function. He showed that such a principle would result in unacceptably large sacrifices to be made by the present generation in that it would impose an unacceptably high savings burden on the present generation. Arrow (1996) confirms this argument by way of a thought-experiment, showing that if the present generation is presented with a one-time-only investment opportunity which provides a small constant income forever, then with no discounting, the optimal decision requires that the present generation invests its entire income, that is, it should have a savings rate equal to 1. Interestingly, Arrow shows that Koopmans's basic argument depends neither on uncertainty about the investment (although uncertainty reinforces the argument) nor essentially on the assumption of an infinite time horizon, by demonstrating that even if the time horizon of the investment is reduced from infinity to say 3000 years and the return to investment is assumed to be as low as 0.01 per cent (one-hundredth of a percentage), without discounting of future returns, the optimality still dictates that the present generation should save and invest almost 90 per cent of its income – too high a rate by any ethical standard.

In other words, what seems to be trivial (all generations must be treated equally) may have unexpected and contradictory consequences (future generations may be worse off).

The conclusion is not only that a positive discount rate would be fair to present generations. As suggested by Farzin (2007), a positive discount rate would also favour future generations:

> Although discounting of future welfare defies the moral principle of treating the welfare of all generations equally, again rather ironically, it may lead to an optimal outcome in which after certain initial periods all future generations will enjoy an equal welfare level.

The role of economics is therefore to highlight paradoxes of this sort. As a consequence, sustainability science badly needs sound economic analyses and modelling.

There are other examples of complex problems that could be highlighted and have been analysed in this book. Consider technical progress. It is certainly a major component of any sustainable development path. Without some drastic innovation, in particular in the energy sector, the world's future economic development can hardly be sustainable. However, the confidence that technical progress may lessen the trade-off between economic growth and environmental protection[1] does not necessarily imply that investments in environment-friendly research and development (R&D) and innovation will be undertaken by firms, or that R&D and innovation can be disseminated to give all countries the opportunity to protect their environment at a low economic cost.

The basic question is then: why do firms invest in R&D? They do so not only to pursue directly new product and process innovation but also to develop and maintain their broader capacity to assimilate and exploit externally available innovation. Behind the 'innovative' reason for R&D are two motivating forces: profitable investment and strategic advantage. Therefore, policies designed to stimulate innovation must provide an opportunity to increase firms' profits and competitiveness.

But do we really need policy? The answer is not trivial, albeit crucial for sustainable development. In the case of technical progress, some failures prevent markets from achieving the first-best adoption and diffusion of innovation.

There are three types of market failure at work when we consider the question of innovation and the environment. The first is the conventional market failure associated with externalities. If innovation results developed by one firm spill over to other firms, there is an incentive for firms to copy innovation rather than to generate it themselves. The second is the conventional static market failure associated with imperfect competition – as patented innovation generates ownership of designs, typically output of goods based on these designs is too low, prices too high. The third is the dynamic market failure surrounding R&D and innovation. It arises fundamentally from the nature of knowledge as a public good, which is expensive to produce, but cheap to reproduce. It is particularly important for basic research, but it also holds for applied research.

This dynamic market failure gives rise to a complex set of questions which involve both innovation and its diffusion: (i) How many firms should engage in R&D? (ii) What information should they share: (a) with each other; (b) with other non-innovating firms? (iii) How much R&D should each of the innovating firms carry out? (iv) What degree of protection of environmental innovation should firms be guaranteed? (v) How can public policy intervene to reduce the negative effects of market failures on innovation?

A partial solution to some of the market failures associated with R&D is the creation of a system of property rights, the most obvious one being patent protection. The problem with this is that it may provide too much protection and so prevents socially beneficial sharing of information. In particular, it prevents a socially efficient diffusion of environmental innovation and hence reduces the environmental benefit that innovation provides. This distortion of the information-sharing aspects of R&D generates further distortions on the decisions about the amount of R&D carried out. For these reasons a lot of the focus of technology policy is now on arrangements like research joint ventures (RJVs) which correct the distortions of the patent system by promoting more information-sharing.

Many sources of inertia also govern the rate at which techno-economic systems change. These include: low capital stock turnover rates in some sectors; the time needed for innovations to incubate; institutional barriers to diffusion; weak mechanisms incapable of translating political or societal imperatives into effective economic signals; and self-reinforcing loops between particular technical options and consumption patterns, which create technological 'lock-in' and discourage radical innovation.

Remedying structural inertia is difficult. Decision-making within complex socio-technical systems takes place at many levels (households, industry, public authorities and so on), all governed by different priorities, and diverting complete systems onto less environmentally harmful technological trajectories is a daunting task. Price signals will undoubtedly have some effect on the technological paths taken by the various actors involved in complex systems, but there are genuine fears that these prices will reflect short-term expediency rather than longer-term societal and environmental needs, and that they will be too low to overcome structural inertia as far as innovation is concerned. There is also the added complication that many parts of complex socio-technical systems are comparatively insensitive to price variations, with decisions on future behaviour driven primarily by other factors, for example cost–speed ratios in the transportation sector, aesthetics in architecture and the price of land in urban planning.

All these domestic, sometimes local, policy issues are crucial for the (global) sustainable development of the world economic system. Economics is therefore crucial to help us understand the mechanisms that enable markets to move towards sustainability and the policies that may be necessary to regulate markets when they fail to move along a sustainable path.

The previous chapters of this book contribute to our understanding of the economic mechanisms governing sustainable development. The authors make two major efforts, assessing the economic determinants of sustainability and modelling the interface between economic and natural systems. This is very important in order to highlight some major sustainability issues. The definition of crucial issues emerging in models of sustainable development is indeed at the core of the second part of the book. Issues such as the use of sustainability indicators, the choice of a unit for measuring policy costs, the role of technical progress, the design of tax revenue recycling schemes, or the way new energy technologies can be modelled, have been analysed in detail and some methodological advances have been proposed.

However, this book is not only about identifying crucial issues. The book also proposes practical development of actual models to include new features that help economic models to capture the various dimensions of sustainability. In particular, the third part of the book contains a detailed overview of models used within the TranSust project. This comprehensive and thorough description provides researchers and policy-makers with a concise and easy-to-consult 'guide' to some of the most used energy–environment–economics models.

There is another feature of the book that needs to be stressed. The TranSust project focused on the economic dimension of 'transition to sustainability'. Transitions are costly and, as emphasized above, need to be guided. Economic analysis can help in identifying mechanisms and paradoxes, but eventually policy needs to be implemented. Several obstacles however soon emerge. For example, over the last 20 years, scientists have stressed the importance of some new phenomena related to the use of the environment: climate change, ozone layer depletion, acid depositions, freshwater pollution, marine pollution, deforestation and the loss of biological diversity. Some of these problems have been more recently discovered (for example the ozone layer depletion); some have acquired importance due to their scale and potential impact (for example climate change, deforestation, or water pollution). Most of the new sustainability problems mentioned above have an intrinsic international dimension due to transnational or global spillovers. The depletion of the ozone layer and climate change depend on global aggregate emissions. Acid depositions and marine pollution usually cross the borders of the polluting country. Even deforestation is an international problem as forests are a sink for CO_2 and provide important support for biodiversity.

The international dimension of the environment is a source of substantial interdependence among nations: each country benefits from using the environment as a receptacle of emissions and is damaged by environmental deterioration. While the benefit for any country is primarily related to domestic pollution alone, the environmental damage is related to both domestic and foreign emissions. This problem is not new to economists, and has been analysed in the area of externalities and public goods. What is new is the context where these problems take place. Currently, the atmosphere and the waters are managed as global common-property goods, and there is no institution which possesses powers to regulate their use by means of supranational legislation, economic instruments, or by imposing a system of global property rights. This fact requires a shift in the analysis, from government intervention to international policy coordination and voluntary agreements among sovereign countries. Again, the economic analysis of international negotiations and institutions can be very helpful in increasing the probability that countries agree on actions to protect the environment and move towards sustainability. This is why this book can also be helpful in the design of sustainability policy.

Finally, it has become widely accepted that development in general, and sustainable development in particular, is a knowledge-intensive activity that continuously evolves over time. If sustainable development is about progress 'to meet the needs of a much larger but stabilizing human population, to sustain the life-support systems of the planet, and to reduce substantially hunger and poverty' (National Research Council, 1999), then sustainability itself can be thought of less as a state or condition and more as a direction or bias for development activities. This puts 'sustainability' in the same camp as other great goals of the last century, such as 'freedom' and 'justice' – goals that we think more about moving toward than we do about achieving. If achieving sustainable development in some ultimate sense may seem problematic, promoting a transition toward sustainability should not.

An even more important reason for the shift of emphasis in sustainability thinking from 'target' toward 'process' is simply that we have so much to learn. Understanding sustainability is understanding a complex, dynamic system of nature–society interactions. Sustainable development thus becomes viewed as a process of adaptive management and social learning in which knowledge plays a central role. The science of sustainability, and above all the economics of sustainability, is taking its first steps. This book is a preliminary contribution to a research process and knowledge development to which many researchers are contributing. We do hope that future results can be developed from the ones proposed in this book.

NOTE

1. This trade-off is especially difficult with regard to greenhouse gases (GHGs) where the magnitude of future environmental damages is unknown and where estimated abatement costs are likely to be significant and borne by current generations.

REFERENCES

Arrow, K.J. (1996), 'What does the present owe the future?', The Grace Adams Tanner Lecture in Human Values, University of Oxford, 11 April.
Farzin, Y.H. (2007), 'Sustainability and optimality in economic development: Theoretical insights and policy prospects', mimeo.
Koopmans, T.C. (1956), 'Objectives, constraints, and outcomes in optimal growth models', *Econometrica*, **35**, 1–15.
National Research Council (1999), *Our Common Journey: A Transition Toward Sustainability*, Washington, DC: National Academy Press.

Ramsey, F.P. (1928), 'A mathematical theory of saving', *Economic Journal*, **38**, 543–59.

Stavins, R., A. Wagner and G. Wagner (2002), 'Interpreting sustainability in economic terms: Dynamic efficiency plus intergenerational equity', mimeo, Harvard University.

WCED (World Commission on Environment and Development, The Brundtland Commission) (1987), *Our Common Future*, Oxford: Oxford University Press.

Index